THE GALILEAN ECONOMY IN THE TIME OF JESUS

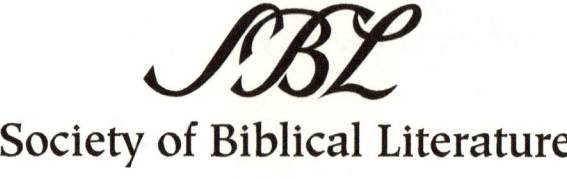

Society of Biblical Literature

Early Christianity and Its Literature

Gail R. O'Day, General Editor

Editorial Board

Warren Carter
Beverly Roberts Gaventa
Judith M. Lieu
Joseph Verheyden
Sze-kar Wan

Number 11

THE GALILEAN ECONOMY IN THE TIME OF JESUS

THE GALILEAN ECONOMY IN THE TIME OF JESUS

Edited by
David A. Fiensy and Ralph K. Hawkins

Society of Biblical Literature
Atlanta

THE GALILEAN ECONOMY IN THE TIME OF JESUS

Copyright © 2013 by the Society of Biblical Literature

All rights reserved. No part of this work may be reproduced or transmitted in any form or by any means, electronic or mechanical, including photocopying and recording, or by means of any information storage or retrieval system, except as may be expressly permitted by the 1976 Copyright Act or in writing from the publisher. Requests for permission should be addressed in writing to the Rights and Permissions Office, Society of Biblical Literature, 825 Houston Mill Road, Atlanta, GA 30329 USA.

Library of Congress Cataloging-in-Publication Data

The Galilean economy in the time of Jesus / edited by David A. Fiensy and Ralph K. Hawkins.
    p. cm. — (Early Christianity and its literature ; number 11)
    ISBN 978-1-58983-757-7 (paper binding : alk. paper) — ISBN 978-1-58983-758-4 (electronic format) (print) — ISBN 978-1-58983-785-0 (hardcover binding : alk. paper)
    1. Galilee (Israel)—Antiquities. 2. Galilee (Israel)—Economic conditions. I. Fiensy, David A. II. Hawkins, Ralph K. III. Series: Early Christianity and its literature ; no. 11.
    DS110.G2G367 2013
    330.933'4505—dc23   2013007486

Printed on acid-free, recycled paper conforming to
ANSI/NISO Z39.48-1992 (R1997) and ISO 9706:1994
standards for paper permanence.

Contents

Preface vii
Abbreviations ix

Introduction
   David A. Fiensy 1

People, Land, Economy, and Belief in First-Century Galilee and
   Its Origins: A Comprehensive Archaeological Synthesis
   Mordechai Aviam 5

City and Village in Lower Galilee: The Import of the Archeological
   Excavations at Sepphoris and Khirbet Qana (Cana) for Framing
   the Economic Context of Jesus
   C. Thomas McCollough 49

Revisiting Jesus' Capernaum: A Village of Only Subsistence-
   Level Fishers and Farmers?
   Sharon Lea Mattila 75

Execrating? or Execrable Peasants!
   Douglas E. Oakman 139

Assessing the Economy of Galilee in the Late Second Temple
   Period: Five Considerations
   David A. Fiensy 165

Contributors 187
Ancient Sources Index 189
Modern Authors Index 191
Subject Index 196

Preface

In March of 2009, at the business meeting of the Southeastern affiliate of the American Schools of Oriental Research, we were discussing ways to come up with a dynamic program for the next year's meeting, and we zeroed in on this issue of the socioeconomic situation of the Galilee during the time of Jesus. We had accrued about $1,500 in our treasury, and we decided that we should spend it on a "big-name" speaker whom we would invite to deliver a plenary address and to whom we would invite other speakers to respond. James R. Strange, who was the president at the time, suggested four or five archaeologists who were doing important work in the field whose work might generate excitement. Since I was the incoming vice president in charge of the next year's program, I jotted these names down and immediately began contacting them to discuss the possibility of their participation in the 2010 program. To our delight, Mordechai Aviam agreed to come and discuss his findings at Yodefat and their importance for understanding the Galilean economy during the time of Jesus. We decided that, since much of this data is unpublished elsewhere, it would make an excellent topic for a plenary address. David Fiensy, Tom McCollough, and Doug Oakman, all of whom have been at the forefront of the discussion about Jesus and the archaeology of the Galilee, were invited to serve on a panel as respondents. Sharon Mattila presented a paper in another of our sessions, and it made important contributions to the conference's theme of the Galilean economy during the time of Jesus.

Afterwards we all agreed that the conference had been a great success and that the papers should be published. I asked David Fiensy to serve as a co-editor with me. Together we express our thanks to our graduate student, David Hunter, who assisted with several of the essays. The contributors and I all hope that these essays will further the discussion not only about the Galilean economy during the time of Jesus but about the socioeconomic background of Jesus and the nature of his message and ministry.

Ralph K. Hawkins
Averett University

Abbreviations

BTB	*Biblical Theology Bulletin*
CurBR	*Currents in Biblical Research*
ETS (A)	Eastern Terra Sigillata Ware
GCW	Galilean Coarse Ware
IAA	Israel Antiquities Authority
JRA	*Journal of Roman Archaeology*
LA	*Liber Annus*
NEAEHL	*The New Encyclopedia of Archaeological Excavations in the Holy Land*. Edited by Ephraim Stern. 4 vols. Jerusalem: Israel Exploration Society & Carta, 1993

Introduction

David A. Fiensy

Scholars of classical history are going through a revolution in their thinking about the ancient economy. In particular, they are debating the usefulness of certain classicists' (e.g., Moses Finley's[1]) assumptions and methods for understanding and researching the Greco-Roman world. Those studying the economy of Galilee in the late Second Temple period are also involved in this debate but often unaware of its counterpart in classical scholarship. This volume will highlight areas of disagreement at play in the study of the economy of the Roman Empire which also play a role in the current debate over the historical Galilee.

In the contemporary quest for the historical Jesus, the socioeconomic background of Jesus and its impact on his message and ministry is the subject of intense debate. Among many, it is accepted that the Galilee in which Jesus was born and raised was plagued by grinding poverty, that his followers were primarily poor people, and that his audience was made up of the masses of the poor.[2] Others, however, have argued that Galilee was an egalitarian and economically prosperous society.[3] These contradictory

---

1. Moses I. Finley, *The Ancient Economy* (Berkeley: University of California Press, 1985).

2. John Dominic Crossan, *The Historical Jesus: The Life of a Mediterranean Jewish Peasant* (San Francisco: HarperSanFrancisco, 1991); idem, *The Birth of Christianity: Discovering What Happened in the Years Immediately after the Execution of Jesus* (San Francisco: HarperSanFrancisco, 1998); and Richard A. Horsley, *Galilee: History, Politics, People* (Valley Forge, Pa.: Trinity Press International, 1995).

3. J. Andrew Overman, "Jesus of Galilee and the Historical Peasant," in *Archaeology and the Galilee* (ed. Douglas R. Edwards and C. Thomas McCollough; Atlanta: Scholars Press, 1997) 67–74; Douglas R. Edwards, "The Socio-economic and Cultural Ethos of the Lower Galilee in the First Century: Implications for the Nascent Jesus Movement," in *The Galilee in Late Antiquity* (ed. Lee I. Levine; New York: Jewish Theo-

viewpoints make it clear that the current quest for the historical Jesus is also by necessity a search for the historical Galilee.[4] The geographical and cultural location of Jesus' youth may help us understand his later message and/or his pattern of ministry. Certainly scholars of the past have thought as much; the current group seems to have the same opinion.[5]

The current quest for the historical Galilee is a study in contrasts: (1) Some look at Galilee through the lenses of cultural anthropology and macro-sociology; others look at Galilee through the lenses of archaeology and reject the use of social theories. (2) Some maintain that the relations between rural villages and the cities were hostile; others propose that the relationship was one of economic reciprocity and goodwill. (3) Some suggest that Galilee was typical of other agrarian societies with poor peasants who lived in the rural areas and exploitative wealthy people who lived mostly in the cities; others respond that life was pretty good for everyone in Galilee and that it was an egalitarian society. (4) Some regard Galilee as so hellenized that there were Cynic philosophers running around; others retort that Galilee was thoroughly Jewish. (5) Some think that the Galileans were politically and religiously radicalized and resistant not only to the Romans but also to the Judeans to the south. The essays that follow will at various points interact with these points of view.

In chapter 1 Mordechai Aviam, the experienced archaeologist, will set up much of the debate with his archaeological overview of Galilee. He will present to the reader not only his methodology (he will use archaeology but not the social sciences) but also his conclusions: Galilee was economically prosperous, and the Galileans did not have it too badly because of their vigorous manufacturing and trade. Further, the Galileans were not radicalized but were sympathetic with and basically identical to the Judeans in religion and politics. They were thoroughly "Jewish,"

---

logical Seminary, 1992), 53–74; and Dennis E. Groh, "The Clash between Literary and Archaeological Models of Provincial Palestine," in *Archaeology and the Galilee* (ed. Douglas R. Edwards and C. Thomas McCollough; Atlanta: Scholars Press, 1997), 29–37.

4. Seán Freyne, "The Geography, Politics, and Economics in Galilee and the Quest for the Historical Jesus," in *Studying the Historical Jesus: Evaluations of the State of Current Research* (ed. Bruce Chilton and Craig Evans; Leiden: Brill, 1994), 76; and Halvor Moxnes, "The Construction of Galilee as a Place for the Historical Jesus," *BTB* 31 (2001): 26–37, 64–77.

5. See the surveys in Moxnes, "The Construction of Galilee"; and Mark Rapinchuk, "The Galilee and Jesus in Recent Research," *CurBR* 2 (2004): 197–222.

that is, Judean in ideology, and were experiencing good times economically. He will cite many archaeological reports on many cities and villages but will lean most heavily on his own work at the village of Yodefat. The rest of the chapters will interact with one or more of his conclusions and will align with or reject Aviam's claims according to the author's own methods and evidence.

C. Thomas McCollough, also an experienced archaeologist, will follow Aviam's point of view in chapter 2 but restrict his argument primarily to two sites, Sepphoris and Khirbet Qana (Cana), the sites he has personally helped excavate. McCollough will support the claim that Galilee was economically prosperous though with a bit more caution than Aviam. The village residents were not destitute, but much of the architectural grandeur of Galilee came in the second century C.E., not in the first. Although several preliminary reports on the excavations at Khirbet Qana have already appeared in print, some of McCollough's information about Khirbet Qana is being presented to the general public for the first time.

In chapter 3 Sharon Mattila will challenge past analyses of Capernaum as a subsistence-level fishing village. She will argue that there was economic stratification and that at least some residents had attained a level of wealth. Her chapter follows Aviam and McCollough but is even more geographically restricted in making the general argument than McCollough, since she focuses on only one village. Mattila will press for the view that "at least some of the villagers in Jesus' Capernaum probably lived at a level significantly above subsistence." She will present four arguments for her thesis.

In chapter 4 Douglas Oakman will take issue with the first three chapters. His essay will revisit the question of "peasants." Oakman challenges Aviam's dismissal of the term and the category and urges caution in any belief in the higher standards of living proposed by Aviam, McCollough, and Mattila. Oakman will urge the use of the social sciences and their models (where appropriate) in understanding the Galilee of the late Second Temple period. He will offer two tables of comparison between peasants and modern farmers to explicate his definition. He will then present a sociological model to illustrate his thinking on how the ancient Galilean economy worked.

Finally, David Fiensy in the last chapter seeks to map five considerations in the contemporary debate about the ancient economies. These dimensions are evident or implied in each of the first four chapters. Very often scholars simply make assumptions about one or more of these considerations without defending their assumptions. He will thus seek to contextualize Aviam's (and in turn each of the other authors') work. Fiensy will appeal to scholars to use critically both archaeology and social science models in the complex task of constructing the ancient economy. This essay stands ideologically rather midway between the first three and Oakman's chapter.

Bibliography

Crossan, John Dominic. *The Birth of Christianity: Discovering What Happened in the Years Immediately after the Execution of Jesus.* San Francisco: HarperSanFrancisco, 1998.

———. *The Historical Jesus: The Life of a Mediterranean Jewish Peasant.* San Francisco: HarperSanFrancisco, 1991.

Edwards, Douglas R. "The Socio-economic and Cultural Ethos of the Lower Galilee in the First Century: Implications for the Nascent Jesus Movement." Pages 53–74 in *The Galilee in Late Antiquity.* Edited by Lee I. Levine. New York: Jewish Theological Seminary, 1992.

Finley, Moses I. *The Ancient Economy.* Berkley: University of California, 1985.

Freyne, Seán. "The Geography, Politics, and Economics in Galilee and the Quest for the Historical Jesus." Pages 75–121 in *Studying the Historical Jesus: Evaluations of the State of Current Research.* Edited by Bruce Chilton and Craig Evans. Leiden: Brill, 1994.

Groh, Dennis E. "The Clash Between Literary and Archaeological Models of Provincial Palestine." Pages 29–38 in *Archaeology and the Galilee.* Edited by Douglas R. Edwards and C. Thomas McCollough. Atlanta: Scholars Press, 1997.

Horsley, Richard A. *Galilee: History, Politics, People.* Valley Forge, Pa.: Trinity Press International, 1995.

Moxnes, Halvor. "The Construction of Galilee as a Place for the Historical Jesus ." *BTB* 31 (2001): 26–37, 64–77.

Overman, J. Andrew. "Jesus of Galilee and the Historical Peasant." Pages 67–74 in *Archaeology and the Galilee.* Edited by Douglas R. Edwards and C. Thomas McCollough. Atlanta: Scholars Press, 1997.

Rapinchuk, Mark. "The Galilee and Jesus in Recent Research." *CurBR* 2 (2004): 197–222.

1
People, Land, Economy, and Belief in First-Century Galilee and Its Origins: A Comprehensive Archaeological Synthesis

Mordechai Aviam

What was the economic standard of living in Galilee in the first century C.E., the time of Jesus? Were the rural village dwellers very poor, exploited by wealthy, urban aristocrats and close to revolution? Or were the country people living in small villages relatively happy with their lives and their prosperity? Were the Galileans similar or dissimilar religiously to the Judeans? Did the Galileans resent the Judean laws and religious regulations, or were they observant of them? The answers to these questions are today vigorously debated. In this chapter, I will attempt to provide the best answers based on recent archaeological evidence. We will first survey the settlement of Galilee. Next, we will examine Galilean daily life in the first century C.E. Finally, we will take a look at the sociopolitical and religious attitudes and behavior of the Galileans before the Revolt of 66–73 C.E.

Archaeological Overview of the Late Second Temple Period

Recent archaeological finds may be able to offer some preliminary answers to these questions. But first, we need to place our questions into an appropriate background.

Galilee before the Hasmoneans

Archaeological evidence over the last decade has demonstrated that ethnic and religious changes occurred in the Galilee at the end of the second century B.C.E. One instance of such change was evidenced by the identification of "Galilean Coarse Ware" (GCW; see fig. 1), a type of clay vessel that was probably produced by the pagan population of the Galilee during the Persian and Hellenistic periods.[1] This group of ceramic ware has been found (although not yet thoroughly analyzed) in a large number of sites in mountainous Galilee, mainly in Upper Galilee but also in the northern part of Lower Galilee, as far south as the Tur'an ridge and Tiberias. They are found at large sites such as Beer Sheba of the Galilee (about 12.5 acres) located at the border valley between Lower and Upper Galilee and in tiny sites like the one on the peak of Mount Hod in Upper Galilee (about 0.125 acres). By the end of the second century B.C.E., most of these small sites were abandoned, and GCW did not continue in use into the next period.

Of particular interest are the finds from Mount Mizpe Hayamim. The preliminary report shows that a temple on the summit of the mountain probably functioned as a regional cult-center. Bronze and stone Phoeni-

Figure 1. Galilean coarse ware jar (center), Yodefat. Photo by Mordechai Aviam.

---

1. Mordechai Aviam, "The Galilee, the Hellenistic to Byzantine Periods," *NEAEHL* 2:453–58; Rafael Frankel, Nimrod Getzov, Mordechai Aviam, and Avi Degani, *Settlement Dynamics and Regional Diversity in Ancient Upper Galilee: Archaeological Survey of Upper Galilee* (Jerusalem: Israel Antiquities Authority, 2001); and Mordechai Aviam and Aharoni Amitai, "Excavations at Khirbet esh-Shuhara" [Hebrew], *Eretz Zafon* (2002): 119–34.

cian figurines, most of which are of Egyptian origin, were found, as well as a large quantity of GCW, all belonging to the Late Persian and Hellenistic periods. According to the excavator, the site, dated by a mid-second century B.C.E. coin, was abandoned at the end of the second century B.C.E. as a result of a violent event, during which the statues and figurines were desecrated. Frankel suggests that the destruction happened during the Hasmonean conquest.[2]

Equally important was a large amount of GCW and three bronze figurines found during the survey of Beer Sheba of the Galilee. One half of a rectangular base of Apis (5 x 3 cm) was identified by the front hoof of the bull (fig. 2). Around the base, there are three inscriptions in three languages. On the front, an inscription in Aramaic reads קרב (qrb), or "sacrifice." On one long side is a hieroglyphic inscription that, based on its engraving style, appears to be original. The third inscription is unreadable but looks as if someone copied Greek letters without knowing the language. This object, which originally had only the hieroglyphic inscription, was probably imported from Egypt; the two other inscriptions were probably added at Beer Sheba. The date of the piece is probably Hellenistic, judging by the Greek inscription. Based on the Aramaic inscription, the figurine was brought to a temple as a donation.

The second figurine found in the survey is a bronze torso (5 cm) of a nude female, possibly Aphrodite. It also appears to date to the Hellenistic period, as this design of a nude female's body is not typical to the Persian period (fig. 3).

The third small figurine (2 cm) depicts a well-known amulet of "Horus the infant." This figurine could be worn as a pendent as it has a small loop on its back. It could also be placed upright as suggested by its bottom, which is designed to be affixed to a base. It is almost identical to a Horus figurine found at Gamla, where no Persian period pottery has been found, and at Yavne Yam.[3] Thus, this Beer Sheba figurine also dates to the Hellenistic period. The assemblage of these figurines points to the existence of a sacred place in this fortified settlement during the Hellenistic period.

---

2. Rafael Frankel, "The Sanctuary from the Persian Period at Mizpe Yamim," *Qadmoniot* 113 (1997): 46–53.

3. For Gamla, see Shemaryahu Gutman, *Gamla: A City in Rebellion* [Hebrew] (Tel Aviv: Miśrad ha-biṭaḥon, 1994), 48. For Yavne Yam, see Moshe Fischer, "Yavneh-Yam. 1992–1999—Interim Report" [Hebrew], *Qadmoniot* 123 (2002): 2–11.

Figure 2. Apis figure, Beer Sheba. Photo by Mordechai Aviam.

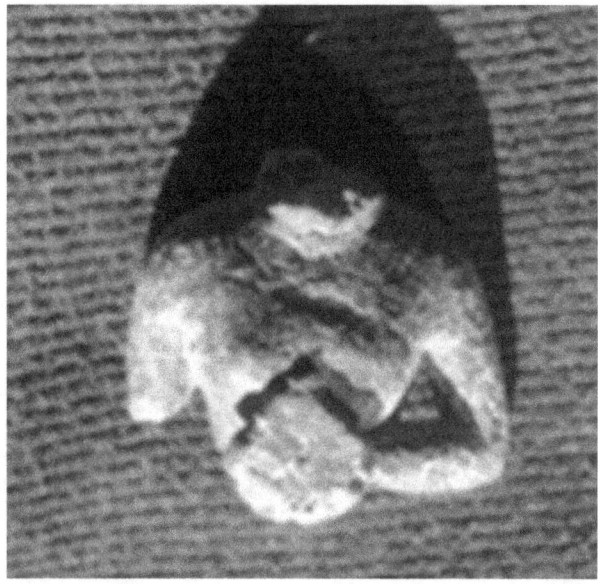

Figure 3. Bronze torso of nude female, Beer Sheba. Photo by Mordechai Aviam.

In the excavations at Yodefat, remains of the earliest settlement were discovered in three different areas. The most important one is located in the northwest side of the hill which was covered by a massive wall. Here are two or three rooms, probably basements, where two complete GCW *pithoi* and an imported, stamped, amphora were found together on the ash-covered floor. The date of this Rhodian *amphora* is the second half of the second century B.C.E.[4] In an associated locus, as well as on the bedrock nearby, two typical Hellenistic period oil lamps were found, decorated with erotic figures. During the late second century B.C.E., Jews in Judea did not use this type of oil lamp, as the biblical law prohibiting figurative art was strictly observed.

A Hellenistic period farmstead was discovered during the excavations at Esh-Shuhara, on the Northern Road of Israel. On one of the floors a complete GCW *pithos* was found, as well as many potsherds, coins, and two arrowheads. Some of the coins are from the Hasmonean dynasty. This site was probably conquered during the Hasmonean conquest of the Galilee.[5]

Excavation at Tel Qedesh over the last few years has focused mainly on a large administrative building at the southern edge of the tel. The building was probably established during the Persian period and was expanded and enlarged in the Hellenistic period. A hoard of more than two thousand bullae, as well as storage rooms and rooms decorated with stucco and fresco, showed that the building had been of great importance.[6] One of the bullae carried the Greek name of the site, "Qedesh," and others carried Phoenician inscriptions and deities. This discovery confirms Josephus's description of Qedesh: "this Kydissa was a strong Mediterranean village of the Tyrians" (*J.W.* 4.104). It was the southernmost administrative presence of Tyre in the Galilee, and until the Hasmonean activity in the Galilee it was a local Phoenician, pagan settlement and stronghold. Many of the storage jars found in the storeroom are of the GCW style, although the excavators decided on a different nomenclature. The build-

---

4. The stamp was read by Donald T. Ariel.

5. Aviam and Amitai, "Excavations at Khirbet esh-Shuhara"; Danny Syon, "Coins from the Excavations at Khirbet esh-Shuhars" [Hebrew], *Eretz Zafon* (2002): 123–34. In his report, Syon developed a different understanding of the site.

6. Sharon C. Herbert and Andrea M. Berlin, "A New Administrative Center for Persian and Hellenistic Galilee: Preliminary Report of the University of Michigan/University of Minnesota Excavations at Kedesh," *BASOR* 329 (2003): 13–59.

ing was destroyed by fire in the mid-second century B.C.E., and the excavators suggested that it was the result of the Seleucid-Hasmonean battle of the Hazor plain.

A site that is associated with Qedesh is the Hellenistic period fortress at Qeren Naftaly. Atop a high hill, 2 km east of Qedesh, are the remains of a large, well-preserved fortress which was partially excavated.[7] It was built during the third or second centuries B.C.E. and used probably by the same authorities who operated the administrative building at Qedesh. In the second half of the second century B.C.E., the site shifted hands and a typical Jewish *miqweh* (ritual bath) was built into the foundation of one of the rooms of the former fort (fig. 4). Some Hasmonean coins were also found, which, together with the *miqweh*, point to the ethnic change at the site and across all of the Galilee.

Figure 4. *Miqweh* at Qeren Naftaly. Photo by Mordechai Aviam.

---

7. Mordechai Aviam, "Yodefat, a Case Study in the Development of the Jewish Settlement in the Galilee during the Second Temple Period" (Ph.D. diss., Bar Ilan University, 2005) 59–89.

The Arrival of the Hasmoneans

The Hasmonean annexation of the Galilee could have occurred in two stages—the first at the time of Hyrcanus I (135–105 B.C.E.), and the second during the reign of Jannaeus (104–78 B.C.E.), whom we know conquered the central Golan. These one or two events shaped the northern border of their kingdom. The annexation is probably reflected in the ethnic border mentioned in the "Baraitha of the bounderies" (t. Shevi'it 4:14).[8] Another short list of the "Fortified towns from the time of Joshua Ben Nun" mentioned four sites in the north: "The Old Castle of Zippori, the Acra of Gush Halav, Old Yodefat and Gamla" (m. Arakhin 9:6). When discussing this list, Adan-Bayewitz suggested that these sites were mentioned as fortified towns because, when Jews settled this area after the Hasmonean conquest, they found these sites already fortified from the Hellenistic period.[9] Lately, Liebner[10] adopted this approach and used it to support his suggestion that there were no Jews in Galilee and that Zippori was not a Jewish site before the Hasmonean annexation.

My conclusions are different (see fig. 5). First, the analysis of the stratigraphy of Yodefat proved that the first fortification of the hill is from the Hasmonean era. The Gentile settlement atop the hill had no wall. Second, Gamla had no Hellenistic fortifications. If the round tower is Hellenistic (as suggested by its construction of only "header" stones, which is typical of Hellenistic fortifications), it was the only fortified element and is therefore not a wall. The excavations at Gush Halav yielded no fortifications of the Hellenistic period, only what seems to be a fortifying earthen-ramp that could be the fortifications of John of Gush Halav from the first century C.E. Recent excavations on the northern slope of the hill (excavations of M. Hartal for the IAA) yielded a Hellenistic private courtyard that was covered by the early Roman earthwork. At Zippori, no evidence for Hellenistic fortifications was found. To sum up, there is neither reason for Adan-Bayewitz's identification of these sites as Gentile fortified sites nor

---

8. See Mordechai Aviam, *Jews, Pagans and Christians in the Galilee* (Rochester, N.Y.: University of Rochester Press, 2004), 11–13.

9. David Adan-Bayewitz, "The Tannaitic List of 'Walled Cities' and the Archaeological-Historical Evidence from Iotapata and Gamla" [Hebrew], *Tarbiz* 66 (1996–1997): 449–70.

10. Uzi Liebner, *Settlement and History in Hellenistic, Roman, and Byzantine Galilee* (Tübingen: Mohr Siebeck, 2009).

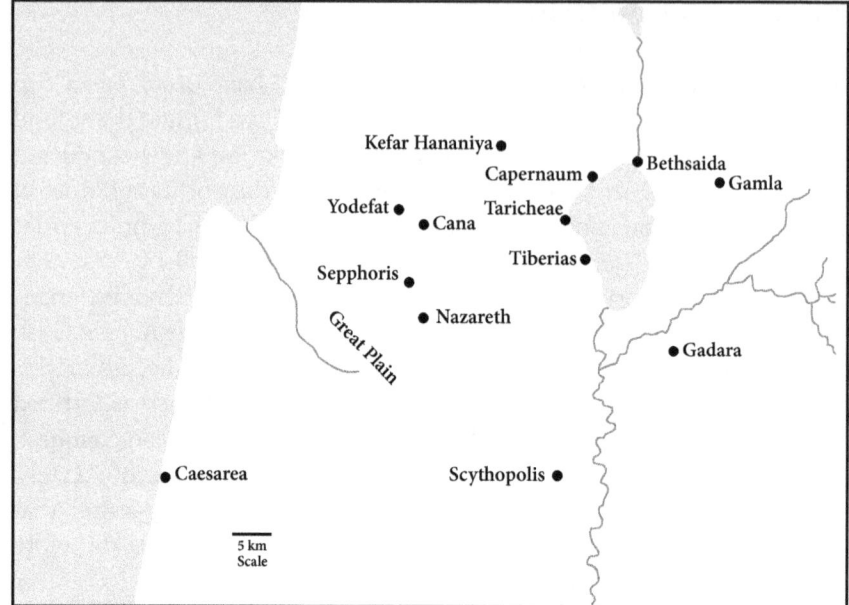

Figure 5. Galilee and environs.

Liebner's support for it. I am back to my 2004 suggestion, which strengthens Richard Horsley's thesis[11] that this list preserves a roster of Hasmonean strongholds or military settlements, all of which continued to evolve into villages in the early Roman period.

These finds from the various sites are clear evidence of the destruction and abandonment of late Hellenistic period sites that demonstrate pagan presence. Three of the sites (Mizpe Yamim, Yodefat, and Esh-Shuhara) were destroyed at the end of the second century B.C.E., probably during the Hasmonean conquest of the Galilee. Two sites had Hasmonean coins in the destruction layers or in the superimposed layers.

As a result of this evidence, I can suggest that most of the population in Upper Galilee and in the northern half of Lower Galilee were pagans. The use of a mixture of Phoenician and Egyptian cult objects and symbols is typical of the Phoenician population.[12]

---

11. Richard A. Horsley, *Archaeology, History and Society in Galilee* (Valley Forge, Pa.: Trinity Press International, 1996), 26.

12. Ephraim Stern, *The Material Culture of the Land of the Bible in the Persian Period* (Jerusalem: Bialik Institute, 1973), 230.

Scholars have long debated the presence of the Itureans in the Galilee, and this debate has continued into the present. As there is no convincing evidence for Iturean existence in the Galilee, I will maintain my conclusion, supported lately by Liebner,[13] that the Itureans lived on the Hermon ridge and in the northern Golan and did not occupy the Galilee.

Galilee under the Hasmoneans

At the turn of the first century B.C.E., the Galilee was conquered by the Hasmoneans. Whether they forced the native population to convert to Judaism or whether part of the population was happy to convert is unknown. The religious motivation of the Hasmoneans, to "purify" the Land of Israel from any idolatry and to enlarge the territory of their kingdom to the borders of the kingdom of David, created a Galilee of some abandoned, pre-Hasmomaean, Gentile sites and many reestablished or continuous sites now inhabited by a Jewish population.

Was there a royal investment in the newly occupied territories? Some years ago, I suggested that the knowledge of the industrial olive press was exported from Judea, where it was well known (for example, the dozens of olive presses from Marisa), to the Galilee at this time. There was a rapid growth in the number of installations in the Galilee since that time, and it reflects an increase in the number of olive plantations in the area.[14]

New settlements were established, as suggested by Liebner.[15] According to his intensive survey, Arbel and Migdal were first built in the Hasmonean period (fig. 6). At Migdal, where two large excavations have been conducted in recent years, it was proven that the site was first built in the Hasmonean period.[16] An important discovery was made by De Lucca and his team when they uncovered a massive, well-preserved stone pier of a harbor, including some mooring stones (anchoring stones) protruding out of the wall toward the lake.[17] Its earliest stage is dated to the Hasmonean

---

13. Liebner, *Settlement and History*, 319–29. Liebner suggested that the entire story of Timagenes about the circumcision of the Ituraeans never actually happened.

14. S. De Luca, oral information.

15. Liebner, *Settlement and History*, 329–31.

16. Stefano De Luca, "La città ellenistico-romana di Magdala/Taricheae: Gli scavi del Magdala Project 2007 e 2008: Relazione preliminare e prospettive di indagine," *LA* 49 (2010): 342–562.

17. Ibid.

Figure 6. Aerial view of Magdala/Migdal excavations. Photo courtesy of Stefano De Luca, archaeologist, of the Magdala Project. In the center, the square frame is the Franciscan excavations. The harbor is under the tree. To the left are the IAA excavations, with residential areas and the synagogue.

period and the second stage to the Herodian period (probably Antipas). It is the first evidence for the royal investment in the Galilee.

Liebner rightly suggested identifying Khirbet Abu Shusheh, in the Gennesar Valley, as ancient Gennesar (Ginosar), based on what the pottery shows us about the long period of occupation. He suggests that when Jonathan Maccabeus marched his troops toward the Hazor plain to fight Demetrius, he passed near "the water of Gennesar" and that the lake got its name from the important site near its shore.[18]

Reinforcing both Liebner's identification and his suggestion that Migdal took its preeminence from Gennesar is the discovery of the Hasmonean harbor at Migdal. Here we have a series of royal initiatives around the Sea of Galilee indicating that it was an important economic factor in the life of Jewish Galilee. Shortly after the conquest of the Galilee at the end of the second century B.C.E., it was Gennesar which was the "Capital" of the region. The Hasmoneans, in an attempt to show their social and eco-

---

18. Liebner, *Settlement and History*, 180–91.

nomic interest in the "new" Jewish region, decided to establish a new, local capital. Migdal was established with a "modern," functional royal harbor. It was not long after that, about a hundred years later, that another dynasty took over, and Herod Antipas established a new, modern city, probably with a harbor itself, named Tiberias, and it replaced Hasmonean Migdal as the most economically important city in the region.

If we combine the evidence from the four sites of Hasmonean Galilee and Golan (the fortress at Qeren Naftali, the establishment of Gamla with its late Hasmonean olive press, and the citadel of Zippori and Migdal with its harbor), we will come to an understanding of the large investments of the Hasmoneans. It was a crucial part in building the new Jewish life in the Galilee. I believe that authorities encouraged people to emigrate from crowded Judea to the new open territories, and that they encouraged veterans of the Hasmonean armies to settle there, joining the minority of the local population which was, in my eyes, a mix of remnant Jews and converted gentiles.

The new Jewish life all over Galilee is attested by the large quantity and wide distribution of Hasmonean coins.[19] Hasmonean *miqwā'ôt* were also found in three corners of the Galilee—Zippori, Gamla, and Qeren Naftali—a new phenomenon clearly associated with the change in ethnicity and the distribution of Jews in the region.

Galilee under King Herod: Years of Negligence

With the decline of the Hasmonean kingdom, loyal Galileans, supporters of the Hasmonean family, rose up against Herod's attempt to conquer and rule the Galilee. According to Josephus, there were battles at Arbel (*J.W.* 1.307–313) and Sepphoris (*J.W.* 1.303), as well as a battle at a fortress in northern Galilee (*J.W.* 1.328) in which alien forces were involved. The evidence points to the identification of this fortress with the fortress of Qeren Naphtali.[20] A siege complex circling the mountain evinces the battle and the conquest of the Hasmonean garrison's fortress. Moreover, the *miqweh* at the site was intentionally filled and possibly desecrated when it was used as a dump pit for pigs and other hunted animal bones. The finds of

---

19. Danny Syon, "Tyre and Gamla: A Study in the Monetary Influence of Southern Phoenicia on Galilee and the Golan in the Hellenistic and Roman Periods" (Ph.D. diss., Hebrew University, 2004).

20. Aviam, *Jews, Pagans and Christians*, 59–89.

many oil lamps, decorated with figurative art, as well as the evidence of the "nonkosher" animal bones and the disuse of the *miqweh*, all point to non-Jewish occupation of the fortress at the second half of the first century B.C.E. According to Josephus, Herod used Roman legions as well as "mountaineers" from Lebanon in his campaign against the Galileans who, I believe, took over this fortress.

At Gamla, in area B/D (the "Hasmonean Quarter") the ceramic and numismatic evidence, as well as the skeletons of two horses at the olive press, point to a sudden abandonment of the quarter at the end of the first century B.C.E. or the very beginning of the first century C.E. (fig. 7).[21] We should assign the abandonment of this quarter, located on the upper northeastern side of the hill, to the early years of Herod's activity in the north and his battles against the Jews, the supporters of the Hasmonean dynasty.

Herod never forgot the Galileans' attitude toward him. According to Josephus, during Herod's long reign he never conducted a building project in the Galilee, a claim that seems to be supported by an absence of archaeological remains.[22] Even the "Royal Palace" mentioned by Josephus (*Ant.* 17.271) is not necessarily a palace built by Herod but was rather the "Old Palace" of the Hasmoneans, which was used by the young Herod when he was king of Galilee. The closest Herodian investment in the Galilee was the temple dedicated to Augustus "near the place called Paneas," which was not built for Jews. In contrast, as if to pay the Galileans back for their hostile attitude, it was built on the very edge of Galilee, on the lands of Zenodoros. Although Sepphoris was the capital of Galilee and an administrative center, there is no historical or archaeological evidence, yet, for any Herodian official building there.

Herod Antipas: Ethnarch of the Galilee

A great change took place in the Galilee in the first century C.E. When Herod Antipas assumed the tetrarchy, he chose Sepphoris as his capital. This was an obvious and natural step as it was the most important Jewish

---

21. Andrea M. Berlin, *Gamla I: The Pottery of the Second Temple Period* (IAA Reports 29; Jerusalem: Israel Antiquities Authority, 2006), 64.

22. Peter Richardson expresses a bit of hesitation while discussing Herod's building activities in the Galilee (see *Herod, King of the Jews and Friend of the Romans* [Columbia: University of South Carolina Press, 1996], 175–76). In my opinion, Herod avoided serious investments in the Galilee.

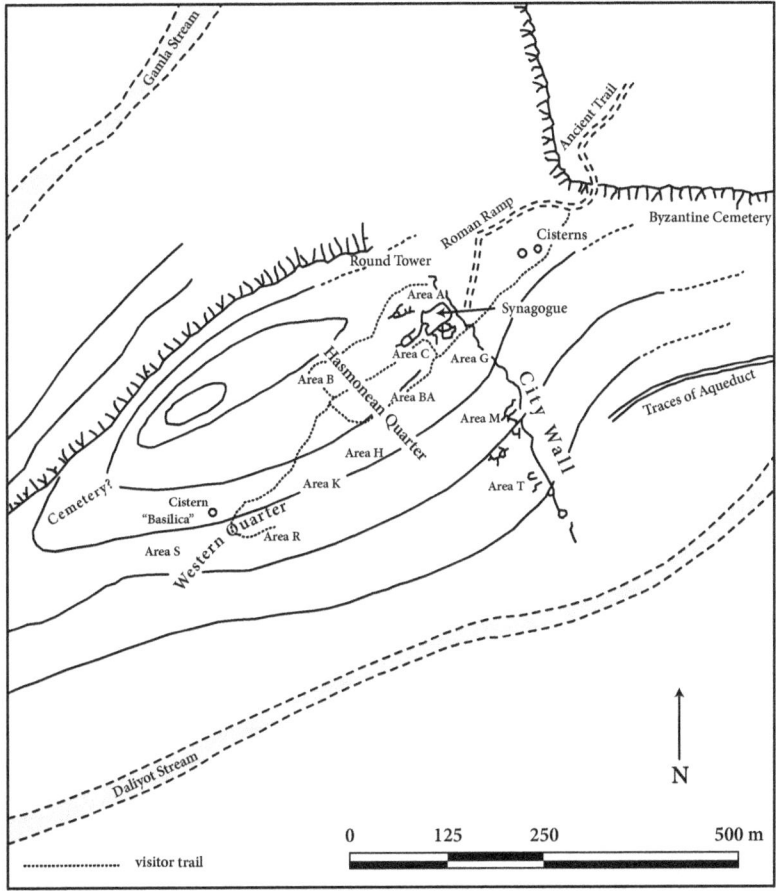

Figure 7. Gamla, topographical plan. Courtesy of Danny Syon.

city in the center of his territory. According to Josephus he adorned it to be "the jewel of all Galilee" (*Ant.* 18.27). As he was following in his father's footsteps, he probably built Sepphoris as a "Hellenistic-Roman" style city. At the end of the second decade, just as his father had done, he established the new capital city of Tiberias (*Ant.* 18.36).

At Sepphoris, although no final reports have yet been published, it seems as if the course and foundation for the *cardo* were outlined in the first century, probably at the time of Antipas.[23] The first stage of the aque-

---

23. Douglas R. Edwards and C. Thomas McCollough, *Archaeology and the Galilee* (Atlanta: Scholars Press, 1997), 139.

duct to Sepphoris was dated by Tsuk to the first century C.E.[24] There is a debate as to the date of the Sepphoris Theater (see photo in chapter 2 of this volume). According to Strange and McCollough, the theater was built in the first half of the first century C.E. (oral information), but according to Weiss it was only established in the second century C.E.[25]

The Sepphoris theater's history may be paralleled by the theater at nearby Tiberias (fig. 8). During the last couple of years, the theater of Tiberias has been completely excavated. It appears that the theater at Tiberias had two stages of building similar to the Bet-Shean/Scythopolis theater,[26] the first stage of which was built in the mid-first century C.E., the time of Emperor Tiberius.[27] Perhaps then a similar date would be appropriately assigned to the theater at Tiberias. If this is the case, it could support a date in the first century C.E. for the theater at Sepphoris as well.

Other evidence for these building activities came to light with the important discovery of the Antipas stadium,[28] which was discovered on the shore of the Sea of Galilee, exactly as described by Josephus (*J.W.* 3.10). If a stadium was built as mentioned by Josephus, there is no reason why a theater could not also have been erected, as was the case in Caesarea where Herod the Great built both structures (fig. 9).

At Tiberias, the famous monumental ceremonial gate with two round towers has been re-excavated and is now on public display (fig. 10). The area of the former excavation was enlarged and a monumental bridge was discovered.[29] It seems as if the location for the gate, on the northern bank of a small creek, was chosen to use as a defensive, moat-like structure. From the gate, the *cardo* leads to the north. Although the *cardo* was dated

---

24. Tsvika Tsuk, "The Aqueducts to Sepphoris" (M.A. thesis, Tel Aviv University, 1985), 61.

25. Zeev Weiss, "Josephus and Archaeology on the City of the Galilee," in *Making History: Josephus and Historical Method* (ed. Zuleika Rodgers; Leiden: Brill, 2007), 387–414.

26. Walid Atrash, oral information.

27. Gabriel Mazor and Walid Atrash, *Nysa-Scythopolis: The Southern and Severan Theatres. Final Report. Bet She'an 3* (IAA Reports; Jerusalem: IAA, forthcoming).

28. Moshe Hartal, "Tiberias, Galei Kinneret," *Hadashot Arkheologiyot—Excavations and Surveys in Israel* 120 (2008). Online: http://www.hadashot-esi.org.il/report_detail_eng.asp?id=773&mag_id=114.

29. Moshe Hartal, "Tiberias," *Hadashot Arkheologiyot—Excavations and Surveys in Israel* 122 (2010). Online: http://www.hadashot-esi.org.il/report_detail.asp?id=1574&mag_id=117.

Figure 8. Tiberias, theater. Photo by Mordechai Aviam.

Figure 9. Tiberias, southern edge of stadium. Photo by Mordechai Aviam.

Figure 10. Tiberias, Antipas's Gate. Photo by Mordechai Aviam.

to the second century C.E. (by the excavation near the bathhouse), it seems that its beginning, near the gate, and probably the entire course, even if not yet paved, is from the first century.[30] The remains of a lavish, first-century building with an *opus sectile* floor were found—presumably the palace of Herod Antipas, over which the later basilica was superimposed—as well as the remains of Second Pompeian style frescoes.[31] To these remains we should add the theater and stadium that were discussed above, as well as clear, new evidence for an early aqueduct identified by Tsuk within the remains of the later one.[32] Thus we have a panoramic view of a great royal investment in establishing a local capital city.

Our historical survey demonstrates that when the Jewish leaders of Galilee began to rule (with the exception of Herod the Great) they made significant financial investments in the region. These building projects provided employment, stimulated trade, and in general raised the level of prosperity.

---

30. Morten Hørning Jensen, *Herod Antipas in Galilee* (Tübingen: Mohr Siebeck, 2006), 139–40

31. Ibid., 141–44.

32. Tsuk, personal communication.

Evidence from Yodefat and Gamla for First-Century Daily Life

In this section we will trace the development of the Galilean settlements from their establishment in the Hasmonean era into the first century C.E. (fig. 11).[33] Since both Yodefat and Gamla were destroyed and abandoned in the year 67 C.E., and since their outlines are relatively clear, both sites can be used as test cases for this important investigation. At Gamla, the excavation of areas B and D, located on the upper slope at the northeastern edge of the hill, yielded mainly Hellenistic and Hasmonean houses, pottery, and coins. The excavators noted that the number of Hellenistic and Hasmonean pottery and coins decreases as one moves down the hill or continues along the slope to the southwest.

Yodefat

At Yodfat we succeeded in gaining more information. We dated the early wall of the site to the Hasmonean period and identified it as surrounding only the top of the hill, an area of approximately 3 acres. As was mentioned

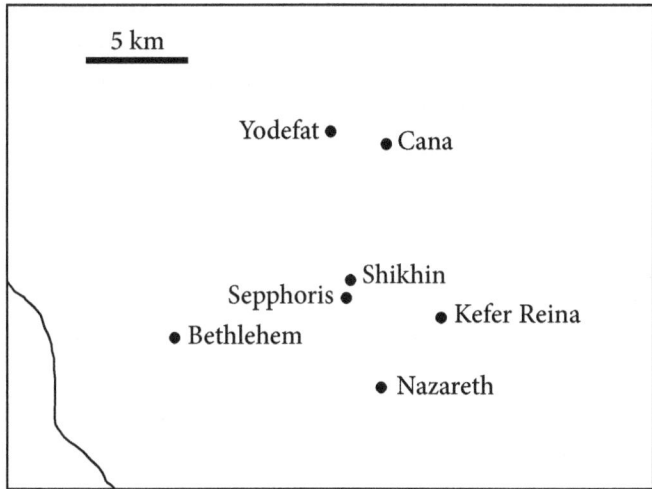

Figure 11. Map 2: Lower Galilee centered around Sepphoris.

---

33. An attempt was made by Liebner (*Settlement and History*) to estimate the size of settlements according to pottery in the survey. In my opinion, this method is good primarily to establish the maximum spread of the site but much less so for estimating the size of the village in its different stages.

earlier, we believe it was a Hasmonean stronghold. Within the frame of this wall we surveyed a specific type of cistern. It has a wide square opening and a spiral fleet of steps along the wall leading down to the bottom. This type of cistern is well known from Hellenistic sites such as Marissa.[34] The second type of cistern probably developed from the first. It has a square opening with only two or three steps, as well as a place to stand when pulling up the vessel after having filled it with water. This type of cistern was found along the second level, outside the Hasmonean wall. The third type is the well-known "bell shaped" cistern. This type is distributed all over the site. I think that one can identify the growth of the town from the top of the hill down: The upper level would include the pre-Hasmonean village, the Hasmonean stronghold, and the Herodian period settlement. The second level would be comprised of the fresco house, which dates to the third quarter of the first century B.C.E. (and which will be described later). Remains dating to the time of Herod Antipas make up the lowest level.

In addition, the present author analyzed the distribution of coins at Yodefat. Areas XIV, XV, and XIX, which are located on the top of the hill, yielded 65 percent Hellenistic coins, 33 percent Hasmonean coins, and only 2 percent Roman period coins. Areas XVI and XI, which are located on the slope (the second level), yielded 31 percent Hellenistic coins, 47.5 percent Hasmonean coins, 12.5 percent Roman coins, and 9 percent other coins. In areas III and VI, which are on the southern plateau (lowest level), there were 12 percent Hellenistic coins, 10.5 percent Hasmonean, 37 percent Roman period coins, and 59 percent other coins. It is very clear, though, that the town developed from the top, along the slopes and to the southern plateau, until its destruction in the year 67 C.E.

The Yodefat excavations[35] reveal the entire formation of a first-century Galilean rural town (fig. 12). The area of the town is about 47 dunams (13 acres), room for about two thousand inhabitants. The houses are simple:

---

34. Amos Kloner, *Maresha Excavations Final Report I: Subterranean Complexes 21, 44, 70* (IAA Reports 17; Jerusalem: Israel Antiquities Authority, 2003), 34–35.

35. The Yodefat excavations were conducted during seven seasons from 1992 to 1997 and directed by Mordechai Aviam with the help of William Scott Green. In the season of 1992, Douglas R. Edwards from the University of Puget Sound was a co-director. In the seasons of 1992–1994, David Adan-Bayewitz from the Bar Ilan University was a co-director. The first preliminary report has been published: David Adan-Bayewitz and Mordechai Aviam, "Iotapa, Josephus and the Siege of 67: Preliminary Report on the 1992–1994 Seasons," *JRA* 10 (1997): 131–65. There is also a summary of the seven seasons in Aviam, *Jews, Pagans and Christians*.

Almost no ashlars were used as building materials and most of the floors are made of packed soil or smoothed rock (only one or two are made of natural pavers, and they are in open courtyards). Two houses include small, simple *miqwāʾôt*. A small, elite community probably occupied the higher eastern slope of the town's hill where they lived in large, beautifully decorated mansions. At this part of the town, which is built on a steep slope, three large and massive terraced walls were built that supported two- or three-story buildings.

Mansion of a Wealthy Family

We excavated a portion of one of these buildings (fig. 13). The walls are covered with beautiful frescoes of the Second Pompeian style, and there are chunks of beautifully designed stucco originating from the upper part of the walls. A unique feature was also uncovered: the floor was covered with frescoes designed as *opus sectile*. The only parallel to such a fresco floor is the painted floor at the early stage (Herodian date) of the *orchestra* at the theater at Caesarea. Similar wall paintings are known mainly in Herodian palaces[36] but also in very rich mansions like the one at Caesarea, beneath the Byzantine period *palestra* of the bathhouse[37] and the wealthy houses on the Western hill of Second Temple period Jerusalem.[38]

Some other finds in this excavated area pointed to a wealthy lifestyle. Many shards of gray "knife-pared" oil lamps (fig. 14), including some parts of a multi-nozzle oil lamp, were found. This type of multi-nuzzle oil lamp is rare in archaeological excavations and considered a luxurious object.[39] A small fragment of a rectangular, stone table, similar to some of those found at Jerusalem, was also found. Until now, no stone table has been published from first-century Galilee.

---

36. See, for example, Herodium: Virgilio C. Corbo, *Herodion, gli edifgice della reggia-fortezza* (Jerusalem: Franciscan Printing Press, 1989) 46, pl. II:1.

37. Yosef Porath, "The Caesarea Excavation Project—March 1992—June 1994: Expedition of the Antiquities Authority," *Excavations and Surveys in Israel* 17 (1998): 39–49.

38. Silvia Rosenberg, "Wall Painting Fragments from Area A," in *The Finds from Areas A, W and X-2: Final Report* (vol. 2 of *Jewish Quarter Excavations in the Old City of Jerusalem Conducted by Nahman Avigad, 1969–1982*; ed. Hillel Geva; Jerusalem: Israel Exploration Society, 2003).

39. Dan Barag and Malka Hershkovitz, "Lamps from Masada," in *Masada IV* (Jerusalem: Israel Exploration Society, 1994), 1–78.

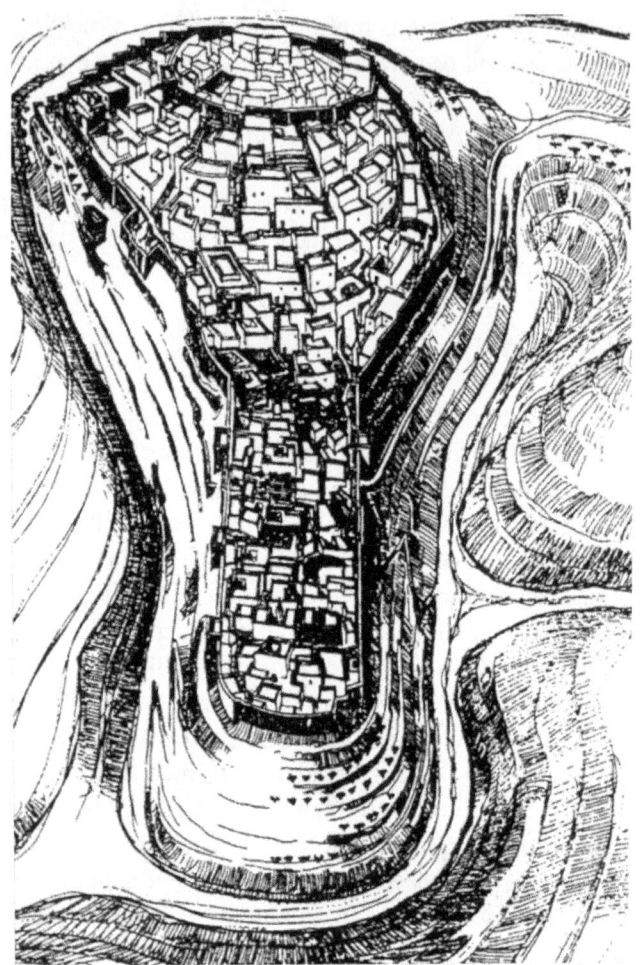

Figure 12. Yodefat, reconstruction by Brian Lalor.

Small Luxury Items

Although not found in the same area, some other objects retrieved from the soil of Yodefat point to wealth in the town. The first is an iron door-key, a type known throughout the Mediterranean from the Roman period. Such a locking device and a key from a locksmith was expensive and implies that there was valuable property to lock behind the door (fig. 15).

The second is a set of two plates of bronze measuring scales coated with zinc (fig. 16). The diameter of each is 8 cm, which would have made

Figure 13. Yodefat, Pompeian house display at the Hecht Museum, University of Haifa. Photo by Mordechai Aviam.

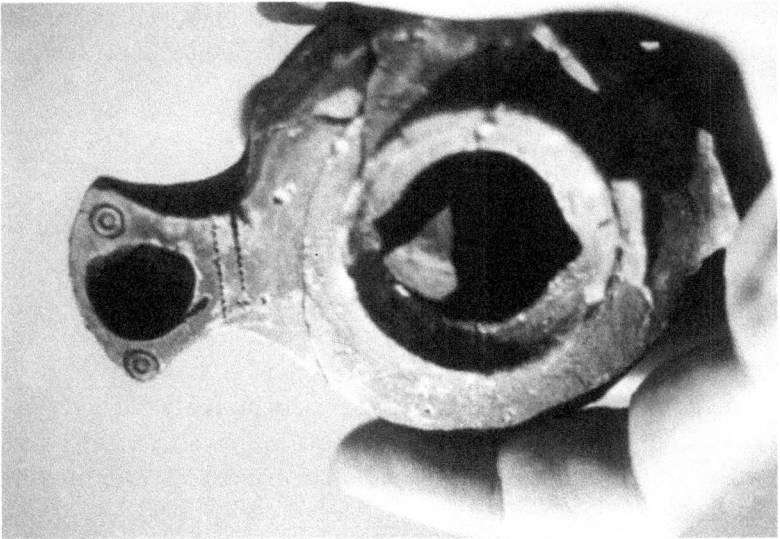

Figure 14. Yodefat, knife-pared lamp. Photo by Mordechai Aviam.

Figure 15. Iron door-key. Photo by Mordechai Aviam.

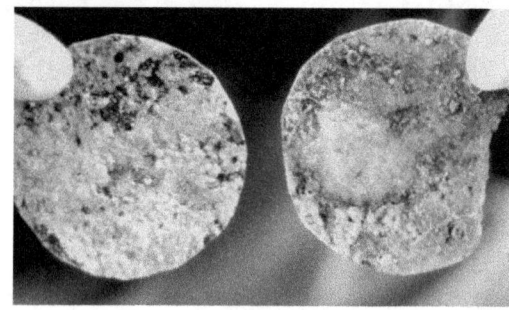

Figure 16. Bronze scales. Photo by Mordechai Aviam.

them most appropriate for use in weighing gems, gold, incense, or expensive powders. The coating, which would have prevented oxidation of the bronze when in contact with the powder, probably suggests that it was used for weighing powders. Two decorated gems which were once inlayed in rings and one golden ring were found as well. Similar finds were made at Gamla: an iron door-key and a few engraved gems.

Industry in Yodefat

Although most of the other houses which were excavated at Yodefat were much more modest, made of field stones or covered with mud plaster and with packed soil or smoothed rock floors, two houses in this area had *miqwāʾôt* in them. These houses, neighboring the town's wall, are located closest to an oil press which was built in a cave on the upper part of the eastern slope. The owners of these houses were probably the operators of the oil press and produced oil in purity (hence the *miqwāʾôt*), a well-known phenomenon in the Second Temple period. A *miqweh* was excavated at the olive-press building at Gamla.

Apart from the olive oil production, two more industries were identified at Yodefat during the excavations. The first is the clothing industry.

Many spindle whorls, as well as a spindle rod, were found in different houses. But what was very impressive was the large number of fired-clay loom weights. More than 250 of these pyramidal loom weights (10–15 cm. in height) were found in and around the destroyed houses. It is the largest number of loom weights ever found in residential areas in the land of Israel from the Roman period. At Gamla for example, where the excavated area is twice as large, only about ninety loom weights were discovered. There is no doubt that this reflects a vigorous home industry of wool materials. Supporting evidence is the analysis of animal bones, made by C. Copp.[40] According to her study, not only are there more sheep bones than goat bones, but most of the sheep were killed at an older age. The bone evidence suggests that sheep were grazed for wool and milk rather than meat only.

The second industry, which was a great surprise, was the potter's quarter, located in the southernmost part of the town. Four pottery kilns were discovered in four excavated squares. The first two kilns are preserved to a very low level, and they are within the frame of a house, probably a courtyard. Among the large amount of potsherds found around the kilns were some wasters of cooking pots.

The third kiln was discovered at the southeastern edge of the town on the beginning of the slope. Because of its location, it was demolished by the builders of the defensive wall, which was erected as preparation for the war against the Romans during the year 67 C.E. There was much pottery in and around the kiln, and some of the sherds were wasters from the potter's work. One of them was the rim of a storage jar, a well-known type in the Galilee during the early Roman period. After the kiln went out of use as a result of the building operation, another small kiln was built beside it. This one was probably never used, as the war and siege came upon the town. It was destroyed and abandoned forever.

The discovery of the "potter's quarter" led to a study of the types of vessels which were produced at the site. In addition to the storage jars mentioned above, there were also different kinds of cooking vessels produced in the town, most of which are identical to the group called "Kefar Hananya ware." It is clear now that during the early Roman period in the Galilee cooking vessels were not produced only at Kefar Hananya, but also

---

40. A report on the animal bones from Yodefat was delivered by Copp to the author. A summary appears in Aviam, *Yodefat: A Case Study*, 214–15.

at Yodefat and probably at other Galilean villages. The potters of Yodefat had a least one advantage over their competitors from Kefar Hananya: they were much closer to the markets of Sepphoris.

Agriculture

In order to better understand the economic life of the inhabitants of Yodefat, and through it that of the entire Galilee, the present author surveyed the entire agricultural territory of Yodefat. First an imaginary line was created, based on topography and the distance to other first-century villages in the vicinity, which was then checked step by step. The first important conclusion was that about half of the land is not arable land. It is rocky, and, for the most part, there are no signs of terracing. This part of the agricultural land was probably used for grazing. Another important observation was that there are many water cisterns in open land, which is very different from many other areas surveyed in the Galilee. I believe that these cisterns were used to keep rain water for the herds, as there is not even one natural spring in the entire territory. Surprisingly, only two rock-cut wine presses were found in this area, and in one of them, the plaster was dated to the Byzantine period, which indicates that wine production was not a central product of the inhabitants of Yodefat.

Gamla

Let us return now briefly to Gamla in the Golan. In the first century C.E., the Golan was under the rule of Herod Phillip and Agrippa, and the volcanic rocks there created different types of agriculture and led to special building methods. However, the discoveries there are important for the purposes of this essay, because the inhabitants were Jews of the same origin and from the same period of settlement as at Yodefat and, when the revolt erupted, the Golan likewise came under the government of Josephus Flavius together with the Galilee.

There are many similarities between the two towns. Gamla was almost twice as large, and all of its houses were built of basalt stones. For this reason, the stones are cut (it is much harder to build walls from basalt field stones than to do it from limestone). In area R, a large and impressive olive press was uncovered with one crushing and two squeezing installations. A house containing two to three large flour mills was unearthed nearby, and it seems as if there were few workshops in this quarter. In the debris of a private house near the olive press, many chunks of frescoed plaster and stucco were found. The fresco is of the same type which was found *in situ* at Yodefat.

Some luxurious objects were also found at Gamla, including a few decorated gems, a door key, and some fragments of a multi-nozzled oil lamp. A hoard of twenty-seven silver coins was found near the olive press and four small golden jewels.

Our summary of the excavations of Yodefat and more briefly of Gamla has shown that villages in Galilee (Yodefat) and Golan (Gamla) could have wealthy persons living in them. The excavations brought to light expensively constructed houses and luxury items. Further, the presence of industries such as olive oil pressing, clothing manufacture, pottery production, and flour milling indicate that the village residents were not simply dependent on farming small plots of ground but were engaged in vigorous trade with other villages and with nearby cities. Archaeology does not confirm the picture of a half-starved peasant as the typical Galilean.

Galilean Religious and Political Beliefs and Behavior

It is sometimes affirmed that the Galileans resented the Judeans and their religious regulations. They disliked, it is stated, sending their tithes to the temple. They felt exploited economically by the wealthy elites in Jerusalem. But were the Galileans generally radicalized and hostile to the wealthy, the Romans, and even the Judeans? Were they "going their own way" in terms of religion and politics? The archaeological data below will show that they were obedient to the Judean political authorities and that they shared the same religious scruples and practices of the Judeans.

Sociopolitical Attitudes

Either at the very end of 66 C.E. or the very beginning of 67, the Jewish rebel "government" in Jerusalem declared a revolt against the Romans by canceling the Roman governorship over the Jewish territories on both sides of the Jordan River (*J.W.* 2.562–568). Jewish governors were appointed, having the authority to collect taxes, establish courts (including the power of life and death) and to build walls and fortify settlements.

Many scholars over the years have hesitated and usually rejected Josephus's description of his activity in the Galilee in which he claims to have fortified nineteen settlements. Some suggested that these events never happened, that there were no fortifications at all, and that Josephus's narrative is a complete fiction. During the last twenty years opinion has slowly changed, but even today, one can sense a touch of hesitation.[41]

We can, however, learn more about the Galilean society in these days through the stone walls of Galilean towns and villages. On the one hand, from Josephus's narrative of Galilean society, we know of a few political/social parties such as the zealots, the group who followed John of Gischala, the party of the sailors and the poor, a group that followed Justus of Tiberias, the people who followed Flavius himself, and, probably, people who did not favor any political party. A crucial point is to determine who the majority were and who established the tone in Galilee.

Of the nineteen settlements in Galilee and Golan which are mentioned by Josephus as being fortified on his orders, both Sepphoris and Gischala (Gush Halav) conducted the work by themselves. Yet no evidence of walls has been found at either site (at Gush Halav, I suggested identification of a protective earth ramp). Two sites in the Golan are not conclusively identified. At one of these, Yehudiya (identified with Sogane), there are some signs of fortifications, but these have not been verified. Clear remains of fortifications were found at Yodefat, Gamla (both excavated and conclusively dated to the revolt), Beer Sheba of the Galilee, Mount Tabor, and Mount Nitai, including the fortified cave on the cliff of Arbel (suggested to be "the caves of Arbel" or "the caves around the Lake Gennesar").

A moat and sparse evidence of walls were found at Zalmon and Meroth. It is evident today that, at about half of the sites that are mentioned by Josephus, we have remains of a serious investment of fortification even if walls from earlier periods were used. In the only two sites on which heavy battles took place, Yodefat and Gamla (which were besieged, conquered, and destroyed), walls were hurriedly built shortly before the war, but it was still a serious operation.

---

41. Liebner says, "Thus Josephus' activity, *if any*..." (*Settlement and Pattern*, 341). Liebner is minimizing the finds at Yodefat in an attempt to put the weight on the earlier fortifications. In my study on Yodefat (*Yodefat: A Case Study*, 43–61) I tried to pinpoint and prove that the wall, which is about 1 km long, was built for (and only a short time before) the war. But in the north, it is built on earlier, Hasmonean foundations. Even there, however, it was fixed and reorganized. So is the case at Gamla. The only earlier, possible fortification is the round tower at the upper part of the wall.

At Yodefat, the total length of the wall is more than 1 km, and at Gamla it is about 200 m. At Mount Nitai, the wall is about 120 meters long, and on top of Mount Tabor, it is more than two kilometers. Even if these fortifications were built on earlier foundations, reconstructing, strengthening, and arranging them for an actual defense was not a simple task. It was not an act of farmers or even the organization of the village or town by itself. Such a task must be organized, financed and executed by a central authority and leadership, and the only candidate for it is Josephus Flavius. Although Josephus is trying to show in his account of the war that he is the "initiator" and the "inventor" of this fortifying system, it seems clear that it was the order of the revolutionary government in Jerusalem that initiated the wall building and that each one of the governors appointed to the different districts operated the same way. One of the best indications of such organization is the fortification of Machairos in Transjordan, where the village was surrounded with a wall and the citadel, the Hasmonean-Herodian palace, was reorganized for the war.

The fact that at least half of the sites have yielded archaeological evidence for the fortification process proves that most of the Galileans collaborated with Josephus. The fortified sites are spread from the Golan (Gamla and possibly Yehudiya) to the eastern Galilee (Mount Nitai), as well as to central (Mount Tabor and Beer Sheba) and western Galilee (Yodefat). Josephus traveled in the Galilee, as its governor, from Tiberias in the east to Yodefat in the west, and even visited at Gabara, which collaborated with John of Gush Halav.

In salvage excavations at Qiryat Ata, new evidence recently came to light which was identified by D. Barag (and supported by me) as Kafrata of Josephus Flavius. In the excavations, evidence for first-century Jewish life was provided by the discovery of some stoneware vessels and possibly the remains of the wall.[42] These finds at Qiryat Ata, and my confirmation of Barag's identification, stretch the Jewish territory even farther southwest to the edge of the Acco Plain.

RELIGIOUS BEHAVIOR AND CONNECTION TO JERUSALEM

The archaeological discoveries during the last twenty-five to thirty years in the Galilee shed new and important light on the religious behavior of the

---

42. Barag, personal communication.

Galileans and the place of Jerusalem and the temple in their daily activities.

Ritual Baths (*Miqwā'ōt*)

We have already discussed the introduction of the *miqwā'ōt* installations into the Galilee—at Qeren Naftali, Gamla, and Sepphoris—after the Hasmonean annexation. From that time on, these installations became part of the daily life of Galileans. First century *miqwā'ōt* were found at the city of Sepphoris, the towns of Gamla and Yodefat, the villages of Cana, Iblin, Nazareth, and Yaphia, the cliffs of Arbel, and even in tiny villages or farmsteads such as Mount Kamon, Bet Zarzir, and, most recently, Suaed Humeira, above the Zippori stream on the western edge of Lower Galilee.

This wide distribution of *miqwā'ōt* in cities, villages, and even in hamlets or farmsteads clearly tells us that religious purification in water was a very common practice in Galilee, just as it was in Judea. The presence of the installations may also point to a measure of wealth, since poor people did not have the ability to build *miqwā'ōt*. The existence of *miqwā'ōt* near olive presses at Yodefat and Gamla points to another important religious practice: producing oil in purity. The oil was probably manufactured in purity for Jews who ate their daily food in purity. This kind of religious custom was very common in Jerusalem society and probably spread all over the Jewish territory during the last decades of the Second Temple period. The Galilee took part in it as well.

Stoneware Vessels

The discovery of stone vessels in the Galilee is probably another indication of the religious behavior of Galilean Jews. Dozens of sherds of stoneware vessels were discovered at Yodefat as well as at Gamla. Most of the vessels are cups, small and large, some of which are pitchers (fig. 17). The second type of vessel is the semi-global bowls. The large, tall containers, called the *kallal*, are missing from the repertoire at both sites but they were found at Sepphoris and at Kefar Otnai (Legio). What is even more important is the discovery of local workshops for the production of stoneware vessels. Two had been known for some years as a result of the discovery of quantities of stone cup cores which were found at Bethlehem of the Galilee and near the village of Reina. But some five years ago, a cave was discovered northeast of Nazareth containing hundreds of stone cup cores. Since the excavations

Figure 17. Stone cups from Yodefat. Photo by Mordechai Aviam.

were very limited and have not yet been published, the cave awaits further study. Probably the stone containers were not used as daily vessels. As a matter of fact, there are no parallels for these shapes among known clay vessels, which suggests their identification as cultic vessels.

The mugs could be used for washing hands before meals,[43] but since the mugs and cups with spouts are designed to pour liquids slowly (the handle and the spout are arranged perpendicularly), I suggest that they were used to fill up the oil lamps (see below). The capacity of the small pitchers is similar to the capacity of regular clay oil lamps and the capacity of the large pitchers is similar to large lamps or multi-nozzle lamps.

The bowls are ancient drinking vessels. Berlin showed that there were some changes in the dining behavior from first century B.C.E. to first century C.E. at Gamla[44] and one of the changes was fewer pottery drinking bowls and more use of stone bowls. At Yodefat in the first century C.E., we have similar numbers of clay and stone drinking bowls. As stone vessels are much more expensive, I think it is more logical to assume that the stone bowls were used for sacred drinking (e.g., wine with the Shabbat meal).

Oil Lamps

An interesting result came to light during the study of the oil lamps found at Yodefat. There were only three types of oil lamps in use at Yodefat during

---

43. Berlin, *Gamla I*, 150–51.
44. Berlin, *Gamla I*, 133–56.

the first century c.e. The first is the "discus" lamp, which is the common type in most of the Gentile cities, such as Dor.[45] Of this type, only five fragments were found, representing 1.7 percent of all lamps. The second is a local type, presumably manufactured at the site, but known from other Galilean sites. It has the shape of a boot with a high rim around the eye of the lamp. This type is already known as a Galilean type,[46] and it accounts for 19.6 percent of all Yodefat lamps. The third is the "knife-pared" or "Herodian" oil lamp (see fig. 14 above), which is well known all over Israel and Transjordan and dated to 25 b.c.e.–125 c.e.[47] Similar data came from Gamla. When we carried out a petrographic analysis on some of these lamps, the results showed that all of them were made in Jerusalem. It was not the first time such results had come to light,[48] but the percentage was a great surprise, since the oil lamps in the "Jerusalem" group amounted to 78 percent of all lamps, which is similar to the situation at Gamla!

Why did the residents of Yodefat and Gamla use such a high percentage of Jerusalem lamps? There is no better reason for such a phenomenon than a Halakhic or religious explanation. Their frequency of use has to do with religious scruples. I would like also to suggest that there was a mystical, emotional, and spiritual connection between the holiness of Jerusalem and light. For Jews, Jerusalem and the temple at its center were the light of life and were symbolized by the flame rising from the candle's spout; it could even represent the light from the menorah in the temple. Although the Galilean Jewish potters produced oil lamps by themselves and could easily have manufactured knife-pared oil lamps, they preferred importing them in vast quantities from Jerusalem.

In 2008 Adan-Bayewitz and others published a large, detailed, and learned article in which they chemically checked knife-pared oil lamps from Jewish and non-Jewish sites, especially in the north, and proved, from another point of view and another field of science, that the majority of the knife-pared oil lamps in the northern Jewish towns and cities

---

45. Renate Rosenthal-Heginbottom, "Imported Hellenistic and Roman Pottery," in *Excavations at Dor, Final Report IB (Qedem Reports 2)* (ed. Ephraim Stern; Jerusalem: Israel Exploration Society, 1995), 183–250, esp. 243.

46. Varda Zussman, "The Lamp," *Atiqot* 19 (1990): 97–98.

47. Barag and Hershkovitz, "Lamps from Masada," 24–58.

48. Jan Gunneweg and Isadore Perlman, "The Origin of the Herodian Lamp," *BAIAS* 3 (1984): 79–83.

came from Jerusalem.[49] As one of their final conclusions, they suggested, as I have, that the reason for importing Jerusalem oil lamps was religious. They propose that it was used as "Erev Shabbat," or Friday evening, light. It is a reasonable suggestion, but it does not make a lot of sense to import almost 80 percent of your lamps from Jerusalem if you use them on only one night out of every seven. Therefore, I see the popularity of the Jerusalem lamps as being connected with a more regular daily (or nightly) activity that involves the religious and spiritual place of light. It is also interesting to note that almost all of the oil lamps found in first to second century Jewish tombs are of the "knife-pared" type. In this case, people are being buried or brought for burial in the holy light of the temple and the holy city.

Coins

As Syon has pointed out, Hasmonean coins were found on the living surfaces of both Yodefat and Gamla, as well as on other floors of dwellings dated to the first century C.E.[50] It seems as if these old coins were still in circulation at the time of the First Revolt. This was probably an inner Jewish circulation, and by using these historic, nationalistic coins, Jews could keep among themselves not only memories from more "glorious" days, but also coins which carried with them some "fragrances" of holiness from Jerusalem, their minting place.

The Gamla coin demonstrates to a high degree the relationship between daily life, money, secularity, nationalism, and holiness. Samples of this unique Revolt coin were found only at Gamla (with one exception, probably carried away by refugees of the town). On one side it bears a Paleo-Hebrew inscription of *lg'lt* ("for the redemption") and on the other side *yršlm hq...* ("holy Jerusalem"). According to Gutman and Syon,[51] it was minted at Gamla, one of the last fortified towns that stood in the north against Vespasian's troops, as a nationalistic slogan that connects the Galileans directly to the safe redemption and holiness of Jerusalem and the temple.

---

49. David Adan-Bayewitz, Frank Asaro, Moshe Wieder, and Robert Giauque, "Preferential Distribution of Lamps from the Jerusalem Area in the Late Second Temple Period (Late First Century B.C.E.–70 C.E.)," *BASOR* 350 (2008): 37–85.
50. Syon, *Tyre and Gamla*, 116–22.
51. Gutman, *Gamla*; Syon, *Tyre and Gamla*.

Burials

A surprise was waiting for us, the excavators of Yodefat, in two of the ancient cisterns in the town. At the bottom of the first one, surrounded by a low, one-course wall, was a heap of human bones and skulls. Our anthropologist concluded that these were not articulated skeletons but rather a heap of gathered bones of a man, a woman, and a child. As it was in one of the first seasons of excavation, we did not yet know how to interpret this find.

It was only after the second dig in another cistern that we came to a full understanding of this discovery. While digging in this large cistern, we discovered the top of a simple, thin wall, and behind it we uncovered a large heap of gathered human bones. Our anthropologist identified the bones of some twenty different humans, most of whom were children of different ages, but also adults, both men and women. Two of the skulls carried marks of blows, probably by a heavy object that could have caused their deaths. Some tibia bones bore cut marks, perpendicular to the bone, typical of someone trying to defend himself from a striking sword.

Since the bones were gathered together, surrounded by a wall and the entire cistern was filled with debris that was dated no later than the first century C.E., we could prove that these were the bones of the people of Yodefat, either natives or refugees from neighboring villages who found shelter behind the walls of the town. They were all killed or died during the siege of the summer of 67 C.E. In some cases we discovered scattered human bones on the floor of the destroyed houses.

While digging the "fresco house," on its fresco floor, we found the leg bones of an adult male surrounded by arrowheads (see reconstruction in fig. 13). We had questions regarding who the bones belonged to and when they were buried. Since there was not even one complete skeleton found in the cistern or in the destroyed houses, since the bones were collected and organized in the cisterns, and since we have evidence that they were killed by violent acts, we can be sure that when the town was conquered with its heavy massacre, the Romans punished the people of Yodefat and the Galileans and sought to generate fear in the other fortified towns by not letting the survivors bury their dead. The Romans probably knew the importance of burial in the Jewish religion and used it as a punishment.

Because burial is such an important religious duty, the Jewish residents returned in order to carry it out. We cannot say exactly when, but a year or two after the destruction, Jews came back, searched among the debris, collected the bones (mainly skulls and long bones), went down into the empty cisterns, piled up the bones, surrounded them with a wall, and filled the cistern with soil and stones. This was an act of emergency burial.

On the importance of burial we can learn not only from the Torah and Talmud but also from the description of Josephus himself during the revolt. In *Jewish War* 3.27–28, there is the story about the Jewish commander Niger of Peraea, who lost a battle and took shelter in a cave while the fort in which he was hiding earlier was set on fire. He was saved and trapped in the cave, while he could hear his friends who were "looking for his corpse for burial." On the other hand, during the civil war in Jerusalem, the fighting factions prevented their rivals from burying their dead. Josephus writes: "in their impiety as to cast out the corpses without burial, although the Jews are so careful about funeral rites that even malefactors who have been sentenced to crucifixion are taken down and buried before sunset" (*J.W.* 4.316–317).

Synagogues

The topic of first-century synagogues was for many years heavily debated among scholars. Yet in the last twenty years the debate lost its intensity as slowly more and more buildings from this period identified as synagogues have been discovered. However, because only one synagogue has been found in the north (at Gamla; fig. 18), some scholars raised questions as to whether the building at Gamla is a unique phenomenon and, as such, is not a synagogue. Where are the other Galilean synagogues? For years, I have been claiming that finding a synagogue in the Galilee is only a question of "archaeological luck," which is connected with the number of excavations being carried out in the region.

If we take Masada and Qiryat Sefer as models of the Second Temple period's synagogues, then there is no doubt that the building at Gamla is a synagogue: it is a large, public building, the gathering people sat along the walls facing the center, and there is a niche in the wall, presumably to house a wooden closet containing the Torah scrolls.

An important discovery was made in 2009 at the ancient site of Migdal. In a salvage excavation by the IAA, a first-century synagogue was unearthed—the first to be found in Galilee. Migdal is a well-known site of historical significance in Galilee. It is mentioned in Josephus and hinted at in the New Testament. This square building with benches around the walls has a footpath, part of which is paved with a mosaic floor, along with walls and pillars covered with frescoes.⁵² The central floor is made of pebbles. If this was the original floor, it was probably covered with rugs or mats. To the west, there is another room with benches that could be used as a smaller study room, similar to the one at Gamla. In the center of the building, standing on the floor on four small legs, is a rectangular stone decorated on the top and on all four sides (fig. 19). This is a unique stone with no parallels in the Jewish archaeology and art of the first century or later.

A closer look at the photos shows that at the four corners of the surface of the stone, there are rough areas which look like places where four legs once stood, whether they were of a wooden table resting on the stone, or whether they were part of the stone and later broke off. In my opinion, this stone served as a base for the Torah reading table.⁵³

The two long sides are decorated with what seems to be an arched colonnade, probably with two rows of columns, one inside the other (fig. 20). At the beginning of each row is a hanging object, which the excavator identifies as an oil lamp. The surface of the stone is completely covered with a group of objects (fig. 21). Six of them are designed as ivy leaves, each pair in different sizes. Six are of geometric design, and they surround a central large rosette in a circle. On both sides of the rosette, there are two objects interpreted by the excavator as palm trees. I would like to suggest that this is a representation of objects from the temple. The surface may represent the table of showbread itself. The twelve objects could represent the twelve showbread loaves. The two objects on both sides are not trees but rather tools like shovels or the *magrefa*. It is possible that the rosette represents another dish on the table or a significant symbol. In this way, the entire rectangular stone, standing on four legs as a base for the Torah reading table, depicts and represents the table of showbread in the temple and the temple itself. The back side of the stone presents the holy of holies.

---

52. The description of the building and its design, as well as the discussion of the decorated stone is from the website of the IAA, lectures given by the excavator Dina Avshalom-Gorni, as well as many websites: "Ancient Hebrew Design," *The Bible Illustration Blog* (February 12, 2011); online: http://bibleillustration.blogspot.com/; Jeffrey Garcia, "The Excavations at Magdala," *Helek Tov* (November 28, 2010); online: http://t0.gstatic.com/images?q=tbn:ANd9GcS0spuy5m5Xqum-lmMcOAEzOtqq7d8gXXSOcMU1iWy-4JEKnczv&t=1. See also http://www.youtube.com/watch?v=VX83jUdeKSE; http://www.lomdim.org.il/photos?album=Migdal.

53. For a full and comprehensive discussion of the decoration of the stone, see, M. Aviam, "The Decorated Stone from the Synagogue at Migdal," *NovT.* 55.4 (2013) (forthcoming).

Figure 18. Gamla synagogue. Photograph by David Fiensy.

Figure 19. Stone table (back side), Migdal. Photo by Mordechai Aviam from the replica.

Figure 20. Side of stone table, Migdal. Drawing by D. Shalem from photos of the replica.

Figure 21. Surface of stone table, Migdal. Drawing by D. Shalem from photos of the replica.

As there was nothing in this room in the Second Temple but the divine spirit, the representation is of the divine chariot, well known from both the Bible and the Apocrypha. Below the wheels are the flames of fire. This is the earliest appearance in Jewish art of this biblical description.

The façade of the stone is the most interesting. In the center, there is an eight-branch menorah standing on what looks like a high platform, flanked by two vases, and they are all in an architectonic frame of two pillars and an arch. I tend to believe that this is a representation of the temple with the menorah inside it. I also believe that the square object at the bottom of the menorah is not a platform but rather a representation of the golden altar. The scene here is the inside of the temple, and it is similar to the representation of these objects in the incised depiction of the temple found in the Jewish Quarter in Jerusalem.[54] The surface probably represents the table of showbread (fig. 22). If this is the case, the full arcade on the sides represent the temple, and the inner arcade on the sides could represent the holy of holies inside the temple.

This is the only first-century menorah found thus far engraved on a stone and the only one from Jerusalem. It is very clear that this stone, whether it was a base for a reading table or was used for other purposes, had an important role in the worship of that synagogue. It no doubt reflects the strong spiritual and physical connections between Galilean Jews and the temple in Jerusalem.

It is also important to note that although the plan of first-century synagogues in Israel—and especially the two of the north, Gamla and Migdal—are alike, there are also some interesting differences. The synagogue at Gamla is much bigger, is built of good ashlars, and had some architecturally decorated fragments but no remains of fresco or mosaic. The one at Migdal is smaller and is decorated with frescoes and mosaics. These differences could be the results of financial investments and urban status.

Summary

This essay has surveyed the archaeological discoveries in the Galilee from the fourth to third centuries B.C.E. to the first century C.E. (a period of more

---

54. Li-hi Habas, "An Incised Depiction of the Temple Menorah and Other Cult Objects of the Second Temple Period," in Geva, *The Finds From Areas A, W and X-2: Final Report*.

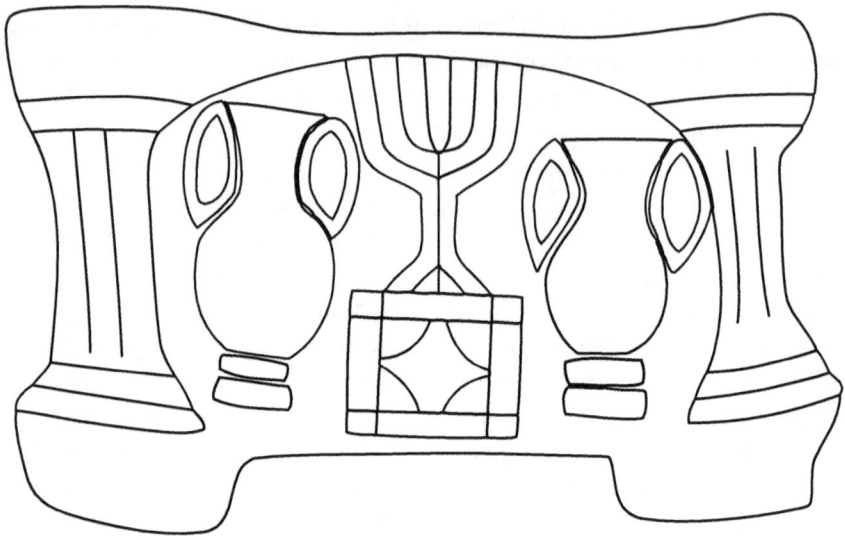

Figure 22. Façade of stone table, Migdal. Drawing by D. Shalem from photos of the replica.

than four hundred years), from large cities such as Acco-Ptolemais, Sepphoris, and Tiberias to small villages or farmsteads such as Mount Kamon, Suaied Hummeir, and Bet Zarzir. A rise in interest in Galilean archaeology, along with an increase in the number of archaeological excavations—especially the large excavations at Gamla and Yodefat, along with those of Tiberias, Sepphoris, and Migdal—has brought to light a great deal of information.

The seeds of the foundation of first-century Galilean Jewry were sown with the Hasmonean conquest. I have attempted to show that there is archaeological evidence for this stage, including:

- the destruction and later abandonment of the administrative center at Qedesh;
- the abandonment of the temple at Mizpe Hayamim and the desecration of its sacred objects;
- the destruction layer at Yodefat and the erection of a Hasmonean wall above it;
- the abandonment of many of the small sites which contained GCW pottery; and
- the appearance of Hasmonean coins throughout the territory of

Galilee (except for the western side, where Acco-Ptolemais, which was not defeated, continued to hold some of the hinterland).

Jews of the Galilee were mostly immigrants from Judea, probably settled by the Hasmonean authorities who subsidized their move into the newly occupied territories. As a result, the Galileans viewed themselves as strong supporters of the Hasmoneans. As such, they resisted Herod the Great and revolted against him, as reflected in the story of Arbel and the discoveries at Qeren Naftali. The Hasmoneans laid the foundations for a strong and solid Jewish Galilee, as reflected by the massive number of settlements mentioned by Josephus Flavius (204 villages, towns, and cities).[55]

I suggested that the archaeological evidence indicates that as a result of the Galilean Jews' attitude toward Herod, he denied them any royal investments. This situation completely changed at the time of Herod Antipas. Investments were made in the first capital city, Sepphoris, and vast investments were again made later in establishing a new capital at Tiberias, dedicated to the emperor but built for Jews. Taxes now flowed not only to Jerusalem for impressive and monumental projects in Judea and for building projects outside of the territory of Israel, but were now invested directly in the Galilee. Utilizing the new evidence from Yodefat and Gamla, I have tried to show that the second wave of Galilean development after the Hasmonean period was during the time of Herod Antipas.

The results of the excavations at Yodefat and Gamla prove that villages in the Galilee were not poor. Galilean villagers were not peasants. Both poor people and rich people lived in cities, towns, and villages. The only place where Josephus mentions poor people is in a city, at Tiberias. He observed that the houses in the small village of Kabul (Chabulon) were "built in the style of those at Tyre, Sidon and Beirut" (*J.W.* 2.503–504). The excavators at Gamla and Yodefat did not discover evidence of poverty (which would probably be very hard to find anyway). Within the walls of Yodefat, in the excavated houses, one gets the impression of a town populated by middle to upper-middle class persons. Wealth might be recog-

---

55. Although there have been many scholars over the years who have disputed Josephus's counting of settlements, H. Ben David succeeded in proving that the number of settlements mentioned by Josephus was probably very realistic; H. Ben David, "Were There 204 Settlements in Galilee at the Time of Josephus Flavius?" *JJS* 62 (2011): 21–36.

nized by the existence of *miqwāʾōt* similar to those found in the houses in Jerusalem. The association of *miqwāʾōt* with olive presses places these producers on a higher level of the social hierarchy of first-century society. The olive press at Gamla, as well as the flour mill, are part of unit 5050, in which white decorated stucco was found, pointing to a residence of high socioeconomic rank. But even wealthier was unit 1900 at Gamla, just west of the olive press, in which chunks of frescoes were found, similar to the frescoes at Yodefat. These houses belonged to very rich families. These families lived in small and large towns in Galilee and Golan and probably in the cities as well. No one should affirm today that "townsmen were rich and villagers were poor peasants."

Galilean villagers in the mountains, such as at Yodefat, were entrepreneurs. In an attempt to overcome the inferiority of the land, they developed some occupations that could increase their income, as in the case of the potters of Yodefat and the wool/clothing production.

The reconstruction of the socioeconomic pyramid in the Galilean society according to archaeological finds places the wool workers (evidenced by the spindle and spindle whorls), weavers (evidenced by the loom weights), and potters (evidenced by the kilns, potter's wheel, and wasters) at the bottom. Owners of shops and workshops (evidenced by the flourmill and olive presses) formed the next socioeconomic level. The owners of the fresco houses formed uppermost level of the pyramid. Who were these people at the top of the pyramid? Josephus tells us that Gamla was the home of Phillipus, son of Jacimus, chief of staff of King Agrippa. This is the kind of family, I would assume, that could live in an elegant mansion such as the one found at Yodefat. High officials, tax collectors, and oligarchic families are the most likely candidates for having built and lived in such houses in villages, towns and cities.

Were Galileans more rebellious, zealous, and radical than Jews in other parts of ancient Israel? If they were, they represented only a few individuals. Can one establish such a conclusion based on archaeological evidence? Drawing on the archaeological evidence for Josephus's fortified towns and cities, I sought to show that such a large-scale operation cannot take place without the wide support of the inhabitants. Josephus's narrative of his travels in Galilee, together with the evidence for construction of fortifications, seem to me to prove that most of the Galileans shared an approach to the revolt similar to that of Josephus, as did the rebel government in Jerusalem, and as did the majority of people in Judea and Peraea. Galileans were no different.

Thanks to archaeological discoveries, we can better understand the Galileans' religious behavior and attitude toward the temple and Jerusalem. As I showed above, *miqwāʾôt* arrived in the Galilee immediately after their appearance in the Hasmonean period, probably together with the conquering armies and as part of the transformation of the Galilee into a completely Jewish land. Shortly after that, sometime at the end of the first century B.C.E., stone vessels appeared in the Galilee and began to be manufactured there, probably very close to the beginning of their production in Jerusalem. Hasmonean coins were in intensive use from the days of the conquest, as were Herodian coins from Jerusalem. Local minting started with Herod Antipas, and these coins bore no human images on them. These imageless coins coincide with an absence of figurative oil lamps. The Galileans kept the second commandment as strictly as the Judeans. In some sites, there is evidence for clear preference of local pottery production on imported vessels, which could hint at some kind of religious motive. The evidence for Galilee's strong connection to Jerusalem is very important for understanding the Galilean's world in the first century.

If the above analysis is correct in that the massive import and use of Jerusalem oil lamps in the Galilee is the result of religious conviction, then this provides a significant contribution to our understanding of the behavior and beliefs of the Galilean people, a subject for which there is little written evidence. Similarly, the stone from the synagogue at Migdal may tell us a great deal about Galilean religious values. Our understanding of Second Temple period synagogues is that they were community gathering places mainly for reading the Torah. This religious custom, although not part of the temple cult, was nevertheless observed at the temple, while Torah reading was the central focus of the synagogues. The connection between the synagogue and the temple through Torah reading is, I think, well exhibited in the stone table (found at Migdal), which was used as a reading table. The synagogue and the Torah scroll, which were surely a part of daily life for at least some of Migdal's residents, symbolize the strong connection to the temple and to its cult.

I would say that the entire collection of archeological discoveries in the last thirty years sheds new and very important light on the Galileans during the Second Temple period, and this light should lead to new ways of studying, researching, and understanding the historical sources.

Bibliography

Adan-Bayewitz, David. *Common Pottery in Roman Galilee.* Ramat-Gan, Israel: Bar-Ilan University Press, 1996–1997.

———. "The Tannaitic List of 'Walled Cities' and the Archaeological-Historical Evidence from Iotapata and Gamla" [Hebrew]. *Tarbiz* 66 (1993): 449–70.

Adan Bayewitz, David, Frank Asaro, Moshe Wieder, and Robert Giauque. "Preferential Distribution of Lamps from the Jerusalem Area in the Late Second Temple Period (Late First Century B.C.E.–70 C.E.)." *BASOR* 350 (2008): 37–85.

Adan-Bayewitz, David, and Mordechai Aviam. "Iotapata, Josephus and the Siege of 67: Preliminary Report on the 1992–94 Seasons." *Journal of Roman Archaeology* 10 (1997): 131–65.

Aviam, Mordechai. "The Galilee, the Hellenistic to Byzantine Periods." *NEAEHL* 2:453–58.

———. *Jews, Pagans and Christians in the Galilee.* Rochester, N.Y.: University of Rochester, 2004.

———. "Yodefat, a Case Study in the Development of the Jewish Settlement in the Galilee During the Second Temple Period." PhD diss., Bar Ilan University, 2005.

Aviam, Mordechai, and Aharoni Amitai. "Excavations at Khirbet esh-Shuhara" [Hebrew]. *Eretz Zafon* (2002): 119–34.

Barag, Dan, and Malka Hershkovitz. "Lamps from Masada." Pages 1–78 in *Masada IV.* Jerusalem: Israel Exploration Society, 1994.

Ben David, H. "Were There 204 Settlements in Galilee at the Time of Josephus Flavius?" *JJS* 62 (2011): 21–36.

Berlin, Andrea M. *Gamla I: The Pottery of the Second Temple Period.* IAA Reports 29. Jerusalem: Israel Antiquities Authority, 2006.

Corbo, Virgilio C. *Herodion, gli edifice della reggia-fortezza.* Jerusalem: Franciscan Printing Press, 1989.

De Luca, Stefano. "La città ellenistico-romana di Magdala/Taricheae. Gli scavi del Magdala Project 2007 e 2008: relazione preliminare e prospettive di indagine." *LA* 49 (2010): 343–562.

Edwards, Douglas R., and C. Thomas McCollough. *Archaeology and the Galilee.* Atlanta: Scholars Press, 1997.

Fischer, Moshe. "Yavneh-Yam. 1992–1999—Interim Report" [Hebrew]. *Qadmoniot* 123 (2002): 2–11.

Frankel, Rafael. "The Sanctuary from the Persian Period at Mizpe Yamim" [Hebrew]. *Qadmoniot* 113 (1997): 46–53.

Frankel, Rafael, Nimrod Getzov, Mordechai Aviam, and Avi Degani. *Settlement Dynamics and Regional Diversity in Ancient Upper Galilee: Archaeological Survey of Upper Galilee.* Jerusalem: Israel Antiquities Authority, 2001.

Gunneweg, Jan, and Isadore Perlman. "The Origin of the Herodian Lamp." *BAIAS* 3 (1984–1985): 79–83.

Gutman, Shemaryahu. *Gamla: A City in Rebellion* [Hebrew]. Tel Aviv: Miśrad ha-biṭaḥon, 1994.

Habas, Li-hi. "An Incised Depiction of the Temple Menorah and Other Cult Objects of the Second Temple Period." Pages 329–342 in *The Finds from Areas A, W and X-2: Final Report.* Vol. 2 of *Jewish Quarter Excavations in the Old City of Jerusalem Conducted by Nahman Avigad, 1969–1982.* Edited by Hillel Geva. Jerusalem: Israel Exploration Society, 2003.

Hartal, Moshe. "Tiberias." *Hadashot Arkheologiyot—Excavations and Surveys in Israel* 122 (2010). Online: http://www.hadashot-esi.org.il/report_detail.asp?id=1574&mag_id=117.

———. "Tiberias, Galei Kinneret." *Hadashot Arkheologiyot—Excavations and Surveys in Israel* 120 (2008). Online: http://www.hadashot-esi.org.il/report_detail_eng.asp?id=773&mag_id=114.

Herbert, Sharon C., and Andrea M. Berlin. "A New Administrative Center for Persian and Hellenistic Galilee: Preliminary Report of the University of Michigan/University of Minnesota Excavations at Kedesh." *BASOR* 329: (2003): 13–59.

Horsley, R. A. *Archaeology, History and Society in Galilee.* Valley Forge, Pa.: Trinity Press International, 1996.

Jensen, Morten Hørning. *Herod Antipas in Galilee.* Tübingen: Mohr Siebeck, 2006.

Kloner, Amos. *Maresha Excavations Final Report I. Subterranean Complexes 21, 44, 70.* IAA Reports 17. Jerusalem: Israel Antiquities Authority, 2003.

Liebner, Uzi. *Settlement and History in Hellenistic, Roman, and Byzantine Galilee.* Tübingen: Mohr Siebeck, 2009.

Mazor, Gabriel, and Walid Atrash. *Nysa-Scythopolis: The Southern and Severan Theatres. Final Report. Bet She'an 3.* IAA Reports. Jerusalem: Israel Antiquities Authority, Forthcoming.

Porath, Yosef. "The Caesarea Excavation Project—March 1992–June 1994: Expedition of the Antiquities Authority." *Excavations and Surveys in Israel* 17 (1998): 39–49.

Richardson, Peter. *Herod, King of the Jews and Friend of the Romans.* Columbia: University of South Carolina Press, 1996.

Rosenberg, Silvia. "Wall Painting Fragments from Area A." Pages 303–28 in *The Finds from Areas A, W and X-2: Final Report.* Vol. 2 of *Jewish Quarter Excavations in the Old City of Jerusalem Conducted by Nahman Avigad, 1969–1982.* Edited by Hillel Geva. Jerusalem: Israel Exploration Society, 2003.

Rosenthal-Heginbottom, Renate. "Imported Hellenistic and Roman Pottery." Pages 183–250 in *Excavations at Dor, Final Report IB (Qedem Reports 2).* Edited by Ephraim Stern. Jerusalem: Institute of Archaeology, 1995.

Stern, Ephraim. *The Material Culture of the Land of the Bible in the Persian Period.* Jerusalem: The Bialik Institute and the Israel Exploration Society, 1973.

Syon, Danny. "Coins from the Excavations at Khirbet esh-Shuhara." *Eretz Zafon* (2002): 123–34.

———. "Tyre and Gamla: A study in the Monetary Influence of Southern Phoenicia on Galilee and the Golan in the Hellenistic and Roman Periods." Ph.D. diss., Hebrew University of Jerusalem, 2004.

Tsuk, Tsvika. "The Aqueducts to Sepphoris." M.A. thesis, Tel Aviv University, 1985.

Weiss, Zeev. "Josephus and Archaeology on the Cities of the Galilee." Pages 387–414 in *Making History: Josephus and Historical Method.* Edited by Zuleika Rodgers. Leiden: Brill, 2007.

Zussman, Varda. "The Lamp." *Atiqot* 19 (1990): 97–98.

2
City and Village in Lower Galilee: The Import of the Archeological Excavations at Sepphoris and Khirbet Qana (Cana) for Framing the Economic Context of Jesus

C. Thomas McCollough

My archaeological efforts have focused on the city of Sepphoris and the village of Khirbet Qana (Cana), which stand some 10 km apart from one another on the eastern and western flanks of the Bet Netofah Valley. This paper focuses on the material culture recovered from these two sites in Lower Galilee.[1] In brief, the material culture that I review buttresses the complex picture of village life that has emerged from the work of Mordechai Aviam and lends further support for the notion that the first stages of the urbanization of Galilee did more to invigorate rather than eviscerate the village economy. Our evidence from Sepphoris argues for an unpretentious urban space in the first decades of the first century C.E. The evidence from Khirbet Qana presents a village growing and thriving in ways similar to Yodefat, with the addition of a public building that is arguably a synagogue. The ceramic and coin profiles from the village suggest a pattern of complementarity in village industry and the outlines of a coherent economic and cultural integration in the early decades of the first century in Lower Galilee. The evidence suggests that villages could

---

1. Having been engaged in archaeological excavations of urban and village sites in Lower Galilee for over twenty years, I have come to know well and have deep respect for the work of Mordechai Aviam. It is, therefore, a real pleasure to put the data I have had a role in recovering and analyzing in dialogue with that which Aviam offers in terms of the issues surrounding the Roman economy of Galilee.

The Urban Dimension: Sepphoris

benefit from, without being overwhelmed by, the arrival of Rome and its urban structures.

I begin with the urban side of the interaction by focusing on Sepphoris, the site chosen by Herod Antipas to build a city from which he could rule Galilee. The results of the excavations of this city have been frequently referenced if only partially revealed. My interest is not to review the whole of the material remains but rather to offer a few images and reflections on architectural elements that I have been involved in uncovering and analyzing and that have implications for assessing the Roman economy of Lower Galilee.

The first of these architectural features is the *Cardo Maximus*, which the University of South Florida excavations as well as the Hebrew University excavations exposed (fig. 1). This beautifully paved north-south street appears to be part of the effort to impose a grid—a Hippodamian grid—on the landscape and thereby give shape to a classic Roman urban space. In an article I wrote with Douglas Edwards, we revealed the results of our excavations into a portion of the *cardo*.[2] After removing a few of the pavers, we found a street below the pavers that was made from crushed limestone (fig. 2).

In the limestone makeup we found only Hellenistic and early Roman sherds and one coin of Herod Archelaus. This suggested that in the first decades of the first century C.E. this city reflected the design of an archetypal Roman city but that the paved *cardo* dated to a later period. As we noted in that article, the excavations made evident that this street "was part of the planned systematic expansion of the city to the east on previously unoccupied territory, probably during the reign of Herod Antipas."[3] This conclusion was reinforced by numismatic evidence when we recovered a Tiberias city coin minted in 119–120 C.E. directly beneath the stone pavers. This sequence correlates with the Roman road chronology offered

---

2. C. Thomas McCollough and Douglas R. Edwards, "Transformations of Space: The Roman Road at Sepphoris," in *Archaeology and the Galilee: Tests and Contexts in the Graeco-Roman and Byzantine Periods* (ed. Douglas R. Edwards and C. Thomas McCollough; Atlanta: Scholars Press, 1997), 135–42.

3. Ibid., 140.

Figure 1. Cardo Maximus (Roman street) at Sepphoris. Photo by David Fiensy.

Figure 2. Excavations below paver of Roman street at Sepphoris. Photo by Tom Longstaff, USF Excavations at Sepphoris.

in other studies of the roads in Roman Palestine.⁴ I think it is also worth noting that the imperial road connecting Ptolemais to Tiberias and the Sea of Galilee was not constructed until after 70 C.E. This evidence suggests that while a Roman grid marked off the streets of Sepphoris in the early decades of the first century C.E., the transportation infrastructure for substantial trade in Lower Galilee marks the landscape of this region only in the later decades of the century.

The second archaeological feature is the Roman theater (fig. 3). The theater is located on the western slope of the acropolis, offering the audience a beautiful view of the Bet Netofah Valley. It was partially built into the hillside, and when both lower and upper seating areas were complete, it could seat approximately six thousand. Our excavations concentrated on the area to the side and back of the stage to clarify the construction of the stage area, and perhaps more importantly, to recover evidence of the phases of construction.⁵ Our recovery of the phases of construction would help answer a question that is now frequently woven into discussions of the historical Jesus: Could one say with any confidence that this theater was part of the landscape of Galilee that Jesus would have encountered?⁶ We also wanted to try to determine whether the building materials used in the earliest phases of the construction of the city were imported or local, as this could have a bearing on the impact on the local economy and could speak to the splendor of the early Roman city.

Our analysis of the data argues that the theater at Sepphoris was built in two stages. Based on the architectural and ceramic evidence we recovered, the founding date for the theater was in the first decades of the first century C.E. This theater was small, encompassing essentially the lower or *ima cavea* and a simple stage lacking a *scaena*. The theater was significantly enhanced and expanded to include a second tier of seating beginning in the second century. The two phases represent the two phases of the

---

4. See, for example, Benjamin Isaac and Israel Roll, *Roman Roads in Judea 1: The Legio-Scythopolis Road* (BAR International Series 141; London: B.A.R., 1982).

5. In addition to the University of South Florida Excavations (directed by James F. Strange), the theater was also excavated by the Joint Sepphoris Project (a joint effort of Duke University and Hebrew University and directed by Eric Meyers and Ehud Netzer) and Hebrew University (directed by Zeev Weiss).

6. This became an interesting and persistent question in part because of the beguiling article by Richard A. Batey, "Jesus and the Theater," *New Testament Studies* 30 (1984): 563–74.

Figure 3. Partially restored Roman theater at Sepphoris. Photo by David Fiensy.

reception of the theater. This pattern of theater construction is consistent with that discerned by Arthur Segal in his study of the theaters of Roman Palestine.[7] Segal divides the building of theaters into three periods: the Herodian phase that begins in the latter part of the first century B.C.E. and ends in the middle of first century C.E.; the "middle stage" that begins with the end of the first century C.E. and ends in the first decades of the second century C.E.; and the "final stage" that stretches from the latter part of the second century C.E. to the first half of the third century C.E. In the case of the theater at Sepphoris, at the outset it was simply an extension of the interest of Herod Antipas and his retinue. As was true of his father, so also Herod Antipas appears to have built cities with the Roman urban plan in mind (although on a much more modest scale). And as William MacDonald noted, "the theater was essential to a distinctive architectural creation—the Roman town ... this structure was an instrument of architectural colonization symbolic of the ways and claims of Rome."[8] The second

---

7. Arthur Segal, *Theaters in Roman Palestine and Provincia Arabia* (New York: Brill, 1995).

8. William MacDonald, *An Urban Appraisal* (vol. 2 of *The Architecture of the*

phase expressed a municipal interest and investment in the theater. And as in the case of the *cardo*, the architecture takes a turn toward the ostentatious as the city grows in population and is thriving economically. As Segal notes in terms of this second phase,

> Wishing to demonstrate their newly acquired affluence and civic pride, the citizens of the cities turned their energies and funds to construction activities which could satisfy this desire for ostentation, that is, colonnaded streets, triumphal arches, *nymphaea*, and of course theaters.[9]

In terms of construction material, we found that local material was used in the earliest phase of construction. There was no evidence of imported marble or roof tiles and a very small percentage (less than 5 percent) of the ceramics were imported. This pattern would be consistent with Josephus's remark that Sepphoris was well supplied by surrounding villages (*Vita* 38). The material culture recovered from the "surrounding villages" is somewhat puzzling in terms of economic impact. On the one hand, there is evidence of villages expanding and thriving as the city begins to build its monumental structures. This suggests a positive correlation. On the other hand, as noted below, we have very little evidence of increased monetization in the nearby villages in the first decades of the first century and almost no evidence of the use of Roman coinage. It may be that some sort of "trade-in-kind" system was in place that is reflected in the state of the villages, but it is very difficult to verify such in terms of the evidence at hand.

The third structure that bears discussion is the Roman basilica that is located in the lower city and stood at the intersection of the *cardo* and *decumanus* (fig. 4).[10] Here again we have a large (40 x 60 m) and impressive architectural monument that gained its fullest and most magnificent form in the second century C.E. In terms of founding, the ceramic data coming from the probes around the foundations in combination with cer-

---

Roman Empire; New Haven: Yale University Press, 1986), 263.

9. Segal, *Theaters in Roman Palestine*, 22.

10. See the discussion of the plan and possible use of this building in James F. Strange, "Sepphoris and the Earliest Christian Congregations," in *The Archaeology of Difference: Gender, Ethnicity, Class, and the "Other" in Antiquity. Studies in Honor of Eric M. Meyers* (ed. Douglas R. Edwards and C. Thomas McCollough; Annual of the American Schools of Oriental Research 60/61; Boston: American Schools of Oriental Research, 2007), 291–99.

tain architectural features (e.g., typical Herodian bossed masonry) argues for a dating to the period of Herod Antipas. This evidence gives us a second building that would be expected to have some impact on local resources and likewise the local economy, but, once again, the relationship between this construction activity and the village economy is more complex. In the later period, the simple white plaster walls would be covered by frescoes and the white mosaic floors covered by colored mosaics with elaborate designs. The building would eventually have a second story and an interior divided by two rows of columns, as well as an exterior with three, or perhaps four, porches. This architectural pattern is consistent with the other structures discussed and again reveals a transition from a city of relatively modest dimensions to one that presented itself in consequential and rather magnificent terms.

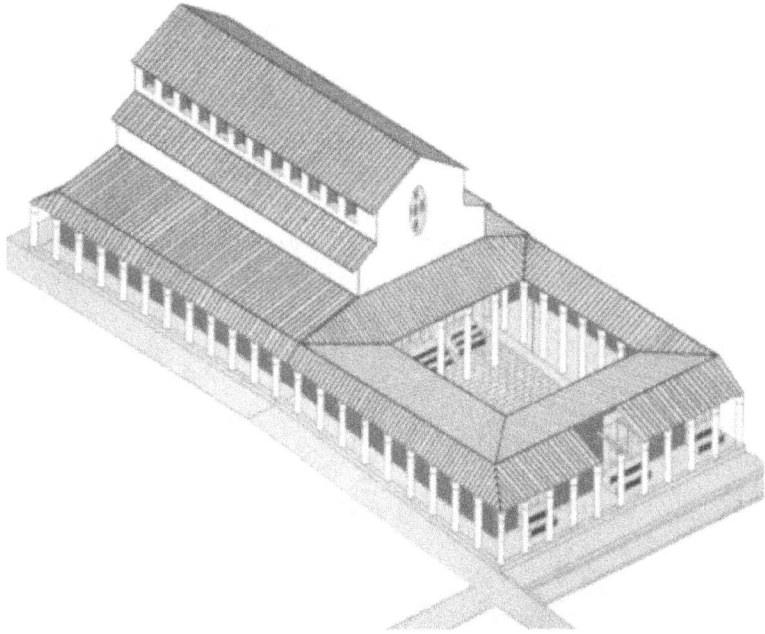

Figure 4. Architectural drawing of Roman basilica at Sepphoris. Drawing by James F. Strange, USF Excavations at Sepphoris.

In sum, the archaeological evidence from Sepphoris that I have introduced does not suggest that the first decades of the first century witnessed the sort of monumental construction that was to define this urban space in the second century. As Richard Horsley has pointed out, Sepphoris was conceived as an administrative center with limited territorial jurisdiction.[11] In this regard, Morten Jensen is surely right to argue that Herod Antipas's impact on Galilee was modest. As Jensen notes,

> It is historically plausible and archaeologically possible that Antipas sponsored a certain amount of building activity in Sepphoris. How much is currently open to question. Nevertheless, even if the theater, the cardo and the basilical building are included, Antipas' Sepphoris was in its "urban infancy" only just deserving the term *polis* in comparison with the surrounding urban areas.... It is thus not warranted to name Antipas a *remaker* of Galilee—instead, the description *modest developer* would be more appropriate.[12]

This is not to suggest that there was an absence of impact on the villages of Lower Galilee. The evidence from Khirbet Qana (and Yodefat) argues for a positive correlation between urban foundation and the village economy. At the same time, the modest dimensions of the urban development limited the extent of the intrusion on village culture and life. As I suggested earlier, Antipas's building efforts did more to invigorate rather than spoil the villages of Lower Galilee in the first decades of the first century.

After the First Revolt, Sepphoris, having not participated, was blessed with Roman patronage (began minting its own coins) and with a swelling of the population (growing from approximately 6,000–8,000 to 12,000–14,000).[13] At this point the city utilized its growing economic resources to undertake such measures as paving the *cardo* in a grand way and enlarging the theater and the basilica. As Eric Meyers noted, "It is during the interwar period, from 68–135 C.E., or at the end of the ER (Early Roman) period, that the character of Sepphoris as a great oriental city became a reality."[14]

---

11. Richard A. Horsley, *Galilee: History, Politics, People.* (Valley Forge, Pa.: Trinity Press International, 1995), 214–15.

12. Morten Jensen, *Herod Antipas in Galilee: The Literary and Archaeological Resources on the Reign of Herod Antipas and Its Socio-economic Impact on Galilee* (WUNT 2/215; Tübingen: Mohr Siebeck, 2006), 162, 257, emphasis original.

13. On the population of Sepphoris, see Jonathan Reed, *Archaeology and the Galilean Jesus: A Re-examination of the Evidence* (Harrisburg, Pa.: Trinity Press International), 62–80.

14. Eric M. Meyers, "The Early Roman Period at Sepphoris: Chronological, Archaaeological, Literary, and Social Considerations," in *Hesed Ve-Emet: Studies in*

The ostentatious, thriving, and profoundly threatening and/or alluring urban centers stood in the foreground not of Jesus but of the Gospel writers. After 70 C.E., the Roman presence was much more substantial and intricate. On the one hand, villagers could more readily access the urban centers because of the roads that were built in the later decades of the century and on the other hand, they had in their foreground striking evidence of the power of Rome in the form of annihilated villages. The growth of the cities and Roman infrastructure in these later decades invariably generated stress points within the villages that led to complex reactions, economic and otherwise. This situation would surely color the Gospel writers' presentation of context far more than it would shape the economic framework of the life of Jesus and the earliest phases of the Jesus movement.

The Rural Dimension: Khirbet Qana

We now shift our focus west and 6 km across the Beth Netofah Valley to the village of Khirbet Qana (fig. 5). The question of whether this site is to be identified with Cana of Galilee featured in the Gospel of John (see fig. 11 in ch. 1) was addressed at length in a paper given by Douglas Edwards shortly before his death in 2008.[15] Edwards offered a compelling case that texts, cartography and archaeology all converge to make this village site the most obvious candidate for New Testament Cana. The importance of this village site for Roman Galilee does not, however, depend on its identification with the New Testament reference. As is true with Aviam's exposure and analysis of the archaeological evidence from Yodefat, so also our recovery of this village offers a splendid opportunity for approaching the dynamics of Roman Galilee from a rural perspective, and its proximity to Sepphoris affords the occasion to reflect upon rural and urban interaction in Lower Galilee.[16]

Honor of Ernest S. Frerichs (ed. Jodi Magness and Seymour Gitin; Atlanta: Scholars Press, 1998), 349.

15. Douglas R. Edwards, "Cana of the Galilee: Quest for a First Century Village," Haywood Lectures, April 2008.

16. For a summary of the results of the first four seasons of excavations at Khirbet Qana, see Douglas R. Edwards, "Khirbet Qana: From Jewish Village to Christian Pilgrim Site," in *The Roman and Byzantine Near East* (ed. John H. Humphrey; Journal of Roman Archaeology Supplementary Series 49; Portsmouth, R.I.: Journal of Roman Archaeology, 2002), 3:101–32; and idem, "Identity and Social Location in Roman Galilean Villages," in *Religion, Ethnicity and Identity in Ancient Galilee* (ed. Jürgen

Figure 5. Aerial view of Khirbet Qana and the Beth Netofah Valley. Photo courtesy of Douglas Edwards, UPS Excavations at Khirbet Qana.

Khirbet Qana shows signs of occupation beginning in the Iron Age. The residue of occupation becomes significant in the Hellenistic period. While to this point we have no identifiable architectural remnants from the Hellenistic period, we have recovered two Tyrian silver coins from the fourth century B.C.E., as well a coin of Antiochus IV (reigned 175–164 B.C.E.). However, the dominant coin evidence from this period is Hasmonean, suggesting a pattern of occupation that will be commented upon at a later point.

Our ceramic finds have also pointed to the late Hellenistic period as the point of origin for an "active" village, as 25 to 30 percent of the ceramic finds date to the late Hellenistic or early Roman periods (fig. 6).

Like most other villages of this period (with the exceptions of Gamla and Yodefat), Khirbet Qana was an unwalled village. It occupied approximately 7 ha and had a population of roughly 1,200. Josephus refers to Cana

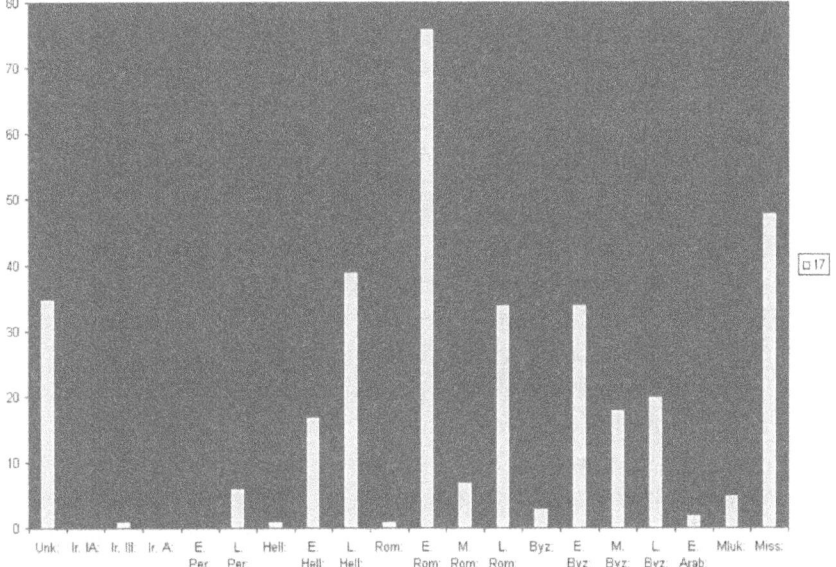

Figure 6. Graph of ceramic data recovered at Khirbet Qana through 2008.

as a village (κωμη) in which he stayed for a short time during the Jewish wars (*Vita* 86). We have no evidence that the village participated in the revolt, and the evidence shows no sign of being assaulted or damaged, as in the case of its close neighbor Yodefat.

In terms of identifying the material culture that could be securely dated to the early decades of the first century, we have been challenged by the disturbance of later structures, frequent instances of founding directly on bedrock, and structures (e.g., cisterns, *miqwāʾôt*) carved directly out of bedrock. To accommodate, we have made extensive use of AMS radiocarbon dating as a supplement to ceramic and numismatic data.[17] Utilizing this method in conjunction with the ceramics and coins, we have identified areas of the domestic quarter, public buildings, and industrial features that can provisionally be dated to the early decades of the first century C.E.

---

17. On the use of carbon-14 dating at Khirbet Qana, see Jason A. Rech, Alysia A. Fischer, Douglas R. Edwards, and A. J. Timothy Jull, "Direct Dating of Plaster and Mortar Using AMS Radiocarbon: A Pilot Project from Khirbet Qana, Israel," *Antiquity* 77 (2009): 155–64.

In terms of houses, remnants of walls that appear to be associated with domestic activities have been exposed on the north, east, and west slopes of the hilltop (fig. 7). The east and west slopes experienced significant Byzantine rebuilding, which included the introduction of large amounts of fill. After removing the Byzantine layers, we were able to expose the walls of early Roman structures and to recover enough ceramic data to establish patterns of housing in the late Hellenistic and into the early Roman periods. The houses on the east and west slopes were small terrace types similar to those exposed at Gamla and Yodefat.[18]

The houses exposed on the northern slope of the hill, where the hill flattens slightly, were larger and included side courtyards. One such courtyard included a stepped pool complex built into the bedrock (fig. 8). This stepped structure has a cistern associated with it, and its steps lead to an area that was well plastered with hydraulic plaster. Carbon dating of the first layer of plaster yielded a date range of 160 B.C.E.–78 C.E. (and 23 C.E.–214 C.E.).[19] Given its form and use of hydraulic plaster, we have identified it as a Jewish ritual bath.

In sum, as at Gamla and Yodefat, the domestic areas of the early Roman period of Khirbet Qana manifest strategies of adapting to topography and display aspects of social and economic differentiation, as well as ethnic/religious identity.

In the early Roman period, the northeast and southwest quadrants of the acropolis were dominated by two large buildings (fig. 9). One of these buildings is evidently a public building, while the other may also be for public use or is perhaps a large and well-decorated house. In both cases, the plaster and mortar samples from foundations that were subjected to radiocarbon analysis established a founding date between 4 and 234 C.E. (95 percent accuracy). The ceramic data from sealed loci beneath plaster floors, from foundation trenches for walls, and from rubble core of walls were forms that have a start date in the late Hellenistic period and an end date in the early second century C.E. We conclude that both buildings have a founding date in the first decades of the first century C.E.[20]

---

18. See the discussion of housing in Peter Richardson, "Khirbet Qana (and Other Villages) as a Context for Jesus," in *Jesus and Archaeology* (ed. James H. Charlesworth; Grand Rapids: Eerdmans, 2006), 120–44.

19. On the two dates, one resulting from the analysis of the acid residue of an olive pit and the other from humic acid, see Rech et al., "Direct Dating."

20. We have few "clean" early Roman loci with identifiable sherds. The sealed loci

Figure 7. Excavated wall of house on E slope of Khirbet Qana. Photo by Douglas Edwards, UPS Excavations at Khirbet Qana.

Figure 8. Excavated wall and stepped pool structure (*miqweh*?) of house on north slope of Khirbet Qana. Photo by Douglas Edwards, UPS Excavations at Khirbet Qana.

The building to the northeast measures approximately 16 meters by 8 meters (including a courtyard). The large room (ca. 12 x 8 m) that borders the courtyard to the south included a pilaster along its north wall made from well-dressed plastered stones with a rectangular capital (possibly to support a second floor). The floor was covered with plaster still *in situ*, and this plaster floor runs up and over part of the south wall. The function of this structure has not been determined with certainty, and Richardson has suggested that instead of a public building, it was "more likely a well-appointed house" (fig. 10).[21]

The building to the southwest included a large room (ca. 20 x 15 m) that had the most distinct and interesting architectural features (fig. 11). The room has a plaster floor, within which were embedded six footers for two rows of columns creating a nave and two aisles. Fragments of the columns were uncovered along with an Ionic capital with scrolls and plaster.

In one corner of the room, a bench was exposed that rested on the plaster floor (fig. 12). This assemblage of features compares very favorably with those of the first-century synagogue at Gamla and has led us to suggest that this building did function as a synagogue. As noted above, the conjunction of radiocarbon and ceramic dating evidence have led us to conclude that founding dates to the early decades of the first century. In short, the existence of these large public (perhaps in one case domestic) structures in the early decades of the first century point to a village that is at once economically stable, if not thriving, as well as sustaining a robust Judaism.

The archaeological excavations have also shown that the village had diversified its activities beyond agriculture. Our excavations have uncovered what appears to be an industrial zone. As at Yodefat, so also at Khirbet Qana, the prevailing west winds led to the utilization of the eastern slope for industrial activity. We have found one—possibly two—*columbaria*, or dovecotes, and based on some glass wasters, perhaps a small glass-making installation. The dating for the *columbaria* and possible glass industry is uncertain but parallels suggest an early first-century date.[22]

---

yielded only body sherds that were identified as probable early Roman sherds. We did have a several identifiable sherds from the wall foundations and rubble core and they were bowls from Kefar Hananya ware 3a, cooking pots from Kefar Hananya ware 4a, and storage jars of the type known from Yodefat and Shikhin.

21. Richardson, "Khirbet Qana," 138.

22. See Boaz Zissu, "Two Herodian Dovecotes: Horvat Abu Haf and Horvat 'Aleq," in *The Roman and Byzantine Near East: Some Recent Archaeological Research* (ed. John

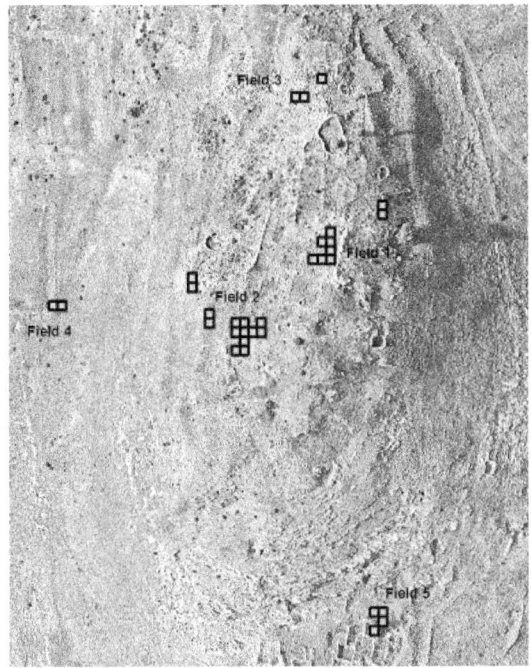

Figure 9. Aerial view of acropolis of Khirbet Qana with areas of public buildings identified (fields 1 and 2). Photo courtesy of Douglas Edwards, UPS Excavations at Khirbet Qana.

Figure 10. Interior of public building or large house with pilaster *in situ* at Khirbet Qana. Photo by Douglas Edwards, UPS Excavations at Khirbet Qana.

Figure 11. Interior of public building (synagogue?) looking south. Photo by Tom McCollough, UPS and Centre College Excavations at Khirbet Qana.

Figure 12. Interior of public building (synagogue?) with capital and benches *in situ* at Khirbet Qana. Photo by Douglas Edwards, UPS Excavations at Khirbet Qana.

Along the southeast side of Khirbet Qana, we have also exposed an interesting and somewhat arcane complex of cells or vats (fig. 13). These structures were cut into bedrock but in some places contain walls composed of cobbles and mortar. The bedrock and the cobble walls were coated in plaster. Integrated into this complex was a small (1.10 m floor to ceiling, 2.10 m opening to back wall, and 1.70 m at widest point) plastered underground chamber with five plastered steps leading down to the entrance (fig. 14). Roughly 3 m down the slope from this complex, we exposed another larger (1.95 m floor to ceiling, 2.87 m opening to back wall, 1. 77 m at widest point) underground chamber with plastered steps (fig. 15).

Both of these stepped complexes appear to be Jewish ritual baths. Plaster samples from each structure was subjected to radiocarbon dating analysis and yielded a date range in line with the public buildings (4–234 C.E.). We speculate that this area was set aside for the production of some product that incorporated the use of liquids (e.g., dyeing, tanning, or a fullery), and this activity raised purity concerns. These discoveries indicate that, like Gamla and Yodefat, Khirbet Qana engaged in industrial activity to complement its agricultural base. It is important to note that at this point, we have found no overlap in the type of industry exposed in these villages. As Aviam has shown, Yodefat engaged in pottery manufacturing and olive oil production. Is this evidence of intentional complementarity? A provisional answer would be yes and in turn points toward a region developing what Richardson termed "a coherent economic unit."[23]

At this point we cannot say with any certainty whether the products being produced at Khirbet Qana were for purely local consumption or were intended in part or in whole to be distributed outside the village. We presume that there was at least some non-village distribution (based on the pattern of pottery distribution from Kefar Hananya and Shikhin), and this presumption in turn raises the question of mode and capacity for such. Before the Jewish Revolt, there is no substantial road that would link this village to other centers of occupation, and in particular, no road that would link it to Sepphoris. Travel outside the village must have been made

---

H. Humphries; Journal of Roman Archaeology Supplement Series 14; Portsmouth, R.I.: Journal of Roman Archaeology, 1995), 56-69; and Mordechai Aviam, "Columbaria in the Galilee," in idem, *Jews, Pagans and Christians in the Galilee* (Rochester, N.Y.: University of Rochester Press, 2004), 31–35.

23. Richardson, "Khirbet Qana," 132.

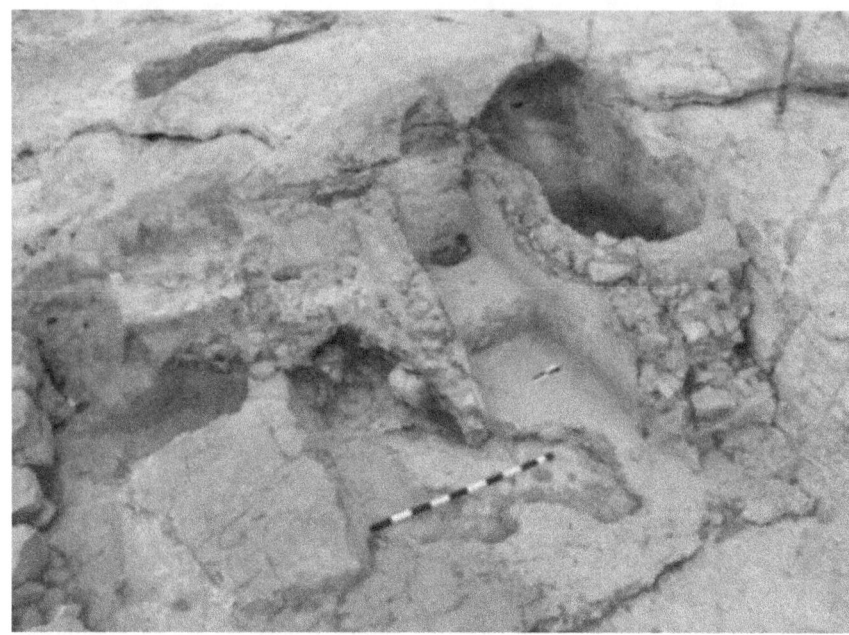

Figure 13. Industrial complex at Khirbet Qana. Photo by Tom McCollough, UPS and Centre College Excavations at Khirbet Qana.

Figure 14. Small stepped underground structure (*miqweh*?) at Khirbet Qana. Photo by Tom McCollough, UPS and Centre College Excavations at Khirbet Qana.

Figure 15. Large stepped underground structure (*miqweh*?) at Khirbet Qana. Photo by Tom McCollough, UPS and Centre College Excavations at Khirbet Qana.

simply by foot or by donkey paths that primarily followed the contours of hills and utilized valleys apart from the rainy season. While these small paths surely inhibited to some degree the development of rural-urban interchange (and the correlate economic interchange), they did facilitate the interconnectivity between villages and towns. As Edwards noted,

> If one plots all the villages discovered and presumed (based on literary sources) today and connects with lines all villages at least 5 km away one can see a maze of interconnecting paths. ... This interconnectivity makes Galilee much more integrated than some would posit.[24]

The ceramic profile from Khirbet Qana (that includes a substantial percentage of wares from Kefar Hananya and Shikhin and only 4 percent Eastern Terra Sigillata) as well as the numismatic profile give strong evi-

---

24. Douglas R. Edwards, "Crossing Boundaries: Trade and Travel in Galilee and Environs," Haywood Lectures, 2008, 26.

dence of such interconnectivity and at the same time offers little evidence of reciprocity with the urban centers. After the First Revolt, as noted earlier, an imperial road connected Acco and Tiberias and that road was connected to Legio via a road running near Sepphoris. This imperial road ran through the Bet Netofah Valley and was 6 kilometers from the village of Khirbet Qana. The benefits that might accrue to the village because of the road could be and appear to be offset by the shift in trading patterns to towns and villages closer to the road. The numismatic pattern suggests that this village did not benefit from or participate in the trade/monetization that such a road would foster. Indeed the evidence points to a village in decline by the end of the second century. As Edwards noted,

> It may be premature to suggest reasons for decline that is not yet proven, but we should consider the possibility that the destruction of Yodefat in the first Jewish Revolt impacted Kh. Qana, in part because it lay on a route connecting Yodefat to Akko/Ptolemais. Further, in the late 1st c. the Romans built a major road connecting Akko/Ptolemais with Tiberias that ran toward Sepphoris along the South side of the valley, some 6 km distant from Khirbet Qana. This occurred following the Revolt and circumvented traditional roads.... Perhaps also the increasing economic and cultural presence of Diocaesarea itself drew resources away from nearby villages ... all we can say so far is that the evidence suggests that Khirbet Qana had difficulty making the transition from the High Imperial period.[25]

In terms of the numismatic data, Aviam's observation that "Jews in Galilee used all kinds of coins that were in circulation—city coins, Tyrian tetradrachms, Roman dinars and Jewish coins"[26] is only partially borne out at Khirbet Qana. As at several other sites in Galilee, there is a striking pattern of the replacement of Seleucid coins with Jewish coinage of the Hasmonean period. As Danny Syon observed in this regard, this pattern is a "dramatic reflection of the historical process of the Hasmonean annexation of Galilee."[27] Of the twelve coins found from the late Hellenistic

---

25. Edwards, "Khirbet Qana," 119.
26. Mordechai Aviam, "First Century Jewish Galilee: An Archaeological Perspective," in *Religion and Society in Roman Palestine: Old Questions, New Approaches* (ed. Douglas R. Edwards; New York: Routledge, 2004), 21.
27. Danny Syon, "Appendix: The Coins," included with Edwards, "Khirbet Qana," 130.

period, only four are non-Jewish coins, and they were identified as quasi-autonomous issues of Akko-Ptolemais dating to the late second to early first century B.C.E. The high percentage of these Jewish nationalistic coins may also bear upon another rather striking aspect of the Khirbet Qana numismatic profile: the paucity of coins from the first three centuries C.E. The only coins from this period are two city coins of Trajan and Hadrian, one of which is countermarked, and both show signs of long wear. Such a pattern suggests that even these coins may not be relevant to the early Roman period in terms of use in the village. There are no city coins from the third century as such. These are coins that are fairly common elsewhere. What is especially interesting is the lack of any coins from neighboring Sepphoris. Sepphoris minted large issues under Trajan and again under Antonius Pius, Caracalla and Elagabalus. Such a paucity of Sepphoris city coins does seem to argue that despite proximity, there was a lack of economic exchange between this village and Sepphoris. Indeed, one might argue that the predominance of Jewish coins is evidence that the village made a conscious choice to use such coinage.

One final artifact of note is an ostracon with the three Hebrew or Aramaic letters: *bêt*, *gîmel*, and *dālet* (fig. 16). Eshel's paleographic study concluded that the inscription should be dated to the end of the first or beginning of the second century C.E.[28] It appears to be either an example of an abecedary or was done for some apotropaic purpose. In either case, the inscription was done before the pot was fired, and given that the pot appears to be similar to Kefar Hananya ware, we can conclude that the inscription was done in Galilee. As Edwards suggested, it does add to our corpus of evidence that points to the continuing use of Aramaic or Hebrew in villages in the early Roman period, and it also suggests a modicum of literacy within the artisan class.[29]

Conclusion

It is surely the case that any attempt to tease out of texts and/or material culture from the ancient world the complex variables that drive an economy is a task fraught with difficulties and dangers. Putting aside the many sticky issues of interpreting texts such as the New Testament or the Mish-

---

28. Esther Eshel, "An Abecedary Inscription," included in Edwards, "Khirbet Qana," 116.
29. Edwards, "Khirbet Qana."

Figure 16. Ostracon with letters for Khirbet Qana. Photo by Douglas Edwards, UPS Excavations at Khirbet Qana.

nah, we know very well that rocks and stones do not speak for themselves. And yet it is one thing for an archaeologist to say that the arrangement of these stones should be interpreted as domestic space; it is quite another challenge to try to deduce from the stones what economic variable or variables the builder of the house had in mind. Thus, as one moves from artifact and architecture to the landscape of economics, one should proceed cautiously in any attempt to frame the economic context of Jesus and the early Jesus movement. In this survey of the evidence from the archaeological excavations of an urban and village site in Lower Galilee, we have noted that among other things one must pay close attention to factors specific to this particular region of Roman Palestine. As Seán Freyne noted in his study of the urban culture of ancient Galilee,

> It is indeed useful to see Galilee or any other region for that matter within the larger context—cultural, social, and economic.... But within such a general perspective more immediate factors which apply to particular regions also need to be articulated in order to present a balanced picture that has the best chance of approximating the real lives of people in that region in a given period.[30]

---

30. Seán Freyne, *Galilee and Gospel: Collected Essays* (Brill: Leiden, 2002), 185. This emphasis on the particularities of this region of Galilee converges with and to

The evidence also makes apparent that one needs to differentiate as carefully as possible the data relevant to the period before and after the First Revolt. The excavations at Sepphoris suggest that while the outlines of monumental structures were in place, the fully realized "oriental city" would not grace the landscape until after the Revolt. At the same time, the ceramic profiles and the building materials do suggest that the rebuilding of the city made use of local resources. The correlation between these finds and the evidence that surrounding villages were growing and thriving in the pre-70 period suggests that the initial phase of the construction of Sepphoris (and Tiberias) had a positive economic impact on Lower Galilee. What is especially interesting is that this economic stimulation seemed to strengthen and benefit interconnectivity between villages rather than fostering strong ties between village and city. These villages could maintain and indeed deepen their identity as Jewish villages even as urban centers grew up in their midst. After the Revolt, the landscape of Lower Galilee was transformed, and I suspect the ability to maintain this sort of cohesive interconnection was much more difficult. After the Revolt, the landscape of Lower Galilee included villages that were annihilated by Roman troops, Roman roads newly constructed, large urban areas, and by the mid-second century, dramatic increases in Roman military presence. This transformation, which brought dramatic increases in militarization, monetization, and mobility to the region, would certainly change the economic climate and perhaps impact the Gospel writers, but it would be a mistake to push such a context onto the earlier decades.

The evidence from Khirbet Qana has reinforced the complex image of village culture and economic activity that Aviam has exposed at Yodefat. The material culture belies any sort of simple description or characterization, such as "peasant villages." These villages have produced evidence that in the early decades of the first century economic stratification and diversification were endemic to village life. Moreover, in both cases, we have material culture that points in the direction of a robust Judaism that did

---

an extent is shaped by the arguments for the importance of 'micro-ecology' in the groundbreaking work of Peregrine Horden and Nicholas Purcell, *The Corrupting Sea: A Study of the Mediterranean History* (Oxford: Blackwell, 2000). Horden and Purcell's use of micro-ecologies for economic and social analogies likewise converges with Eric Meyers's argument for the importance of regional diversity of Galilee for analyzing religious and cultural realities.

not await the flow of refugees from Judea or the coming of Christianity to manifest itself in architecture and practice.

These complex and interconnected villages provide the setting for the life and ministry of Jesus of Nazareth and likewise the most appreciable aspect of the economic framework. The Gospels' imaging of Jesus' context as limited to such village settings may very well reflect the cohesion manifest in the material remains and thus the most obvious and natural choice of a villager like Jesus of Nazareth, rather than a conscious rejection of the nascent urban areas.[31] In so far as this is the case, it suggests that the ongoing efforts to unearth the villages of Galilee hold great promise for gaining greater insight into the impact of the Roman economy on Jesus and the nascent Jesus movement.

Bibliography

Akerlof, George, and Robert Shiller. *Animal Spirits: How Human Psychology Drives the Economy, and Why It Matters for Global Capitalism*. Princeton: Princeton University Press, 2009.

Aviam, Mordechai. *Jews, Pagans and Christians in the Galilee*. Rochester, N.Y.: University of Rochester Press, 2004.

———. "First Century Jewish Galilee: An Archaeological Perspective." Pages 7–27 in *Religion and Society in Roman Palestine: Old Questions, New Approaches*. Edited by Douglas Edwards. New York: Routledge, 2004.

Batey, Richard A. "Jesus and the Theater." *New Testament Studies* 30 (1984): 563–74.

Edwards, Douglas R. "Cana of the Galilee: Quest for a First Century Village." Haywood Lectures, April 2008.

———. "Identity and Social Location in Roman Galilean Villages." Pages 357–76 in *Religion, Ethnicity and Identity in Ancient Galilee*. Edited by

---

31. In George Akerlof and Robert Shiller's recent work on economic decision making, *Animal Spirits: How Human Psychology Drives the Economy, and Why It Matters for Global Capitalism* (Princeton: Princeton University Press, 2009), they argue against the ideas of Adam Smith for the importance of such non-economic factors as stories in shaping economic choices. This may be useful in framing the economic context of Jesus as his "story" is one shaped by village culture and thus his choice to associate with villages is in effect predetermined as the villages he inhabited lacked a story of urban-village interaction.

Jürgen Zangenberg, Harold W. Attridge, and Dale B. Martin. Tübingen: Mohr Siebeck, 2007.

———. "Khirbet Qana: From Jewish Village to Christian Pilgrim Site." Pages 101–32 in vol. 3 of *The Roman and Byzantine Near East*. Edited by John H. Humphrey. Journal of Roman Archaeology Supplementary Series 49. Portsmouth, R.I.: Journal of Roman Archaeology, 2002.

Freyne, Seán. *Galilee and Gospel: Collected Essays*. Brill: Leiden, 2002.

Horden, Peregrine, and Nicholas Purcell. *The Corrupting Sea: A Study of the Mediterranean History*. Oxford: Blackwell, 2000.

Horsley, Richard A. *Galilee: History, Politics, People*. Valley Forge, Pa.: Trinity, 1995.

Isaac, Benjamin, and Israel Roll. *Roman Roads in Judea 1: The Legio-Scythopolis Road*. BAR International Series 141. London: B.A.R., 1982.

Jensen, Morten. *Herod Antipas in Galilee: The Literary and Archaeological Resources on the Reign of Herod Antipas and Its Socio-economic Impact on Galilee*. WUNT 2/215. Tübingen: Mohr Siebeck, 2006.

McCollough, C. Thomas, and Douglas R. Edwards. "Transformations of Space: The Roman Road at Sepphoris." Pages 135–142 in *Archaeology and the Galilee: Tests and Contexts in the Graeco-Roman and Byzantine Periods*. Edited by Douglas R. Edwards and C. Thomas McCollough. Atlanta: Scholars Press, 1997.

MacDonald, William. *An Urban Appraisal*. Vol. 2 of *The Architecture of the Roman Empire*. New Haven: Yale University Press, 1986.

Meyers, Eric M. "The Early Roman Period at Sepphoris: Chronological, Archaeological, Literary, and Social Considerations." Pages 343–56 in *Hesed Ve-Emet: Studies in Honor of Ernest S. Frerichs*. Edited by Jodi Magness and Seymour Gitin. Atlanta: Scholars Press, 1998.

Rech, Jason A., Alysia A. Fischer, Douglas R. Edwards, and A. J. Timothy Jull. "Direct Dating of Plaster and Mortar using AMS Radiocarbon: a Pilot Project from Khirbet Qana, Israel." *Antiquity* 77 (2009): 155–64.

Reed, Jonathan. *Archaeology and the Galilean Jesus: A Re-examination of the Evidence*. Harrisburg, Pa.: Trinity Press International, 2000.

Richardson, Peter. "Khirbet Qana (and Other Villages) as a Context for Jesus." Pages 120–44 in *Jesus and Archaeology*. Edited by James H. Charlesworth. Grand Rapids: Eerdmans, 2006.

Segal, Arthur. *Theaters in Roman Palestine and Provincia Arabia*. New York: Brill, 1995.

Strange, James F. "Sepphoris and the Earliest Christian Congregations." Pages 291–99 in *The Archaeology of Difference: Gender, Ethnicity,*

Class, and the "Other" in Antiquity. Studies in Honor of Eric M. Meyers. Edited by Douglas R. Edwards and C. Thomas McCollough. Annual of the American Schools of Oriental Research 60/61. Boston: American Schools of Oriental Research, 2007.

Zissu, Boaz. "Two Herodian Dovecotes: Horvat Abu Haf and Horvat 'Aleq." Pages 56–69 in *The Roman and Byzantine Near East: Some Recent Archaeological Research*. Edited by John H. Humphries. Journal of Roman Archaeology Supplement Series 14. Portsmouth, R.I.: Journal of Roman Archaeology, 1995.

3
REVISITING JESUS' CAPERNAUM: A VILLAGE OF ONLY SUBSISTENCE-LEVEL FISHERS AND FARMERS?

Sharon Lea Mattila

INTRODUCTION

In the study of the historical Jesus and his ancient Galilean context, it is only in the last two decades or so that New Testament scholars have begun to give due weight to the "dialogue between text and spade, between literary analysis and archaeological analysis," urged by archaeologists of Roman Galilee.[1] The time is right, therefore, for a reappraisal of the village known from the gospels as Jesus' base of ministry.

THE NEED TO REVISIT A DIFFICULT TOPIC

Given the great relevance of Capernaum to the question of the historical Jesus, the excavations that have been conducted at this site have attracted the attention of New Testament scholars, with the lengthiest treatment having been that of Jonathan L. Reed in *Archaeology and the Galilean Jesus: A Re-examination of the Evidence*.[2] Reed's treatment of the site has been further promulgated in another book, jointly authored with the

---

1. Eric M. Meyers, "Jesus and His Galilean Context," in *Archaeology and the Galilee: Texts and Contexts in the Greco-Roman and Byzantine Periods* (ed. Douglas R. Edwards and C. Thomas McCollough; Atlanta: Scholars Press, 1997), 61.

2. (Harrisburg, Pa.: Trinity Press International, 2000), 139–69. For a convenient table outlining the various Synoptic and Johannine references linking Jesus to Capernaum, see Willibald Bösen, *Galiläa: Lebensraum und Wirkungsfeld Jesu* (Vienna: Herder, 1998), 84.

influential John Dominic Crossan, entitled, *Excavating Jesus: Beneath the Stones, Behind the Texts*.[3]

Unfortunately, Reed's characterization of the Capernaum site is very misleading, as are those of other New Testament scholars such as Richard A. Horsley, Seán Freyne, and James H. Charlesworth. This is despite the fact that a sufficient number of detailed reports have been published on the site to make possible the kind of close analysis I present here in *refutation* of such characterizations. The time has come for these misleading characterizations of Jesus' Capernaum to be set aside. This is the goal of this essay.

Accomplishing this goal, however, is a difficult task. This is because Capernaum is not a site like Gamla or Jotapata, neither of which was reoccupied after their destruction by Rome in the late 60s C.E. and whose first-century C.E. remains were thus left relatively undisturbed. Unlike Gamla and Jotapata, Capernaum was continuously occupied for centuries after Jesus' time, reaching its zenith in Byzantine times (ca. 324-640 C.E.). After this, the village moved northward and eastward, having been inhabited continuously throughout the Arab and later periods up to 1033 C.E.[4] Hence, the vast majority of the standing remains that can be viewed at the site today date to centuries after Jesus lived.

This is the case for both sides of the site — the western side, belonging to the Catholic Franciscan order, where intensive excavations began already in 1968; and the eastern side, which belongs to the Greek Orthodox Church, where serious digging began only in 1978. See figure 1 for an aerial photograph of both sides of the site. Thus far, only the much later strata (dating from the early seventh century C.E. to 1033 C.E.) of the Greek Orthodox excavations have been fully published.[5] There is as yet no full

---

3. (San Francisco: Harper, 2001), 119-35. Crossan and Reed have recently published a "revised and updated" edition of this study with HarperCollins, New York, whose copyright date is still printed, in a most confusing manner, as 2001, although in this edition they discuss at some length the James Ossuary and its exhibit at the Royal Ontario Museum in Toronto, Canada, in the fall of 2002. With the exception of their discussion of this ossuary, most of the text of the first edition is reproduced in this "new and updated" edition verbatim. All page references provided in this essay are therefore to their first edition of this book.

4. See, conveniently, the entries on the site of Capernaum by Stanislao Loffreda and Vassilios Tzaferis in *NEAEHL* 1:291-95, 295-96.

5. Vassilios Tzaferis, *Excavations at Capernaum, Volume I: 1978-1982* (Winona Lake, Ind.: Eisenbrauns, 1989).

Figure 1. Aerial view of the Capernaum site in the 1970s, looking east. Permission of the Studium Biblicum Franciscanum, Jerusalem.

The modern divider wall seen in this photograph separates the western side of the Capernaum site belonging to the Franciscan Order of the Roman Catholic Church from the eastern Greek Orthodox side of the site. Along the central axis of the Franciscan excavations are, from south to north: (1) the remains of the octagonal shrine in the Insula Sacra (the "Sacred Insula") and of the structures beneath it; (2) the remains of private houses in Insula 2; and (3) the fine limestone synagogue, partially reconstructed.

report on the Roman-Byzantine strata, but only a brief preliminary report with a small scaled diagram.[6] It is thus the more fully published Franciscan side of the site that I discuss here. Before I outline how New Testament scholars have misleadingly characterized it, I first provide a brief introduction to its main features.

A Brief Survey of the Franciscan Side of the Capernaum Site

Because the village of the Franciscan side reached its zenith in Byzantine times, the large majority of the remains that can be viewed there today are late Roman to Byzantine in date (third to early seventh centuries C.E.).[7] See the reconstruction in figure 2 of the most magnificent structure unearthed by the Franciscans: Capernaum's famous limestone synagogue, perhaps the most impressive in Israel (fig. 4). The limestone out of which this synagogue was constructed was not available locally and had to be brought into the village "from sites not less than 10 km away, such as Mount Arbel. The import of building material from outside sources is not recorded at any other Galilean synagogue, and it is extremely rare even in the excavated areas of Tiberias."[8]

This limestone synagogue did not stand until long after Jesus lived, regardless of whether it was constructed in the second to third centuries C.E. (a minority view) or much later in the fifth century (the majority view).[9] Nevertheless, underneath its main hall there may have been a

---

6. John C. H. Laughlin, "Capernaum: From Jesus' Time and After," *BAR* 19.5 (1993): 55–61, 90. Thus, at this point nothing conclusive can be argued either way concerning whether or not there was a Roman-style bath house in the village at the time of Jesus. Reed argues that this bath house "was constructed in a newly developed area to the east of the town" only in the second century C.E. (*Archaeology and the Galilean Jesus*, 155). Laughlin, however, suggests that it may indeed date back to Jesus' time ("Capernaum," 56–57).

7. See figure 2 for a three-dimensional reconstruction of these remains, generated by AutoCAD on the basis of the excavation plans, and figure 3 for a close-up view of the reconstruction of Insula 2, which I discuss in some detail further on in this essay.

8. Zvi Uri Ma'oz, "The Synagogue at Capernaum: A Radical Solution," in *The Roman and Byzantine Near East: Some Recent Archaeological Research* (ed. John H. Humphry; 3 vols.; Portsmouth, R.I.: Journal of Roman Archaeology, 1995–2002), 2:137–48, here 139.

9. For the late dating of the synagogue, see most recently Stanislao Loffreda, "Coins from the Synagogue of Capharnaum," *LA* 47 (1997): 223–44. For the earlier

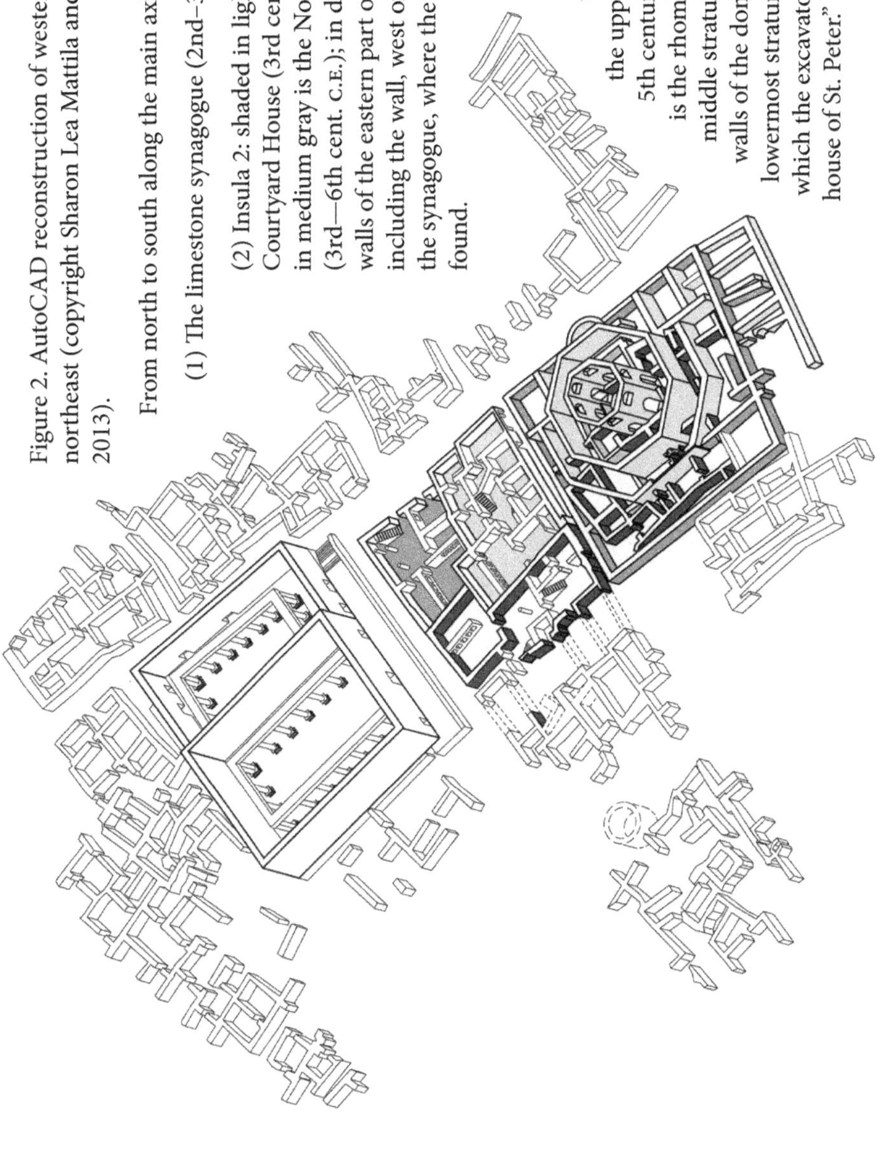

Figure 2. AutoCAD reconstruction of western Capernaum, looking northeast (copyright Sharon Lea Mattila and George Yanchula, 2013).

From north to south along the main axis are:

(1) The limestone synagogue (2nd–3rd or 5th century C.E.).

(2) Insula 2: shaded in light gray is the Triple Courtyard House (3rd century–ca. 450 C.E.); in medium gray is the Northeastern House (3rd—6th cent. C.E.); in dark gray are the ER walls of the eastern part of the Western House, including the wall, west of the modern pathway to the synagogue, where the set of ER glassware was found.

(3) The Insula Sacra: shaded in light gray is the octagonal shrine of the uppermost stratum (4th–5th century C.E.); in medium gray is the rhomboidal shrine of the middle stratum; in dark gray are the walls of the domestic structures of the lowermost stratum (200 B.C.E.–135 C.E.), which the excavators have designated "the house of St. Peter."

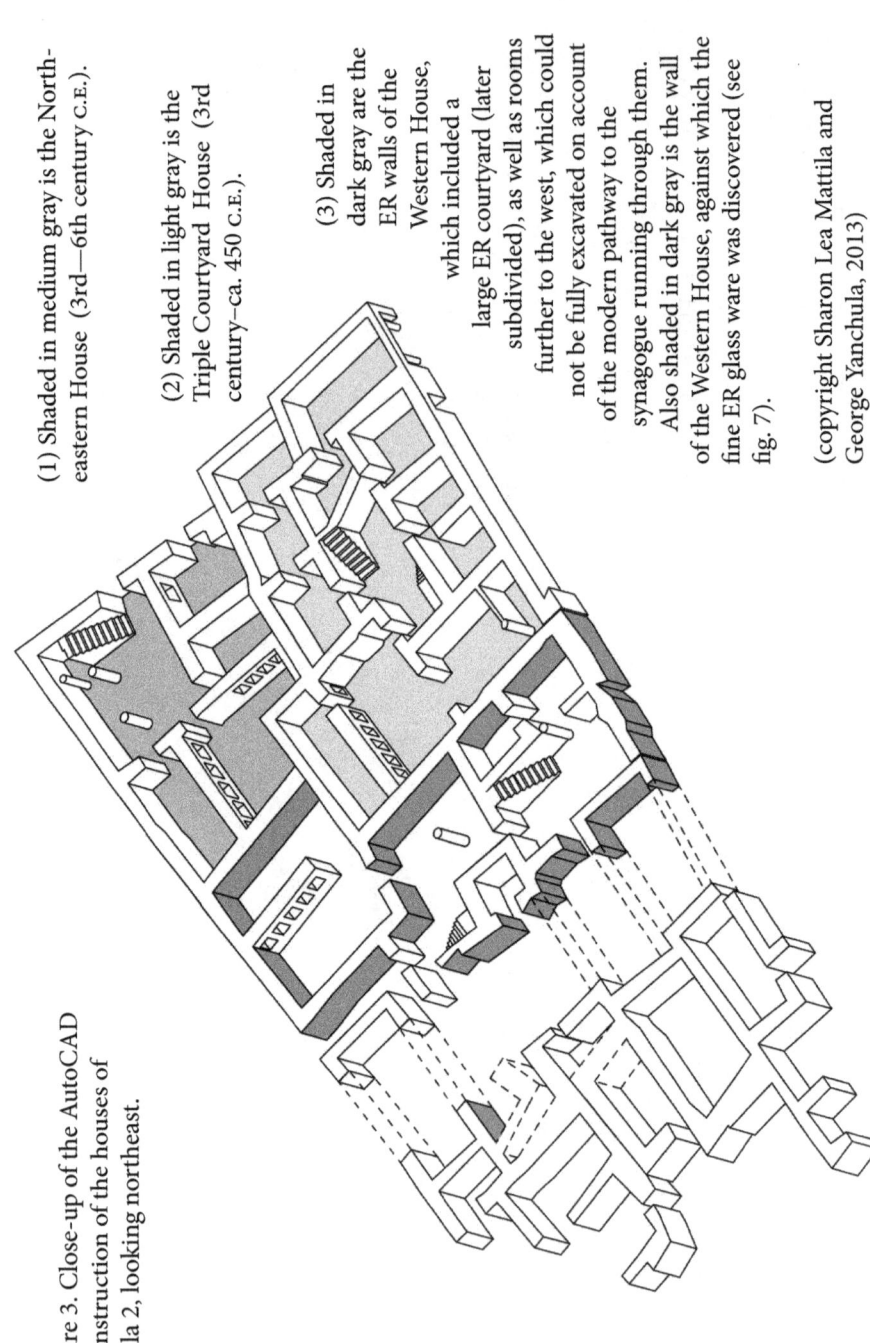

Figure 3. Close-up of the AutoCAD reconstruction of the houses of Insula 2, looking northeast.

(1) Shaded in medium gray is the Northeastern House (3rd—6th century C.E.).

(2) Shaded in light gray is the Triple Courtyard House (3rd century–ca. 450 C.E.).

(3) Shaded in dark gray are the ER walls of the Western House, which included a large ER courtyard (later subdivided), as well as rooms further to the west, which could not be fully excavated on account of the modern pathway to the synagogue running through them. Also shaded in dark gray is the wall of the Western House, against which the fine ER glass ware was discovered (see fig. 7).

(copyright Sharon Lea Mattila and George Yanchula, 2013)

Figure 4. View of the synagogue's masonry and finely worked pillars, made of imported limestone (copyright Sharon Lea Mattila, 2002).

first-century basalt-stone synagogue, as Virgilio Corbo, James F. Strange, and Hershel Shanks have argued.[10] This argument, however, has been

---

dating, see Yoram Tsafrir, "The Synagogues at Capernaum and Meroth and the Dating of the Galilean Synagogue," in Humphrey, *The Roman and Byzantine Near East*, 1:151–61; and Gideon Foerster, "Notes on Recent Excavations at Capernaum (Review Article)," *IEJ* 21 (1971): 207–11. Alternative explanations have been offered by Hanswulf Bloedhorn ("The Capitals of the Synagogue of Capernaum: Their Chronological and Stylistic Classification with Regard to the Development of Capitals in the Decapolis and in Palestine," in *Ancient Synagogues in Israel, Third-Seventh Century C.E.* [ed. Rachel Achlili; Oxford: Oxford University Press, 1989], 49–54) and Ma'oz ("The Synagogue at Capernaum," 137–48). For a good survey of this debate, see John J. Rousseau and Rami Arav, *Jesus and His World: An Archaeological and Cultural Dictionary* (Minneapolis: Fortress, 1995), 39–47.

10. Virgilio Corbo, "Resti della sinagoga del primo secolo a Cafarnao," in *Studia Hierosolymitana III* (ed. Giovanni Claudio Bottini; Jerusalem: Franciscan Printing Press, 1982), 313–57; James F. Strange and Hershel Shanks, "Synagogue Where Jesus Preached Found at Capernaum," *BAR* 9.6 (1983): 24–31.

challenged.¹¹ While this debate is certainly relevant to the socioeconomic character of Capernaum in Jesus' time, I do not seek to resolve it here (if indeed it can be resolved). Instead, my aim is more carefully to interpret the *domestic* remains and finds of the site than New Testament scholars hitherto have done. It is certain that the area underneath the synagogue was occupied in Jesus' time and earlier,¹² but the precise nature of this occupation remains unclear.

In addition to the synagogue, the insula (or village block) that has attracted the most scholarly attention is the southernmost one near the lake shore, which the excavators have designated the *insula sacra*, or "sacred insula." It is most clearly marked by the remains of the octagonal shrine that was erected there in its last phase of occupation (see fig. 2), which is now covered by a modern commemorative shrine of the same octagonal shape. Three main archaeological strata were uncovered in this insula (see fig. 2). The fine shrine of the uppermost stratum, which consisted of three concentric octagons with rich mosaic floors (represented in gray in fig. 2), was erected in the fifth to sixth century C.E. The middle stratum of the insula, exposed underneath, was a rhomboidal "house church," or shrine (represented in medium gray in fig. 2), built in the early fourth century C.E. The lowermost stratum consists of the remains of private domestic structures (represented in dark gray inside the medium-gray rhomboidal structure in fig. 2), dating to the late Hellenistic and early Roman periods (200 B.C.E. to 135 C.E.). These the Franciscan excavators have ascribed to the "House of Saint Peter," although it is of course not certain that Jesus' famous disciple himself once lived there.¹³

---

11. Tsafrir, "The Synagogues at Capernaum and Meroth," 151–61. See Rousseau and Arav for a good survey of this debate (*Jesus and His World*, 39–47).

12. See, for example, Stanislao Loffreda, "Ceramica ellenistico-romana nel sottosuolo della sinagoga di Cafarnao," in Bottini, *Studia Hierosolymitana III*, 273–312.

13. For a description of the buildings of the *insula sacra* and the excavators' arguments in support of the domestic remains having been Peter's house, see Virgilio Corbo, *The House of St. Peter at Capharnaum* (trans. Sylvester Saller; Jerusalem: Franciscan Printing Press, 1969), 53–71; idem, *Cafarnao I: Gli edifici della città* (Jerusalem: Franciscan Printing Press, 1975), 25–111, fig. II; idem, "The Church of the House of St. Peter at Capernaum," in *Ancient Churches Revealed* (ed. Yoram Tsafrir; Jerusalem: Israel Exploration Society, 1993), 71–76; and Stanislao Loffreda, *Recovering Capharnaum* (Jerusalem: Edizioni Custodia Terra Santa, 1985), 51–57. The excavators' arguments were questioned by James F. Strange ("Review: The Capernaum and Herodium Publications," *BASOR* 226 [1977]: 68–69, and "Review: The Capernaum and Hero-

It is difficult to determine the precise delineation of these earliest private structures in the *insula sacra* because they were greatly disturbed by the intense public building and rebuilding activity that took place over the ensuing centuries.[14] There is a central area, called the *sala venerata*, or "venerated room," by the excavators (shaded in dark gray in fig. 2), around which both of the later public structures were built. But it is not certain whether the *sala venerata* was originally two enclosed rooms of the "House of Saint Peter," as Virgilio Corbo suggests, or instead a courtyard, as Peter Richardson has recently argued.[15] One can therefore unfortunately only obtain a very rough idea of the delineation of the domestic rooms and courtyards that once existed in this insula.

One finds the best preserved, fully excavated private houses on the Franciscan side of the site in Insula 2, located between the synagogue (to its north) and the *insula sacra* (to its south) (see figs 2 and 3, and fig. 5 for a photograph of Insula 2). For this reason, and because Insula 2 began to be occupied at the same time as the *insula sacra* in the Hellenistic and early Roman periods, this insula deserves careful scrutiny in any attempt to understand the socioeconomic character of the village, either in the late Roman and Byzantine periods, or in Jesus' time. Hence, the arguments I present here include a close *diachronic* analysis of this insula (that is, a close analysis that traces its development through time).

Misleading Characterizations of Jesus' Capernaum and Preliminary Outline of My Counterarguments

Despite the fact that the bulk of data unearthed at Capernaum dates to centuries after Jesus lived, New Testament scholars have still made attempts to reconstruct the village of Jesus' time. As noted above, the most

---

dium Publications, Part 2," *BASOR* 233 [1979]: 63–69), although he more recently has softened his position to tentatively accepting them, albeit without allowing certainty (James F. Strange and Hershel Shanks, "Has the House Where Jesus Stayed in Capernaum Been Found?" *BAR* 8.6 [1982]: 26–37). Joan Taylor has presented the most thoroughgoing challenge to their arguments (*Christians and the Holy Places: The Myth of Jewish-Christian Origins* [Oxford: Clarendon, 1993], 268–94).

14. Corbo, *The House of St. Peter*, 39.

15. See Corbo, "The Church of the House of St. Peter," 71; idem, *Cafarnao I*, fig. X. For the argument that the *sala venerata* was actually a courtyard, see Peter Richardson, "Towards a Typology of Levantine/Palestinian Houses," *JSNT* 27 (2004): 47–68, especially 63.

Figure 5. View of the walls of Insula 2, constructed out of local undressed basalt stone (copyright Sharon Lea Mattila, 2002).

detailed effort has been that of Reed, further promulgated in his jointly authored book with Crossan.[16] The serious inaccuracies to be discussed below notwithstanding, it should be mentioned that Reed has provided an important correction of earlier greatly exaggerated depictions of the village, which construed it as a rather urbane town of 12,000 to 15,000 residents.[17] After all, even early Roman Pompeii, with its impressive urban remains, contained only approximately 8,000 to 10,000 inhabitants![18] Even the Galilean city of Sepphoris in Jesus' time, according to a recent estimate

---

16. Reed, *Archaeology and the Galilean Jesus*, 139–69; Crossan and Reed, *Excavating Jesus*, 119–35.

17. 12,000 to 15,000 is the population for Capernaum cited in Eric M. Meyers and James F. Strange, *Archaeology, the Rabbis, and Early Christianity* (Nashville: Abingdon, 1981), 58, which Reed rightly challenges (*Archaeology and the Galilean Jesus*, 62–99, 139–69). Both archaeologists have since conceded that this figure was much too high. See Meyers, "Jesus and His Galilean Context," 59; and Strange, "First Century Galilee from Archaeology and from the Texts," in Edwards and McCollough, *Archaeology and the Galilee*, 39–48, especially 47.

18. Hans Eschebach, "Erläuterungen zum Plan von Pompeji," in *Neue Forschungen in Pompeji und den anderen vom Vesuvausbruch 79 n. Chr. verschütteten Städten* (ed. Bernard Andreae and Helmut Kyrieleis; Recklinghausen: Verlag Aurel Bongers Recklinghausen, 1975), 331–38.

by one of the site's excavators, may have numbered only 7,500 to 8,000 people.[19] Only at its zenith in the Byzantine period did it attain a population of 15,000 to 20,000.[20] It was likewise not until Byzantine times that the village of Capernaum reached its peak population, at which point it probably still numbered only about 1,500.[21] Hence, Crossan and Reed's estimate is a reasonable one that in Jesus' time the village contained about a thousand people.[22] One can surely accept without reservation their contention that Capernaum was never at any point in its history "a thriving Greco-Roman metropolis," with all the amenities of urban life. To be sure, it "was simply not in the same league as Caesarea Maritima, Caesarea Philippi, Jerusalem, the cities of the Decapolis, or the Galilean cities of Sepphoris and Tiberias."[23]

These rather self-evident facts notwithstanding, Crossan and Reed have not accurately reconstructed the socioeconomic character of Jesus' Capernaum. Reed has asserted that "the archaeological record makes it clear that" in Jesus' time "chiefly the lower levels of society inhabited Capernaum, like most villages in antiquity."[24] He and Crossan have also declared that "the material remains inside the rooms from early Roman layers at Capernaum bespeak a simple existence of fishers and farmers."[25]

---

19. Tom McCollough, personal communication, 2003. Reed himself has been guilty of exaggerated population estimates, at least in the case of the Galilean towns. Until recently, he still endowed first-century Sepphoris and Tiberias with very high populations of 24,000 apiece ("Population Numbers, Urbanization, and Economics: Galilean Archaeology and the Historical Jesus," in *Society of Biblical Literature 1994 Seminar Papers* [Atlanta: Scholars Press, 1994], 203–19, especially 212–15, 219). This would have made these Galilean towns twice the size of Roman Pompeii! These figures Reed has since reduced considerably. He now sets the first-century population of Sepphoris at 8,000 to 12,000 inhabitants (*Archaeology and the Galilean Jesus*, 80), or almost identical in population to Pompeii. This estimate, however, is probably still too high.

20. Zeev Weiss and Ehud Netzer, "Sepphoris during the Byzantine Period," in *Sepphoris in Galilee: Crosscurrents of Culture* (ed. Rebecca Martin Nagy; Winona Lake, Ind.: Eisenbrauns, 1996), 81–89, especially 86.

21. Stanislao Loffreda, *Recovering Capharnaum*, 18.

22. Crossan and Reed, *Excavating Jesus*, 83, 88; compare with Laughlin, "Capernaum," 57.

23. Reed, *Archaeology and the Galilean Jesus*, 166–67; Crossan and Reed, *Excavating Jesus*, 81–85.

24. Reed, *Archaeology and the Galilean Jesus*, 164.

25. Crossan and Reed, *Excavating Jesus*, 85; compare with Reed, *Archaeology and*

Four Arguments Regarding the Understanding of Capernaum

I argue here that these statements, as well as other assertions made in support of them, are in fact not substantiated by the archaeological record of the site. First, I demonstrate that it is simply erroneous that "there were no luxury items or other indications of wealth" found in the Hellenistic and early Roman strata at Capernaum; that "no stamped handles from imported wine amphorae were found"; and that "even the simplest glass forms are lacking."[26]

Second, I challenge their argument that it was not until the Byzantine period that an "influx of pilgrims" first brought Capernaum's inhabitants some wealth beyond subsistence. They base this argument on the substantial quantities of imported Byzantine fine wares found throughout the *insulae* excavated at the site (see fig. 6).[27] These they aptly describe as "elegant fine wares, from well-known kilns in Africa and Cyprus" (as well as from another as yet unidentified production center), fabricated of "fine clay expertly fired into expensive plates, many of which were stamped with crosses."[28] On the one hand, Crossan and Reed are right that these fine

---

the Galilean Jesus, 160. While Crossan has recognized elsewhere that "peasant" societies are generally characterized by marked internal social differentiation (*The Birth of Christianity: Discovering What Happened in the Years Immediately after the Execution of Jesus* [San Francisco: HarperSanFrancisco, 1998], 345–52), this fact has not seemed to have had any impact on the portrait of Capernaum that he paints together with Reed (*Excavating Jesus*, 81–97). For a critique of how the social-scientific concept of "peasants" has been applied uncritically in New Testament scholarship, see my "Jesus and the 'Middle Peasants'? Problematizing a Social-Scientific Concept," *CBQ* 72 (2010): 291–313.

26. Crossan and Reed, *Excavating Jesus*, 85; compare with Reed, *Archaeology and the Galilean Jesus*, 160.

27. On these fine wares, see Stanislao Loffreda, *Cafarnao II: La Ceramica* (Jerusalem: Franciscan Printing Press, 1974), 13, 65–87, 166–74; and Corbo, *Cafarnao I*, 220. It is important to note that many of the imported fine wares that Loffreda dates as "Late Roman" must be classified as Byzantine, according to the chronology used here. According to the Franciscan excavators' rather idiosyncratic chronology (compare with the critique of this chronology in Strange, "Review" [1977]: 66–67), the "Late Roman" period dates from 300–450 C.E. (Loffreda, *Cafarnao II*, 20). As understood here, the Byzantine period begins with Constantine in the early fourth century C.E., only a few decades after the beginning of Loffreda's "Late Roman" period.

28. Reed, *Archaeology and the Galilean Jesus*, 164; Crossan and Reed, *Excavating Jesus*, 85–97.

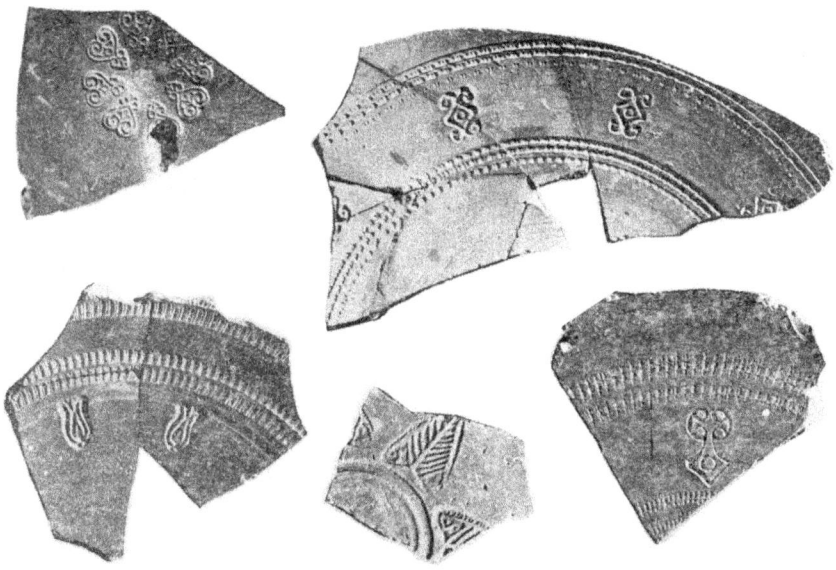

Figure 6. Fragments of Byzantine fine wares recovered at Capernaum. From Stanislao Loffreda, *Cafarnao II: La Ceramica* (Jerusalem: Franciscan Printing Press, 1974), 85, photo 20, nos. 1, 4, and 8; 86, photo 21, no. 1; 87, photo 22, nos. 9, 13, and 14; 88, photo 23, nos. 1 and 7. Used by permission of the Studium Biblicum Franciscanum, Jerusalem.

wares provide clear evidence that many of the inhabitants of Byzantine Capernaum enjoyed prosperity beyond subsistence. On the other hand, I argue here that it is a *non sequitur* that none of the inhabitants of Jesus' Capernaum did.

This particular argument occupies the longest section of this essay because it involves setting the village within its broader context in two very different historical periods, surely an essential task in any effort properly to understand the evidence from Capernaum. I do not pretend to do this *comprehensively* within the confines of an essay, even in a longer section; but I do undertake to highlight in some detail a hitherto insufficiently appreciated and crucial aspect of the cultural, religious, political, and demographic changes that occurred in Palestine at large in the intervening centuries between these two periods, namely, a major shift in trade patterns. On account of this shift and for other cogent reasons, I contend that the presence of Byzantine fine wares, while certainly indicative of wealth beyond subsistence on the part of the individuals who owned them, cannot automatically be associated with an overall increase in *any* site's prosperity in Byzantine times.

My third main argument is against Crossan and Reed's misleading characterization of Capernaum's houses. It is true that Capernaum never resembled a large, Greco-Roman town, planned on a grid system with grand, portico-lined, main streets (usually called the *decumanus* and *cardo maximus*). But this does not mean that the village's domestic remains suggest that "the driving force in Capernaum's layout was ... domestic growth around courtyards, which were encircled as members of extended families added houses, walls, or storage rooms."[29] It goes without saying that Capernaum's insulae (or village blocks) were "certainly not ... [multi-storied] apartment structures ... like those in Rome's port city of Ostia." But this does not mean that one can therefore conclude that the village's houses consisted merely of "a series of rooms clustered around a single courtyard belonging to an extended family."[30]

On this point, it should be noted that Crossan and Reed are by no means alone in describing Capernaum's houses in this manner. Freyne, for instance, declares that these houses "seem to consist of a single room opening onto a courtyard that was shared by several different family units

---

29. Reed, *Archaeology and the Galilean Jesus*, 153.
30. Crossan and Reed, *Excavating Jesus*, 82.

... [meaning] that life for many in a village such as Capernaum was at subsistence level."[31] In a strikingly similar way, Charlesworth asserts that at Capernaum "usually, the houses comprise a single room that opened out to a small courtyard that served more than one family unit. Often the family lived in one room and perhaps in one large bed.... Reed is certainly correct to point out the lack of affluence at Capernaum."[32]

As I show through a close diachronic examination of Insula 2, the layout of the various domestic units and the modifications they underwent over time were a great deal more complex than such assertions imply. As a corrective to what seems to be a relatively widespread misconception of the nature of Capernaum's houses, therefore, this diachronic analysis is especially important. The analysis is also a comparative one, because the village cannot be correctly understood in isolation from its broader Galilean context. It is an analysis that also challenges the rather impressionistic assessment of Joan Taylor, followed unquestioningly by Richard A. Horsley, that the lower classes of Capernaum lived to the west and the more affluent to the east of the modern boundary line between the Franciscan and Greek Orthodox sides of the site (see figure 1 for this boundary line).[33]

My fourth main argument challenges the salience of another point commonly put forward in support of such misleading characterizations of the houses on the Franciscan side of the site. Their walls, built out of undressed local basalt stone using local techniques (see fig. 5), contrast palpably with the dressed limestone walls of the remarkably fine synagogue (see fig. 4). This contrast has frequently been adduced in support of the notion that these houses were those of the subsistence-level poor.[34]

---

31. Seán Freyne, "Archaeology and the Historical Jesus," in *Jesus and Archaeology* (ed. James H. Charlesworth; Grand Rapids: Eerdmans, 2006), 78.

32. James H. Charlesworth, "Jesus Research and Archaeology: A New Perspective," in Charlesworth, *Jesus and Archaeology*, 18. Contrast with the more reasonable assessments of Loffreda, *Recovering Capharnaum*, 20; and Morten Hørning Jensen, *Herod Antipas in Galilee: The Literary and Archaeological Sources on the Reign of Herod Antipas and Its Socio-economic Impact on Galilee* (Tübingen: Mohr Siebeck, 2006), 172, 175.

33. Taylor, *Christians and the Holy Places*, 277; compare with Richard A. Horsley, *Archaeology, History, and Society in Galilee: The Social Context of Jesus and the Rabbis* (Valley Forge, Pa.: Trinity Press International, 1996), 115–16.

34. Examples include: Charlesworth, "Jesus Research and Archaeology," 18; Reed, *Archaeology and the Galilean Jesus*, 151, 159, 164–65; Horsley, *Archaeology, History, and Society in Galilee*, 114–15; Taylor, *Christians and the Holy Places*, 277.

Here I bring in further comparative evidence to suggest that this is not a foregone conclusion.

All the arguments I present here combine strongly to suggest that it is, in fact, unlikely that all of the thousand or so inhabitants of Jesus' Capernaum—fishers and farmers though many of them no doubt were—enjoyed no significant prosperity beyond subsistence. Of course they did not enjoy the same luxuries as did the elite of Jerusalem, Caesarea Maritima, Caesarea Philippi, the cities of the Decapolis, or Sepphoris and Tiberias. But this does not mean that Jesus' Capernaum was a village consisting only of subsistence-level fishers and farmers.

Argument 1. Luxury Items from Hellenistic and Early Roman Contexts

Crossan and Reed's assertion is simply wrong that "there were no luxury items or other indications of wealth" recovered from pre-Byzantine contexts at the site.[35] As a matter of fact, there are indeed luxury items and indications of wealth that have been recovered at Capernaum from contexts that date not only to the early Roman period (63 B.C.E. to 135 C.E.), but even earlier, to the Hellenistic period (323 B.C.E. to 63 B.C.E.).

Imported Vessels

First, Crossan and Reed are mistaken that "no stamped handles from imported" vessels were found at the site.[36] In fact, fragments of imported Rhodian jars were unearthed among the domestic remains of the *insula sacra* and in various other locations where trenches to earlier periods were dug. These include handles stamped with Rhodian months in Greek, and a number of fragments without stamps that apparently belonged to similar jars.[37] Judging from the dates of similar stamped handles found in various other parts of Palestine, the Capernaum handles probably date to the second century B.C.E.[38] Hence, already well before Jesus' time, products were being imported to Capernaum all the way from the island of Rhodes.

---

35. Crossan and Reed, *Excavating Jesus*, 85; compare with Reed, *Archaeology and the Galilean Jesus*, 160.
36. Crossan and Reed, *Excavating Jesus*, 85.
37. Loffreda, *Cafarnao II*, 65, 209–10.
38. For quite up-to-date documentation in support of this dating, see the various

This is not something that subsistence-level fishers and farmers would have been able to afford.

Furthermore, during the eighteenth campaign of digging in 1985, the excavators collected "a quantity of Hellenistic pottery larger than that of all of the preceding campaigns put together." One characteristic of this Hellenistic deposit that the excavators found "of particular interest" and, indeed, "surprising" was "the percentage of elegant imported pottery, exemplified by numerous plates and bowls and cups ... with respect to common pottery." Such a surprisingly large ratio of fine table wares to common wares, they concluded, "clearly indicates the prosperity and openness to commerce of Capernaum already from the Hellenistic period."[39]

The excavators unfortunately do not provide either a precise dating or identification of these Hellenistic table wares. According to Andrea Berlin (who has examined the report and the published diagrams of the forms recovered), they "appear very close to the forms of matte red-slipped tableware manufactured on the coast south of the Carmel, such as those found at Tel Michal, Apollonia, and Dor. Vessels very similar to these have also been found at the site of Kedesh, in the eastern Upper Galilee, and petrographic analysis of those vessels indicates that they were made from coastal clays." Hence, she suggests, "the Capernaum vessels are also early to mid-Hellenistic locally made fine wares," albeit found in a deposit that also contains significantly later items.[40]

These table wares are classified by Berlin as "locally made," as opposed to imported, because they did not need to cross administrative boundaries, nor did they need to travel by sea, in order to arrive at Capernaum. Nevertheless, as the crow flies, the area south of the Carmel is actually farther away from Capernaum than is Tyre, one of the likely main production centers of the finer red-slipped table ware called Eastern Terra Sigillata A (ETSA), dating a bit later to the first century B.C.E., some fragments of which were also brought to light at Capernaum.[41] Hence, while the earlier,

---

reports cited in Mark A. Chancey, *Greco-Roman Culture and the Galilee of Jesus* (Cambridge: Cambridge University Press, 2005), 134 n. 53.

39. Virgilio Corbo and Stanislao Loffreda, "Resti del bronzo medio a Cafarnao," *LA* 35 (1985): 375–90, especially 388–90; translation of the Italian mine.

40. Berlin, personal communication, 2008. Many thanks to Berlin for this identification.

41. See, for example, Loffreda, *Cafarnao II*, 66, 210; and Andrea M. Berlin, "Romanization and Anti-Romanization in Pre-Revolt Galilee," in *The First Jewish*

matte red-slipped Hellenistic table wares probably were not as costly as the later and finer ETSA, there would still have been the mark-up involved in transporting them what was a considerable distance by ancient standards. That is, some prosperity and openness to commerce even in this quite early period is indeed suggested by their presence at Capernaum.

The later and finer ETSA is usually considered an imported ware, and was produced all along the eastern Mediterranean coast, with Antioch and Tyre serving as major production centers, but also with others existing, starting from "just north of Antioch down through the Sharon Plain."[42] Examples of this elegant ware, unearthed at the Jewish village of Gamla in the Golan, are presented in figure 8. The fragments of ETSA are far fewer in number at both Gamla and Capernaum in comparison with the large quantities found at pagan sites, such as Tel Anafa;[43] but this is typical of the general Jewish-versus-pagan ceramic profile of Palestine in the Hasmonean and Herodian periods, as I discuss in the next section.

Indeed, in a recent survey of late Hellenistic and early Roman pottery in Palestine, the excavator most familiar with the Capernaum pottery, Stanislao Loffreda, has expressed some perplexity at the quantity of early fine ware that has been recovered at the site. "It is hardly surprising," he remarks, to encounter such fine ware "in settings such as Machaerus and Herodium, as well as in the sumptuous houses of Jerusalem" (although even in these settings it is nowhere near as abundant as in pagan settings, on which see the next section). However, he asks, why is it also "often present at Capernaum, a modest village in Jesus' time"?[44]

Revolt: Archaeology, History and Ideology (ed. Andrea M. Berlin and J. Andrew Overman; London: Routledge, 2002), 57–73. It is presumably to these fragments of Eastern Terra Sigillata A (ETSA) that Crossan and Reed are referring in their vague statement that "a few ... locally made" imitation fine wares from the early Roman period were found (*Excavating Jesus*, 85). They make no attempt, however, to justify their reinterpretation of these fragments as imitation ware. Berlin does not disagree with Loffreda that these Capernaum sherds are genuine ETSA, although she dates them more precisely to the first century B.C.E., as opposed to Loffreda's early Roman dating ("Romanization and Anti-Romanization," 57–73). Here I am following Berlin's dating.

42. Berlin, personal communication, 2008.

43. See Berlin, "Romanization and Anti-Romanization," 62, fig. 4.1.

44. Loffreda, *Holy Land Pottery at the Time of Jesus: Early Roman Period, 63 BC–70 AD* (Jerusalem: Franciscan Printing Press, 2002), 70–72. Although the title of Loffreda's survey suggests that he discusses only early Roman pottery, he actually also discusses a number of forms that clearly date to the late Hellenistic period.

Figure 7. Early Roman glass ware from Insula 2's Western House. Upper photograph from Stanislao Loffreda, "Vasi in vetro e in argilla trovati a Cafarnao nel 1984. Rapporto preliminare," *LA* 34 (1984): 385–408, figure 15. Lower photograph from idem, *Holy Land Pottery at the Time of Jesus: Early Roman Period, 63 BC–70 AD* (Jerusalem: Franciscan Printing Press, 2002) 103, no. 224. Both reproduced with permission of the Studium Biblicum Franciscanum, Jerusalem. Note the Herodian lamp in the photograph below, recovered *in situ* with the glass ware.

Glass Ware

Finally, Crossan and Reed are mistaken that "even the simplest glass forms are lacking" from early Roman contexts at Capernaum.[45] In fact, a full set of early Roman glassware was discovered against a wall of Insula 2, located west of the modern pathway leading to the synagogue. This wall was part of an early Roman house with a large courtyard (see the diachronic analysis of Insula 2 presented in argument 3, below), incompletely excavated on account of the modern pathway. The wall and the early Roman walls east of it are indicated in dark gray in figures 2 and 3. The set consists of fourteen free-blown vessels—plates, bowls, a goblet, and flasks (see fig. 7 for photographs of this glassware). Loffreda dates it to "not later than the First Jewish War" (ca. 68–70 C.E.).[46] This means that very close to the time that

Figure 8. Examples of Eastern Terra Sigillata from Gamla. From: Andrea Berlin, *Gamla I: The Pottery of the Second Temple Period* (Jerusalem: Israel Antiquities Authority, 2006), 1:13, fig. 2.1. Used by permission of the author.

---

45. Crossan and Reed, *Excavating Jesus*, 85.
46. Loffreda, *Holy Land Pottery at the Time of Jesus*, 103–4. This dating of the glassware differs somewhat from Loffreda's earlier dating of it to the last decades of the first century C.E., or at the very latest the first decades of the second century (idem, "Vasi in vetro e in argilla trovati a Cafarnao nel 1984: Rapporto preliminare," *LA* 34 [1984]: 385–408).

Jesus lived at least one family in the village, residing in a spacious house in Insula 2 with a large courtyard, could afford to purchase a full set of rather elegant-looking glassware.

Nevertheless, it should be mentioned that, elegant-looking though these glass vessels are, they are not as fine as the colored and colorless cast glass vessels and polychrome mosaic vessels that were recovered from the elite quarters of Jerusalem. Whereas the finer vessels required an elaborate and lengthy manufacturing process, free-blown glass was a lot quicker and easier to produce, most likely rendering it the least expensive glass available on the market.[47] It would surely be going too far, however, to take this to mean that a full set of free-blown glass such as the one recovered at Capernaum was affordable to the subsistence-level poor.[48] Once again, it is not my argument here that anyone in Capernaum ever lived in the kind of luxury enjoyed by, for instance, the inhabitants of the "Herodian Mansion" of Jerusalem (where some of the finer glass was found).[49] My contention is simply that at least some of the villagers in Jesus' Capernaum probably lived at a level significantly above subsistence.

The various luxury items mentioned above were owned by residents of the village who lived long before Christian pilgrims made their way there in Byzantine times. This fact gives us one important reason, among others to be discussed in the next section, for seriously questioning Crossan and Reed when they assert that it was only when Capernaum supposedly became a Byzantine pilgrimage center that a sudden increase in wealth occurred in the village.[50]

---

47. For perhaps the most comprehensive survey of the Hellenistic and early Roman glassware recovered from Palestine yet available, see (the title does not reflect the actual breadth of the discussion) Dennis J. Mizzi, "The Glass from Khirbet Qumran: What Does It Tell Us about the Qumran Community?" in *The Dead Sea Scrolls: Texts and Contexts* (ed. Charlotte Hempel; Leiden: Brill, 2010), 99–198. I would like to thank Jodi Magness for bringing this excellent survey to my attention.

48. As Mizzi also emphasizes regarding free-blown glassware in ibid., 106 n. 32.

49. See ibid., 126.

50. Reed, *Archaeology and the Galilean Jesus*, 164; Crossan and Reed, *Excavating Jesus*, 85–97.

Argument 2. A Sudden Increase in Capernaum's Wealth in Byzantine Times? The Village's Broader Context in Two Different Historical Periods

Crossan and Reed are correct that there is considerable evidence that the inhabitants of Byzantine Capernaum enjoyed prosperity beyond subsistence. Substantial quantities of imported fine wares, which date especially to the Byzantine period, were found throughout the insulae excavated at the site (see fig. 6).[51] These fine red-slipped table wares, which have been classified as African Red Slip Ware, Cypriot Red Slip Ware, and Late Roman C Ware, were mass-produced in specialized workshops and appear all over the eastern Mediterranean, starting in the late Roman but especially in the Byzantine period. They became all the rage throughout Palestine and seem to have been afforded by many people in rural areas and in cities alike.[52] As Sean A. Kingsley correctly observes, villagers at Capernaum and elsewhere in Palestine who purchased these popular wares were clearly engaging in a form of "conspicuous consumption" that reveals that they were *not* members of "a peasantry scraping a living from limited subsistence farming, from which no surpluses were retained once taxes had been paid."[53]

The notion that, in contrast, the inhabitants of the Capernaum of Jesus' time were indeed members of such a "peasantry" is, however, a complete *non sequitur*. First, as discussed above, some luxury items from earlier periods were indeed found at the site, including some fragments of imported ETSA and stamped Rhodian amphorae. These imported items are certainly very few, but this is due at least in part to the accidents of preservation and excavation. It must always be recalled that the site reached

---

51. On these fine wares, see Loffreda, *Cafarnao II*, 13, 65–87, 166–74; and Corbo, *Cafarnao I*, 220.

52. See Loffreda, *Cafarnao II*, 67–88, 166–74; Eric M. Meyers, James F. Strange, and Dennis E. Groh, "The Meiron Excavations Project: Archaeological Survey in Galilee and Golan, 1976," *BASOR* 230 (1978): 1–24, especially 10–15; and Dennis E. Groh, "The Finewares from the Patrician and Lintel Houses," in *Excavations at Ancient Meiron, Upper Galilee, Israel 1971–72, 1974–75, 1977* (ed. Eric M. Meyers, James F. Strange, and Carol L. Meyers; Cambridge: American Schools of Oriental Research, 1981), 129–38, especially 138.

53. Sean A. Kingsley, "The Economic Impact of the Palestinian Wine Trade in Late Antiquity," in *Economy and Exchange in the East Mediterranean during Late Antiquity* (ed. Sean A. Kingsley and Michael Decker; Oxford: Oxbow, 2001), 44–68, especially 58–59.

its heyday in Byzantine times and only some trenches were dug down to earlier layers, so that the majority of the finds *of any kind* that were recovered (coins, plain ware, domestic installations, architectural fragments and mosaics of the public buildings, etc.) are Byzantine in date.

EASTERN TERRA SIGILLATA A

Far more importantly, however, the comparatively much smaller number of imported items in the Hasmonean and Herodian periods must be understood within Capernaum's broader historical context at this time, which was very different from what it became centuries later in the Byzantine period. The distinctive features of Hasmonean–Herodian Jewish Palestine, evident in both the archaeological and literary record, are now well known. First, figurative art was scrupulously avoided, as is amply evident in the finds and remains dating to this period.[54] The zeal with which the Jews of the period adhered to the law forbidding images of "any living creatures" (*Ant.* 17.151–152) is illustrated by the two "sages" and their young followers, who paid with their lives for tearing down the golden eagle that Herod the Great had erected over the great gate of the temple (*J.W.* 1.651–655; *Ant.* 17.149–165); and by the burning of Antipas's palace in Tiberias because it contained images of animals (*Vita* 65–66).

Second, a concern for ritual purity spread throughout Jewish Palestine in Hasmonean and Herodian times. The evidence for this includes stepped immersion pools for ritual cleansing (*miqwāôt*), some of which were associated with oil and wine presses, and locally produced stone vessels, insusceptible to impurity, which appear at virtually all Jewish sites beginning in the first century B.C.E. but proliferating especially during the first century C.E.[55] All this archaeological evidence is corroborated by our primary literary sources (the Hebrew Bible, the Dead Sea Scrolls, Josephus, Philo, the New Testament, the Intertestamental and early rabbinic literature), which also attest to a widespread, expansionist—albeit not ubiquitous and certainly not uniform—observance of ritual purity among Jews throughout

---

54. See, e.g, Nahman Avigad, *Discovering Jerusalem* (Nashville: Thomas Nelson, 1983), 154–60; Meyers, "Jesus and His Galilean Context," 59–60. For the few exceptions that prove the rule, see Jodi Magness, *Stone and Dung, Oil and Spit: Jewish Daily Life in the Time of Jesus* (Grand Rapids: Eerdmans, 2011), 221 n. 80.

55. For a brief and well-documented survey of the evidence for *miqwāôt* and the stone-vessel industry, see Magness, *Stone and Dung*, 16–17, 70–74.

Palestine in late Second Temple times.⁵⁶ This included the Galilee, which, after its conquest by the Hasmoneans at the end of the second century B.C.E., had become very much a part of *Jewish* Palestine.⁵⁷ That the Jews of early Roman Capernaum shared this solicitude for purity is clear from the some 150 stone vessel fragments recovered from the site, including a few fragments of expensive, large lathe-turned jars.⁵⁸ The location of the village on the shore of a body of "living water" (suitable for ritual cleansing)—namely, the Sea of Galilee—readily accounts for the absence of *miqwāʾôt* at Capernaum.

---

56. This has been argued quite comprehensively by Thomas Kazen in his *Issues of Impurity in Early Judaism* (Winona Lake, Ind.: Eisenbrauns, 2010) and *Jesus and Purity Halakah: Was Jesus Indifferent to Impurity?* (rev. ed.; Winona Lake, Ind.: Eisenbrauns, 2010). It must nevertheless be mentioned that the extent and nature of Jewish purity observance in late Second Temple times is still the subject of considerable debate. For a basic bibliography on Jewish purity laws representing the spectrum of opinion, see John P. Meier, *Law and Love* (vol. 4 of *A Marginal Jew: Rethinking the Historical Jesus*; New Haven: Yale University Press, 2009), 415–26 (but see Kazen's critique of Meier's own discussion of Jesus and purity halakah [*Issues of Impurity*, 151–67]). For a strong critique of the "minimalist" position in this debate, see John C. Poirier, "Purity beyond the Temple in the Second Temple Era," *JBL* 122 (2003): 247–65.

57. This has been argued quite comprehensively and convincingly by Mark A. Chancey, *The Myth of a Gentile Galilee* (Cambridge: Cambridge University Press, 2002). Whether this occurred on account of the Hasmoneans forcing conversion on non-Jewish Galileans, or the latter's peaceful assimilation, or migrations of Jews from Judea to the Galilee after its conquest, or some combination of all these, Chancey is right that the cumulative evidence quite overwhelmingly points to the Jewish nature of the Galilee by the first century C.E.

58. Most of these fragments have not been published, so I am here relying on the number provided by Reed ("Stone Vessels and Gospel Texts: Purity and Socio-Economics in John 2," in *Zeichen aus Text und Stein: Studien auf dem Weg zu einer Archäologie des Neuen Testaments* [ed. Stefan Alkier and Jürgen Zangenburg; Tübingen: Francke, 2003], 381–401, especially 385, 395–96), who states that Loffreda permitted him "a full examination of all the stone vessels, published and unpublished, found at Capernaum," not counting the very few uncovered on the Greek Orthodox side of the site (ibid., 385, n. 23). In this article, Reed stresses the high cost of the large lathe-turned vessels in comparison to the smaller ones, a point one would surely not wish to dispute. What is interesting is that, while Reed declares the larger vessels to have been "virtually absent" at Capernaum (ibid., 395–96), his fig. 7 (ibid., 395) actually shows that a few fragments of such vessels were indeed found at the site. They account for "less than 2%" (ibid., 395), but why, if Capernaum was the home of only the subsistence-level poor, were *any* expensive large stone jars present in the village?

It is within this broader context that one must understand the significant fact that not only at Capernaum, but at virtually all Jewish sites in this period, ETSA was apparently nowhere near as popular as it was among pagans. For instance, thousands upon thousands of fragments of ETSA (23,756 sherds) were recovered at pagan Tel Anafa, situated 8 km south of Tel Dan in the northern part of the Huleh Valley east of the Jordan. This pagan site reached its *floruit* (128–80 B.C.E.) during the heyday of the independent Jewish Hasmonean kings (134–76 B.C.E.).[59] In striking contrast, this ware is "conspicuous by its absence" from no less an edifice than the Hasmonean palace complex at Jericho. Only a small group of local imitations of ETSA shows up at Jericho in the later stages of the Hellenistic period (ca. 80–31 B.C.E.) prior to the advent of Herod the Great.[60] The "villa" at late Hellenistic Tel Anafa was a fine one, but the Jericho Hasmonean palace complex outshone it architecturally by a good margin.[61] It is true that ETSA would have had to have been transported overland much further inland to reach Jericho than to arrive at Tel Anafa, and this would have driven up the cost of the ware for the Hasmoneans.[62] But it nonethe-

---

59. See Kathleen Warner Slane, "The Fine Wares," in *Tel Anafa II, i: The Hellenistic and Roman Pottery* (ed. Sharon C. Herbert; Ann Arbor, Mich.: Kelsey Museum, 1997), 249–406, especially 255, 261–64, and 272. On the site of Tel Anafa in general, see Sharon C. Herbert, "Introduction," and idem, "Occupational History and Stratigraphy," in *Tel Anafa I, i: Final Report on Ten Years of Excavation at a Hellenistic and Roman Settlement in Northern Israel* (ed. Sharon C. Herbert; Ann Arbor, Mich.: Kelsey Museum, 1994), 1–25, 26–182, especially 16 and 32–33.

60. Rachel Bar-Nathan, *The Pottery* (vol. 3 of *Hasmonean and Herodian Palaces at Jericho: Final Reports of the 1973–1987 Excavations*; Jerusalem: Israel Exploration Society, 2002), 119–20, 197.

61. Compare the plans and photographs of the Tel Anafa "villa" in Herbert, "Occupational History and Stratigraphy," with those of the Hasmonean palace complex in Ehud Netzer, ed., *Hasmonean and Herodian Palaces at Jericho: Final Reports of the 1973–1987 Excavations* (3 vols.; Jerusalem: Israel Exploration Society, 2001).

62. Magness emphasizes the greater cost of overland transport from Phoenicia to Jerusalem and the Jordan Valley versus to the Galilee, in order to explain the absence of ETSA in the former and its presence in the latter in Hasmonean times (*Stone and Dung*, 55–56). This is one point where I must disagree with Magness's otherwise excellent discussion. If the cost of overland transport was the determining factor, why did Galilean Jews stop importing the ware in Herodian times, while the Jews of Judea began to import it? For this phenomenon, see Berlin, "Romanization and Anti-Romanization," *passim*, and my discussion further on in this section. Magness recognizes this phenomenon and rightly ascribes it to increasing purity observance in the

less was surely well within their economic means to have imported it had they so desired. Indeed, during the time of Herod and his descendants (starting in ca. 31 B.C.E.), some sherds of ETSA do show up at Jericho, although it must be underscored that even then their occurrence is still rather limited compared with pagan sites.[63]

The limited quantity of ETSA even in the especially lavish Herodian palaces at Jericho is surely striking,[64] when one considers that at pagan sites it was not only the people at the highest end of the socioeconomic stratum who purchased ETSA. For example, even the new, much humbler early Roman settlers of Tel Anafa—who, after a settlement gap of over half a century, built much simpler dwellings on top of the abandoned late Hellenistic "villa"—continued to import substantial quantities of it.[65]

The same general Jewish-versus-pagan profile also appears, thus far, to be confirmed by the first final report on the fine wares from Jerusalem (although the quantity of fine wares still awaiting publication from the Jewish Quarter does not yet allow certainty). The finds so far examined suggest that ETSA started to arrive at Jerusalem "probably not before the middle of the first century B.C.E.," or not long before Herod's reign, and even afterwards "the ware was not as popular as on sites with Greek and Phoenician connections like Tel Anafa, Samaria and Maresha."[66] This was patently not on account of a comparative lack of purchasing power on the part of elite Jerusalemites, either in Hasmonean or Herodian times. The archaeological remains and finds, which include fine (nonfigurative) mosaic floors, frescoes, glassware, beautifully carved stone tables and other indicators of wealth demonstrate that the inhabitants of Upper Jerusalem

---

Galilee (*Stone and Dung*, 60–61) but does not fully appreciate how it quite undermines the notion that economic factors were determinative in the Jewish-versus-pagan contrast in the distribution of ETSA.

63. Bar-Nathan, *Hasmonean and Herodian Palaces at Jericho*, 119–20, 129, 190–91, 199–203.

64. See the plans and photographs of these in Netzer, *Hasmonean and Herodian Palaces*.

65. Slane, "The Fine Wares," 264; and see fig. 4.1 in Berlin, "Romanization and Anti-Romanization," 62.

66. Renate Rosenthal-Heginbottom, "Chapter 6 (b): Hellenistic and Roman Fine Ware and Lamps from Area A," in *The Finds from Areas A, W and X-2. Final Report* (vol. 2 of *Jewish Quarter Excavations in the Old City of Jerusalem Conducted by Nahman Avigad, 1969–1982*; ed. Hillel Geva; Jerusalem: Israel Exploration Society, 2003), 192–223, especially 214, 219–20.

were very well-to-do and so could have readily acquired greater quantities of ETSA, had they chosen to do so.[67]

Similarly, at Gamla in the Golan, the quantity of ETSA recovered, while significant, also does not come close to matching the quantity unearthed at pagan sites, such as Tel Anafa.[68] Yet, it is clear that well-to-do individuals were living at Gamla, as is revealed by other archaeological indices, such as frescoed walls and luxury items of various types.[69] Likewise, ETSA is totally absent at Yodefat in the Galilee.[70] Yet a mansion was unearthed there that had not only frescoed walls but even a frescoed floor. Also in line with observance of halakah, these frescoes, although imitating Roman designs (with the "Second Pompeian" style on the walls and an imitation of *opus sectile* on the floor), contained no figurative art; and neither did those at Gamla.[71]

It should be noted that there is an interesting discrepancy in the profiles of ETSA at elite Jewish sites in Judea versus in the Galilee and the Golan. Whereas the Judean elite purchased very little, if any, ETSA in the Hasmonean period, they began to acquire some of this ware in the Herodian period. In contrast, as Berlin has shown, the Galilean villages were purchasing this fine ware mostly in the first century B.C.E., with a sharp drop in the amount they acquired in the first century C.E.[72] In all cases and in both periods, however, the occupants of Jewish sites, no matter how affluent, were not buying the ware in the same quantities as were their pagan counterparts.

Indeed, as Berlin has shown, the pagan inhabitants of the "villa" at Tel Anafa in the Hasmonean period purchased over four times as much ETSA

---

67. As a visit to the partially reconstructed Herodian Quarter in the Wohl Museum of Archaeology in the Old City of Jerusalem, or a glance at Avigad, *Discovering Jerusalem*, would immediately make clear.

68. See fig. 4.1. in Berlin, "Romanization and Anti-Romanization," 62.

69. See Danny Syon, "Gamla: Portrait of a Rebellion," *BAR* 18.1 (1992): 20–37, especially 23–24, 33–35; and Shemaryahu Gutman, "Gamala," *NEAEHL* 2, 459–63, especially 462–63.

70. MordechaiAviam, "First Century Jewish Galilee: An Archaeological Perspective," in *Religion and Society in Roman Palestine: Old Questions, New Approaches* (ed. Douglas R. Edwards; New York: Routledge, 2004), 7–27, especially 19.

71. Mordechai Aviam, personal communication, 2003; *idem*, "First Century Jewish Galilee," 17, with photograph. For a photograph of the Gamla frescoes, see Syon, "Gamla," 33.

72. Berlin, "Romanization and Anti-Romanization," *passim*.

than did the residents of Gamla, a relatively large village site. Even the comparatively humbler early Roman settlers of Tel Anafa, while importing less than half as much ETSA than had their wealthier predecessors, still purchased almost twice as much as had the residents of Gamla in the Hasmonean period; and in the meantime the early Roman inhabitants of Gamla who were their contemporaries had virtually ceased buying the ware altogether.[73]

This Jewish-versus-pagan contrast in the profile of ETSA in Hasmonean and Herodian Palestine most likely reflects the widespread Jewish concern for purity, mentioned above.[74] Purity concerns may also lie behind the dramatic decline in numbers, beginning in Hasmonean times, of the imported stamped amphorae of the earlier Hellenistic period at Capernaum, Jerusalem, and other Jewish sites.[75] As was the case for ETSA, some imported amphorae were purchased by the priestly elite of Jerusalem in the Herodian period, but in substantially fewer quantities than at pagan sites.[76]

Neither ETSA nor stamped handles of imported amphorae have thus far been found in any of the excavations of rural settlements in the land of Benjamin, nor in excavations of the town of the Hellenistic period on Mount Gerizim. The large number of coins and substantial industrial installations for the production of wine and olive oil found in the Benjamin settlements surely indicate that the absence of these imported products was likewise not due to economic reasons, but rather to purity concerns;[77]

---

73. See fig. 4.1 in ibid., 62.

74. As has been proposed by, e.g., Bar-Nathan, *Hasmonean and Herodian Palaces*, 197-98; Rosenthal-Heginbottom, "Hellenistic and Roman Fine Ware," 192-223; David Adan-Bayewitz and Mordechai Aviam, "Iotapata, Josephus, and the Siege of 67: Preliminary Report on the 1992-94 Seasons," *Journal of Roman Archaeology* 10 (1997): 131-65, especially 165.

75. As proposed by Donald T. Ariel and Aryeh Strikovsky, "Appendix," in *Imported Stamped Amphorae Handles, Coins, Worked Bone and Ivory, and Glass* (vol. 2 of *Excavations at the City of David Directed by Yigal Shiloh 1978–1985*; ed. Donald T. Ariel; Jerusalem: The Hebrew University of Jerusalem, 1990), 25-29, albeit with some caution.

76. Magness, *Stone and Dung*, 54-58.

77. As observed by Yitzhak Magen, "The Land of Benjamin in the Second Temple Period," in *The Land of Benjamin* (ed. Yitzhak Magen et al.; Jerusalem: Israel Antiquities Authority, 2004), 1-28, especially 18-21. Magen also notes that *miqwāʾōt* were discovered in conjunction with wine and oil presses in this region.

and apparently not only the Jews, but also the Samaritan inhabitants of Mount Gerizim "also strictly observed the laws of purity and impurity."[78]

GALILEAN COARSE WARE

It was not only Gentile luxury products like ETSA and imported wine that were avoided. "Galilean Coarse Ware" (GCW), a locally produced ware which occurs in Persian and pre-Hasmonean Hellenistic pagan contexts over a clearly defined zone in the Upper Galilee and its edges in the northern Lower Galilee, disappears from the region in the Hasmonean period. Some of the GCW sites were abandoned in the wake of the Hasmonean conquest, and others continued to exist but now with Hasmonean coins and no GCW.[79] As Mordechai Aviam has summed it up, the Jews' "avoidance of ... almost all kinds" of imported vessels is "a distinctive phenomenon" of the Hasmonean and Herodian periods, quite akin to the avoidance of figurative art.[80]

If Jewish avoidance of Gentile wares was due to the widespread concern for ritual purity, as all the evidence seems to converge strongly to suggest, then how is it that any ETSA at all turns up at Jewish sites, especially in the mansions of the priestly elite of Herodian Jerusalem, whose *miqwā'ôt*, many stone vessels, and eschewing of figurative art surely demonstrate their own solicitude for Torah observance?[81] Surely political-religious issues have played a role here. As mentioned above, although the

---

78. Ibid., 18.
79. See Mordechai Aviam, "Distribution Maps of Archaeological Data from the Galilee: An Attempt to Establish Zones Indicative of Ethnicity and Religious Affiliation," in *Religion, Ethnicity, and Identity in Ancient Galilee: A Region in Transition* (ed. Jürgen Zangenberg, Harold W. Attridge, and Dale B. Martin; Tübingen: Mohr Siebeck, 2007), 115–32, especially 115–18; and Aviam, "First Century Jewish Galilee," 7–15.
80. Aviam, "First Century Jewish Galilee," 23.
81. It is specifically because ETSA was found in the mansions of the priestly elite that Andrea M. Berlin argues that purity concerns were not the determining factor (*Gamla I: The Pottery of the Second Temple Period* [IAA Reports 29; Jerusalem: Israel Antiquities Authority, 2006], 151). She has accordingly offered an alternative explanation (see ibid., 21–23, 138–40, 142–55, updated from a different explanation she offered earlier in idem, "Romanization and Anti-Romanization," *passim*). In my view, purity concerns remain the best explanation for the Jewish-versus-pagan profile of ETSA, and political-religious issues can explain its presence in the homes of the priestly elite, as I suggest here.

observance of purity was widespread in this period, it was not uniform, with disagreements between the various Jewish factions concerning what precisely it entailed. Perhaps the Sadducean elite, once freed under Herod the Great from the strong Pharisaic influence that had prevailed during Salome Alexander's reign (*J.W.* 1.110–114; *Ant.* 13.401–415), decided that it was not necessary to eat common food in a state of purity as was the practice of the Pharisees,[82] since it is not mandated by Torah which they alone accepted as authoritative (*Ant.* 18.16). Hence, when eating common food they did not scruple to use imported fine ware; whereas when they needed to be in a state of purity for their various sacrificial meals, after having immersed themselves in their *miqwāʾōt* and waited until sunset,[83] they used their stone ware and positively lovely, locally produced Nabatean-style pottery (see fig. 9). In the meantime in the Galilee, the purchase of ETSA dropped off sharply in particular after increased tensions between the Galileans and the Phoenicians began to arise, as recorded by Josephus (*J.W.* 4.104; *Vita* 43–45), as well as during growing anti-Gentile and anti-Roman sentiment in the region in the decades leading up to the Great Revolt.[84]

---

82. Kazen argues in favor of this argument concerning Pharisaic practice, which was made famous by Jacob Neusner, against Ed Sanders's objections to it, although he agrees with Sanders that this practice should not be described as living or eating "like priests" (*Jesus and Purity* Halakah, 68–88, and see his documentation of this debate).

83. Priests wishing to eat their sacrificial meals in purity needed not only to immerse, but also to wait until sunset (see Kazen, *Jesus and Purity* Halakha, 69, 75–77, with biblical and other primary-source references).

84. Hence, I am in partial agreement with Berlin's earlier argument that the reasons for the Jewish-versus-pagan profile of ETSA entailed a political component ("Romanization and Anti-Romanization"), although in my view this was in conjunction with purity concerns. These concerns, however, probably did not entail the notion that the Gentiles themselves were intrinsically ritually impure, a notion that did not develop until tannaitic times and even then inconsistently. See Christine E. Hayes, *Gentile Impurities and Jewish Identities: Intermarriage and Conversion from the Bible to the Talmud* (Oxford: Oxford University Press, 2002), *passim*; Jonathan Klawans, "Notions of Gentile Impurity in Ancient Judaism," *AJS Review* 20 (1995): 285–312; idem, *Impurity and Sin in Ancient Judaism* (Oxford: Oxford University Press, 2000), *passim*; and Saul M. Olyan, "Purity Ideology in Ezra-Nehemiah as a Tool to Reconstitute the Community," *JSJ* 35 (2004): 1–16, on Neh 13:4–9, and also *J.W.* 1.152–153; *Ant.* 14.71–73, which record the ritual defilement by Gentiles of the inner parts of the temple. Nehemiah, however, did not object to Gentiles selling in Jerusalem, except on the Sabbath (13:15–22), and they were allowed in the Second Temple's outer court.

Halakah and Trade

What remains quite clear about late Second Temple times is that it is during this period, perhaps more than during any other period of Jewish history in Palestine, that a widespread regard for halakah gave rise to *deliberately* introverted trade patterns on the part of the Jews. This is probably also reflected in the numismatic record. Significantly, beginning especially during the reign of Alexander Janneus, Hasmonean bronze coins almost entirely displaced those of Gentile origin at Jewish sites throughout Judea, the Galilee, and the Golan.[85] In contrast, there is an almost total lack of Hasmonean coins at pagan sites such as Acco-Ptolemais.[86] The coins in question were bronze Hasmonean *prutot*, or small change, and hence this phenomenon was probably not related to tax collection by the new rulers (the high-value Tyrian shekel remained the standard silver currency in the region and was the coin explicitly required for payment of the temple tax). Instead, the almost complete displacement of Gentile small change with that of the Hasmoneans most likely indicates a corresponding shift in trade relations inward and focused on Jerusalem.[87]

It is crucial to emphasize, however, that the deliberate choice not to import many Gentile products on the part of the Jews of Palestine in the Hasmonean and Herodian periods is *not* an indication of their economic backwardness. Josephus's declaration regarding his people in *Contra Apion* 1.60–61 has too often been cited as evidence for the supposed lack of commercial development of Jewish Palestine in his time.[88] On the one hand,

---

85. For an overview of the numismatic evidence, which amply reflects this displacement in the Galilee, see Chancey, *Greco-Roman Culture and the Galilee of Jesus*, 167–92.

86. Aviam, "First Century Jewish Galilee," 14–15.

87. As underscored by H. S. Kim ("Small Change and the Moneyed Economy," in *Money, Labour and Land: Approaches to the Economies of Ancient Greece* [ed. Paul Cartledge, Edward E. Cohen, and Lin Foxhall; London: Routledge, 2002], 44–51), from the earliest period of monetization, bronze coins were small change, the lowest common denominator in coinage, unlikely to have been used for either tax collection or exchanges solely between members of the upper strata. They were instead used primarily for local economic transactions and only occasionally had a wider distribution.

88. As also observed by Philip A. Harland, "The Economy of First-Century Palestine: State of the Scholarly Discussion," in *Handbook of Early Christianity* (ed. Anthony J. Blasi, Jean Duhaime, and Paul-André Turcotte; Oxford: AltaMira, 2002), 511–27, especially 517–18. For examples, see the references he cites.

this passage does reflect the deliberately more introverted trade patterns on the part of the Jews discussed above. Josephus stresses that his compatriots, who do not live along the Mediterranean coast but reside inland far from the sea, "do not take great pleasure in sea-trade or the mingling with others [engendered] through it." He moreover associates this explicitly with Jewish solicitude for observance of the law and the "peculiarity of our lifestyle." On the other hand, far too much has been made of Josephus's brief comment in this same passage that "[given that] we have been apportioned a good land [or region], it is on this that we focus all our labor."[89] Even if one were to grant (and I cannot) that Josephus intends here to imply that agricultural production was the only economic activity taking place in Jewish Palestine at this time, he would simply be appealing to common aristocratic sensibilities, such as are expressed by "Cato (*Agr.* 1.2–4), Cicero (*Off.* 1.150–51), Varro (*Rust.* 2.10.1–3), and Columella (*Rust.* 1.1–17),"[90] all of whom extol the virtues of landed wealth and investment in agriculture versus investment in trade.

There is no space here to discuss in detail the growing body of evidence for craft and agricultural specialization and local and intraregional trade that took place between the members of the expanding population of Jews in the Hasmonean and Herodian periods.[91] To provide but a few salient examples, the archaeological data indicate that the Hasmoneans had fostered considerable economic growth in the Galilee after their conquest of the region by inaugurating mass production of olive oil, where it had not

---

89. Translation mine. I have translated the Greek word, *emporiai*, as "sea-trade." While this word can sometimes mean business in general, according to *LSJ* it is "mostly used of commerce or trade by sea," whether in the singular or in the plural. It is probably best understood here in this more common sense, especially given the context in which Josephus is using it, which is to explain why the earliest Greek historians were silent about the Jews.

90. Harland, "The Economy of First-Century Palestine," 517–18.

91. For a convenient brief summary of a good part of this evidence, see Douglas R. Edwards, "Identity and Social Location in Roman Galilean Villages," in Zangenberg, Attridge, and Martin, *Religion, Ethnicity, and Identity*, 357–74. Edwards makes a curious error in this otherwise excellent discussion. Without documentation, he declares that "a relatively high proportion" of ETSA was found at Meron (364–65). Groh actually stresses the paucity of early fine wares at Meron ("The Finewares," 136), and, according to Eric Meyers, "you can count them on one hand" (personal communication, 2011). My thanks to Meyers and also to James F. Strange for identifying this as an error.

been an important industry before.[92] By the first century, it is clear that this industry had grown substantially and that significant private interests were also involved, as is indicated by the industrial-scale oil presses in the wealthy quarter of Gamla, found in a well-constructed building also containing a *miqweh*,[93] as well as by John of Gischala's monopoly of the olive oil crop of the Upper Galilean Mount Meiron region during the Revolt, which enabled him to rake in a considerable profit by exporting it at a high premium to fellow Jews in need of pure oil outside of Jewish Palestine (*J.W.* 2.591–592; *Vita* 73–74). Stone vessel production was also a thriving local industry in this period, with a wide distribution all over Jewish Palestine and centers of production at Jerusalem, elsewhere in Judea, and even in the Galilee itself. Some of the stone items produced were of very high quality and no doubt quite expensive.[94]

Also important to mention here are the thriving centers of local Jewish pottery production starting in the first century B.C.E. at Kefar Hananya, Shikhin, and apparently also at Jotapata and elsewhere, while knife-pared oil lamps found at Gamla and Yodefat were imported from Jerusalem.[95] Also produced in Jerusalem were exquisite eggshell-thin bowls with similar features to the fine Nabatean bowls, famous for their thinness and painted motifs, of the same period (see fig. 9). These provide a powerful corrective to any assumption that locally produced fine wares were bound

---

92. Mordechai Aviam, "The Beginning of Mass Production of Olive Oil in the Galilee," in idem, *Jews, Pagans and Christians in the Galilee* (Rochester, N.Y.: University of Rochester Press, 2004), 51–60.

93. A plan of this installation is found in Gutman, "Gamala," 461. Also see the photograph of this installation and that of one of the Hasmonean presses in Aviam, "The Beginning of Mass Production," 55.

94. Yitzhak Magen, *The Stone Vessel Industry in the Second Temple Period: Excavations at Hizma and the Jerusalem Temple Mount* (Jerusalem: Israel Exploration Society, 2002) *passim*; Aviam, "Distribution Maps," 119–20. Aviam mentions "the survey find of a Galilean stone-vessel workshop near Nazareth" ("First Century Jewish Galilee," 20).

95. On Kefar Hananya and Shikhin, see David Adan-Bayewitz, *Common Pottery in Roman Galilee: A Study of Local Trade* (Ramat-Gan, Israel: Bar Ilan University Press, 1993); David Adan-Bayewitz and Isadore Perlman, "The Local Trade of Sepphoris in the Roman Period," *IEJ* 40 (1990): 153–72. On the three pottery kilns uncovered at Jotapata, the storage jar production center found at Yavor, and the results of Neutron Activation Analysis showing that the knife-pared lamps found at Gamla and Yodefat had been produced at Jerusalem, see Aviam, "First Century Jewish Galilee," 18–19.

Figure 9. "Jerusalem Painted Bowls" from Jerusalem. From Stanislao Loffreda, *Holy Land Pottery at the Time of Jesus: Early Roman Period, 63 BC–70 AD* (Jerusalem: Franciscan Printing Press, 2002) 67, no. 140. Used by permission of the Studium Biblicum Franciscanum, Jerusalem.

to be inferior in quality to ETSA.[96] A few samples of these bowls were also recovered at Jericho, and Neutron Activation Analysis has confirmed that Jerusalem was their production center.[97] Since these bowls were unlikely to have been mass produced on the same scale as was ETSA, it is not at all a given that this delicate local ware was cheaper to acquire.

Finally, while purity concerns led to only limited *importing* of Gentile products, some *Jewish* products were *exported*—for instance, from the Galilee to fellow Jews in Syria and Caesarea Philippi, who needed ritually pure olive oil (*J.W.* 2.591–592; *Vita* 73–74; *Ant.* 12.119–124); to the pagan inhabitants of early Roman Tel Anafa in the territory of Herod Philip, who imported a great quantity of foodstuffs from the Lower Galilee and "an astonishing 85% of all recognizable early Roman cooking and

---

96. Avigad, *Discovering Jerusalem*, 179–85.
97. Bar-Nathan, *Hasmonean and Herodian Palaces*, 122–28.

kitchen/utility vessels (excluding jars)" from Kefar Hananya;[98] and to the inhabitants of the region of Tyre and Sidon, who apparently "depended on [Agrippa I's] country for food" (Acts 12:20). There is also the intriguing possibility that basalt Roman millstones produced at Capernaum itself may have been exported all the way to Cyprus, as postulated by the authors of a geochemical analysis, although they do not make clear when in the Roman period this may have taken place.[99] As Douglas R. Edwards has aptly encapsulated the matter, all this evidence implies that "Early Roman Galilean villages ... operated fully within a vibrant economic environment under Herod Antipas," whose complexity, variety of produce, and diversity of activity in individual villages as well as in the cities that has too often been underestimated.[100]

THE BYZANTINE PERIOD

Nevertheless, the Byzantine period does represent the apex of the Galilee's commercial development for the simple reason that the general population of the region had now grown to its peak.[101] A recent archaeological survey of the Upper Galilee (2001), for instance, reports that the number of sites recorded increases from 82 in the Persian period, to 106 in the Hellenistic, to 170 in the Roman, to 194 in the Byzantine.[102] As mentioned above, Capernaum itself also reached its zenith at this time. Indeed, David Goodblatt reports that "there is now a consensus" that Palestine at large

---

98. Berlin, "The Plain Wares," in *Tel Anafa II.i*, 14–15, 22–23, 29, n. 72, 31–32; Herbert, "Introduction," in *Tel Anafa I.i*, 21–22.

99. As mentioned by Edwards, "Identity and Social Location," 366–67. The geochemical study in question is Costas Xenophontos, Carolyn Elliott, and John G. Malpas, "Major and Trace-Element Geochemistry Used in Tracing the Provenance of Late Bronze Age and Roman Basalt Artefacts from Cyprus," *Levant* 20 (1988): 169–83, especially 182; and see 173, fig. 2.4 and 5, for comparative photographs of basalt Roman millstones from Capernaum and Cyprus.

100. Edwards, "Identity and Social Location," *passim*, citation from 373.

101. Aviam notes "an increase in the number of oil presses throughout the Galilee, in both Jewish and Gentile areas," peaking along with the population of the region in the Byzantine period ("The Beginning of Mass Production," 57–58).

102. Rafael Frankel, Nimrod Getzov, Mordechai Aviam, and Avi Degani, *Settlement Dynamics and Regional Diversity in Ancient Upper Galilee: Archaeological Survey of Upper Galilee* (Jerusalem: Israel Antiquities Authority, 2001), 108–16.

"reached its highest population density ever (until the twentieth century) precisely in the Byzantine period."[103]

It must be stressed, however, that this does *not* demonstrate the greater prosperity of the Byzantine inhabitants of Palestine in general or of Capernaum in particular. Increased population requires increased industry to sustain it, and there is not at all a necessary correlation between population/commercial growth and greater prosperity on the part of the *average individual*. As is well known, population growth can outstrip economic growth, producing the opposite effect.[104] As Edwards reminds us, moreover, individual villages were fluid entities, sometimes surviving from one period to the next as new villages were founded, but often not.[105]

What is more, those villages which, like Capernaum, did exist over longer periods "often exhibited changes in their material culture that suggest that cultural changes took place as well."[106] Not only individual villages such as Capernaum but Palestine at large underwent major cultural, demographic, and political-religious changes over the centuries that separated the early Roman from the Byzantine periods, in the wake of the two Jewish revolts and of the likewise pivotal establishment of Christianity as the official religion of the Empire. While there has been much debate over the precise demographic proportions of Jews versus pagans after the two revolts and their fluctuations over time, nevertheless, by Byzantine times "immigration of Christians and the conversion of pagans, Samaritans, and Jews eventually produced a Christian majority" in Palestine at large, so that Jews had now become a minority group (albeit a significant one).[107]

Indeed, it is unclear whether the Byzantine population of Capernaum itself was predominantly Jewish, predominantly Christian, or mixed. As mentioned above, many of the imported Byzantine fine wares recovered

---

103. David Goodblatt, "The Political and Social History of the Jewish Community in the Land of Israel, c. 235–638," in *The Late Roman–Rabbinic Period* (vol. 4 of *The Cambridge History of Judaism*; ed. Steven T. Katz; Cambridge: Cambridge University Press, 2006), 404–30, citation from 406. This demographic growth has been well documented by Ze'ev Safrai, *The Economy of Roman Palestine* (London: Routledge, 1994), 436–58.

104. Indeed, Safrai argues that ultimately this demographic multiplication did outstrip economic growth, causing economic hardship in the region (*Economy of Roman Palestine*, 457–58).

105. Edwards, "Identity and Social Location," *passim*.

106. Ibid., 362.

107. Goodblatt, "Political and Social History," 405–10, citation from 410.

throughout the *insulae* of the village were stamped with crosses (see fig. 6), and the fine limestone synagogue and octagonal Christian shrine coexisted in close proximity to each other in Byzantine times (see fig. 2). On the one hand, Epiphanius declares Capernaum to have been a Jewish enclave intolerant of non-Jews until the fourth century (*Panarion* 30.11.9–10), and on the other, rabbinic sources complain of it having been dominated by "heretics" or *minim* of uncertain identity already by the end of the third century (Qoheleth Rabbah 1.8). Various hypotheses have thus been proposed: (1) that Jews and Christians lived together in harmony in the Byzantine village;[108] (2) that Capernaum was entirely Jewish until the fourth century, and the octagonal basilica was the first Christian structure erected there as a shrine for Christian pilgrims;[109] and even (3) that it was in fact Byzantine Christians at Capernaum who built the synagogue out of gathered remnants of earlier Palestinian synagogues, in order to present it to pilgrims as a relic of the synagogue where Jesus had taught.[110]

While the question of the proportion of Jews versus Christians in Byzantine Capernaum is perhaps irresolvable, what *is* quite clear is that by Byzantine times all these changes had produced in the archaeological record of the Galilee a number of distinctive features that are markedly different from those that distinguish the Hasmonean and Herodian periods. As Mark Chancey has aptly framed it, after the two revolts "[e]vidence for Greco-Roman culture multiplies exponentially in the second and following centuries."[111] Beginning already with the reign of Trajan (98–177 C.E.), coins minted at Sepphoris and Tiberias no longer eschewed busts of

---

108. E.g., Eric M. Meyers, "Early Judaism and Christianity in the Light of Archaeology," *BA* (1988): 69–79; and Peter Richardson, "What Has Cana To Do with Capernaum?" *NTS* 48 (2002) 314–31.
109. E.g., Taylor, *Christians and the Holy Places*, 288–90.
110. E.g., Ma'oz, "The Synagogue at Capernaum," 137–48; and Rousseau and Arav, "Capernaum," 44–45.
111. Chancey, *Myth of a Gentile Galilee*, 181. I think he overstates the "Hellenistic culture so prevalent in the environs of Jerusalem" already prior to the second century C.E., however, and I do not think these changes in the Galilee should be attributed to the Jewish refugees who migrated there in the wake of the two revolts (ibid.). The Roman conquests and subsequent occupations of Jerusalem and other parts of Jewish Palestine quite suffice as an explanation for the inauguration of these changes which, while *comparatively* rapid (which is why I cite Chancey here), would not have happened overnight.

emperors, pagan gods, or other figurative art.[112] In middle and late Roman and Byzantine layers of Jewish settlements, the floors of many houses, public buildings, sarcophagi and even of synagogues depict not only human and animal figures, but even representations of the zodiac, pagan deities, and other pagan themes; although the Upper Galilee appears to have been more conservative in this regard.[113] Eagles were ubiquitous figures as ornaments in the synagogues of late antiquity.[114] Even the rabbis developed a more lenient attitude towards figurative art.[115] Synagogue architecture borrowed a great deal from both pagan public buildings and church architecture.[116]

The political components of these marked changes in the archaeological record are not hard to find. With the exception of the Gallic Revolt of 351–352, which was minimal in its long-term effects, there is abundant evidence for Jewish collaboration with Roman rule after the defeat of Bar Kochba, and even the participation of some Jews in imperial and municipal offices.[117] And while the rabbis tried to prohibit Jews from purchasing certain Gentile products, there is also much evidence in rabbinic texts of Jewish-Gentile market exchange.[118] It is moreover unclear how wide-

---

112. Chancey, *Myth of a Gentile Galilee*, 81–82, 91–93.

113. For an overview, see Lee I. Levine, "Jewish Archaeology in Late Antiquity: Art, Architecture, and Inscriptions," in Katz, *The Late Roman–Rabbinic Period*, 519–55. For the rich figurative art from Middle Roman–Byzantine layers at Sepphoris, including the famous Dionysus Mansion with its striking pagan motifs, see the various essays in Rebecca Martin Nagy, ed., *Sepphoris in Galilee: Crosscurrents of Culture* (Winona Lake, Ind.: Eisenbrauns, 1996). For Meyers's discussion of the apparent greater cultural conservatism that was preserved in the Upper Galilee, see "Galilean Regionalism: A Reappraisal," in *Studies in Judaism and Its Greco-Roman Context* (vol. 5 of *Approaches to Ancient Judaism*; ed. William Scott Green; Chico, Calif.: Scholars Press, 1985), 115–31.

114. In a slide presentation on the synagogues of late antiquity at the Givat Ram campus of the Hebrew University of Jerusalem in 2003, Gideon Foerster expressed his particular bewilderment at the ubiquity of these eagle figures.

115. For the rabbinic references, see Meyers and Strange, *Archaeology, the Rabbis, and Early Christianity*, 152–54.

116. Levine, "Jewish Archaeology in Late Antiquity," 541.

117. Goodblatt, "Political and Social History," 410–16.

118. As Hayes has emphasized, there is in fact "no conflict between the existence of a wealth of [rabbinic] regulations that govern interaction between Jews and Gentiles and evidence of extensive commercial, business, legal, and even social interactions." This is because, "by setting out certain required standards and issuing precautionary

spread among the general Jewish population was the influence of rabbinic interdictions at this time (the infamous 'am-ha'arets, who were clearly Jews themselves, are frequently decried in rabbinic texts for their laxity of observance).[119] In sum, Jewish-Gentile trade relations and cultural exchange had become substantially more open, not only in Capernaum but throughout Palestine.[120]

It is thus not at all surprising that by Byzantine times imported Gentile fine ware had become all the rage throughout the villages and towns of Palestine, whether Jewish, Christian, or mixed.[121] Even in the Byzantine period, however, it is dangerous automatically to associate the appearance of these imported fine wares at a site with an increase in its prosperity. This is impressively illustrated by the case of the Upper Galilean village of Meiron. As at Capernaum, only a handful of ETSA was found, whereas a large quantity of the same late Roman and especially Byzantine fine wares was unearthed.[122] Meiron flourished economically between 250 and 360

---

criteria, the rabbis actually *facilitated* relations with Gentiles by assuring the observant Jew that his dealings were legitimate so long as they conformed to stated regulations" (*Gentile Impurities*, 141–42, emphasis hers).

119. Hayim Lapin has recently summarized the new understanding of the rabbinic movement among many scholars "as part of an ongoing cultural struggle by a segment of a Roman provincial population in a political and administrative setting where they would have had no official authority and possibly little popular appeal" ("The Origins and Development of the Rabbinic Movement in the Land of Israel," in Katz, *The Late Roman–Rabbinic Period*, 204–29, citation from 225).

120. This has been argued at length by Safrai, *Economy of Roman Palestine*, 415–35, 453–56. While I agree with Safrai's basic argument about the later period, I disagree in part with his characterization of the earlier Second Temple economy as "closed" (222–23, 453). By "closed" he means that "the Land of Israel was for the most part self-sufficient and most farmers produced for their own needs" (453). While I agree with the first part of this statement, that Jewish Palestine as a *region* was mostly self-sufficient in this period, I do not think that individual farmers or even villages generally produced solely for their own needs, for the reasons outlined above. In my view, it is more accurate to characterize the economy of the late Second Temple period as *deliberately* more *introverted*, not "closed" in the sense that Safrai uses this term.

121. It should be noted, however, that the number of imported items at Jewish sites remained relatively low prior to the late Roman period (Meyers, "Jewish Art and Architecture in the Land of Israel, 70–c. 235," in Katz, *The Late Roman–Rabbinic Period*, 174–90, especially 188).

122. Groh, "The Finewares," 129–38. As mentioned in n. 91 above, Edwards is mistaken that "a relatively high proportion" of ETSA was found at Meiron ("Identity and Social Location," 364–65). Groh stresses their paucity ("The Finewares," 136),

C.E. but then, reflecting the fluid nature of individual villages underscored by Edwards, underwent a severe economic decline in the Byzantine period.[123] Yet the major part of the imported fine wares unearthed at Meiron belong to forms that are Byzantine in date, or that appeared in Palestine after 360 C.E. That is, not only do they *not* date to the period of Meiron's greatest prosperity. They actually date to a period of its economic decline.[124] Hence, there is in fact a *negative* correlation between the appearance of the majority of these fine wares and Meiron's relative overall prosperity.

In sum, the appearance of substantial quantities of imported Byzantine fine wares at Capernaum is not an indication of a sudden increase in prosperity at the site. It is simply a reflection of the marked shift in trade patterns that occurred in Palestine at large on account of the very different religious, political, and demographic realities of the Hasmonean and Herodian periods on the one hand, and the Byzantine period on the other. The many stone vessel fragments recovered from Capernaum indicate that its inhabitants shared the purity concerns of the late Second Temple period. Hence, along with the Franciscan excavators of the site, one might well conclude that what is surprising about a modest-sized village like Capernaum is the fact that some imported ETSA and stamped Rhodian amphorae were indeed recovered at the site.

ARGUMENT 3. A DIACHRONIC AND COMPARATIVE ANALYSIS OF INSULA 2

As explained above, the best preserved, fully excavated private houses on the Franciscan side of the site are in Insula 2, located between the synagogue (to its north) and the *insula sacra* (to its south) (see figs. 2, 3, and 5). While the houses of Insula 2 began to be occupied at the same time as those of the *insula sacra* in the Hellenistic and early Roman periods, they

---

and according to Meyers, "you can count them on one hand" (personal communication, 2011).

123. Eric M. Meyers, James F. Strange, and Carol L. Meyers, eds, *Excavations at Ancient Meiron, Upper Galilee, Israel 1971–72, 1974–75, 1977* (Cambridge: American Schools of Oriental Research, 1981), xix, 23–41, 50–51, 54; Joyce Raynor and Yaakov Meshorer, *The Coins of Ancient Meiron* (Meiron Excavation Project Series 4; Winona Lake, Ind.: Eisenbrauns, 1988), 1, 82–83, 89.

124. As Groh explains ("The Finewares," 129–38), most of the sherds were unearthed from the unsealed, upper-level loci in the vicinity of the Patrician and Lintel houses and were also severely water-washed. They seem to have originated from an as-yet unexcavated Byzantine part of the site located up the hill from these houses.

did not likewise give way to public structures in later periods. Instead, they continued to be domestically occupied well into Byzantine times, right up until sometime in the fifth to sixth centuries C.E.[125] Insula 2 was thus not subjected to the intensive building activities that took place in the *insula sacra*, meaning that its domestic structures can be much more clearly delineated. Despite this fortuitous fact, the insula did undergo modifications over time and thus the plans of the houses in later centuries are the ones that can most clearly be determined from the extant remains. It is very useful to examine carefully these later houses, however, because it is possible to trace backwards in time from the later to the earlier structures, on the basis of the general trends of development inside the insula.

This diachronic analysis of Insula 2 is based on Corbo's division of the insula into independent houses in his detailed locus-by-locus description,[126] in which he follows the same general principle followed by most archaeologists. As an archaeologist of Pompeii has succinctly put it, "the independence of a unit is defined in terms of its own entrance from the street and the lack of accessibility from other units," a principle that is also used by excavators throughout Palestine.[127] The main entrances from the streets in Insula 2 were "built of ashlars with locking installations," whereas the "door frames between rooms inside the house" for each independent domicile "were usually made with less care" and "lacked closing mechanisms."[128]

Two of the insula's houses have been excavated to their full extent. Their clearest plans are late Roman and Byzantine in date—that of the southeastern Triple Courtyard House (highlighted in light gray in figs. 2 and 3; reconstructed in fig. 10), dating from the third century to approximately

---

125. Corbo, *Cafarnao I*, 174–75, 216–17, fig. XIII.

126. Ibid., 176–94.

127. Felix Pirson, "Rented Accommodation at Pompeii: The Evidence of the Insula Arriana Polliana VI.6," in *Domestic Space in the Roman World: Pompeii and Beyond* (ed. Ray Laurence and Andrew Wallace-Hadrill; Portsmouth, R.I.: Journal of Roman Archaeology, 1997), 165–81, especially 175; compare with Andrew Wallace-Hadrill, *Houses and Society in Pompeii and Herculaneum* (Princeton: Princeton University Press, 1994), 72. Also see Yizhar Hirschfeld's broad survey of Palestinian housing in the Roman–Byzantine periods, based on many archaeological reports (*The Palestinian Dwelling in the Roman-Byzantine Periods* [Jerusalem: Israel Exploration Society, 1995]).

128. Hirschfeld, *Palestinian Dwelling*, 254, summarizing Corbo, *Carfarnao I*, 77, 177.

Figure 10. Comparative reconstructions of the Meron Patrician House (3rd–4th century C.E.) and the Capernaum Triple Courtyard House (3rd century to ca. 450 C.E.)

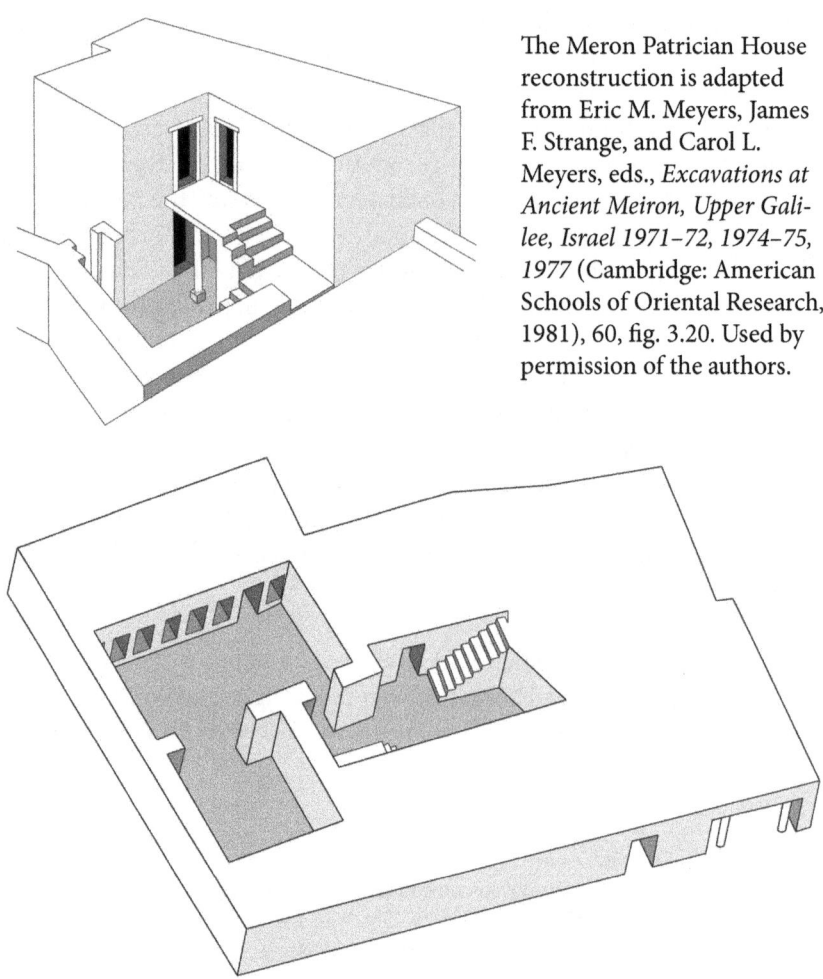

The Meron Patrician House reconstruction is adapted from Eric M. Meyers, James F. Strange, and Carol L. Meyers, eds., *Excavations at Ancient Meiron, Upper Galilee, Israel 1971–72, 1974–75, 1977* (Cambridge: American Schools of Oriental Research, 1981), 60, fig. 3.20. Used by permission of the authors.

The Capernaum Triple Courtyard House was reconstructed using AutoCAD.
Copyright George Yanchula and Sharon Lea Mattila, 2011.

450 c.e.; and that of the Northeastern House (highlighted in medium gray in figs. 2 and 3), dating roughly to the third to sixth centuries c.e. The Western House, which once occupied the western side of the insula, could not be fully excavated on account of the modern pathway running through this house up to the synagogue. The block of rooms excavated directly west of this pathway is therefore included in Insula 2 by the excavators, given the likelihood that some of its easternmost rooms belonged to the Western House (see figs. 2 and 3).

There is one structure associated with the Triple Courtyard House, which has no access to the house proper and a main entrance of a style dissimilar to all the other main entrances of the insula, being wide and adorned in a somewhat pretentious manner with double pillars. Two factors indicate that it was part of the Triple Courtyard House complex: the fact that stairs from one of the inner courtyards led to the structure's roof (see figs. 3 and 10), and its construction history. The two rooms protruding eastward into the street and the diagonal wall separating the southernmost of these new rooms from the rest of the house were erected at about the same time.[129] This newly separated structure was likely a shop. Shops at Pompeii likewise typically had "a wide entrance onto the street" and no direct access to the larger buildings to which they usually were attached.[130] Indeed, it is fascinating to note the extent to which this Capernaum shop, with its back room, resembled the typical ground plan of a Pompeiian shop with back room.[131] Even the size of this shop was almost identical to the average size of such shops at Pompeii.[132]

It is less certain that the structure associated with the Northeastern House, created by dividing the house's original southeastern room in two and providing the new room with its own doorway of ashlars to the street, was a shop.[133] This structure's continued connection with the Northeast-

---

129. Corbo, *Cafarnao I*, 178–81.

130. Pedar W. Foss, "Watchful Lares: Roman Household Organization and the Rituals of Cooking and Eating," in Laurence and Wallace-Hadrill, *Domestic Space in the Roman World*, 197–218, especially 205.

131. For this typical ground plan in Pompeii, see "Type 1: shop and back room (I, 6, 10)," in "Figure 4.11. House types by quartile," in Wallace-Hadrill, *Houses and Society in Pompeii*.

132. The average size of these shops is provided as 25 m² in "Table 4.2," in ibid. The area of the Capernaum shop attached to the Triple Courtyard House was about 23.8 m² (see n. 144 for how this area was measured).

133. As suggested by Corbo, *Cafarnao I*, 176–77, 193–94.

ern House is indicated by its window looking into the house's northeastern courtyard (see fig. 3).[134] If instead it had been divided off as separate living quarters, then this may be evidence of differentiated housing at Capernaum, such as described by Richardson for Khirbet Qana, Yodefat, and Gamla.[135] This tiny dwelling would have been much smaller than the other houses in the insula. Its close association with the Northeastern House and its related construction history, however, make this interpretation likewise uncertain. It may instead have indeed also been a shop.

It is instructive to measure the sizes of the two fully excavated Capernaum houses, including their attached structures, on the basis of their scaled excavation plans, and to compare them with that of the only house at Meiron whose full extent has been excavated, namely, the Patrician House.[136] This Meiron house also happens to be roughly contemporaneous with the late Roman occupation of the two Capernaum houses, dating to the third to fourth centuries C.E. (see the reconstruction of this house in fig. 10). The very name assigned to the Patrician House by its excavators suggests that its inhabitants were relatively well-to-do. Indeed, New Testament scholars such as Horsley have also declared it to be the home of "modestly wealthy" individuals, while stressing the supposed poverty of the houses on the Franciscan side of Capernaum.[137]

Yet in size the Meiron Patrician House compares quite unfavorably to Capernaum's Triple Courtyard House. The Patrician House's internal surface area (or the total area enclosed within its external walls), taking into account both of its two stories and its courtyard, is only 130 m² (the ground floor plan is 79 m²). In contrast, the internal surface area of the

---

134. Ibid.
135. Peter Richardson, "First-Century Houses and Q's Setting," in *Christology, Controversy and Community: New Testament Essays in Honour of David R. Catchpole* (ed. David G. Horrell and Christopher M. Tuckett; Leiden: Brill, 2000), 63–83, especially 68–71; and idem, "Khirbet Qana (and Other Villages) as a Context for Jesus," in *Jesus and Archaeology* (ed. James H. Charlesworth; Grand Rapids: Eerdmans, 2006), 120–44, especially 133–35.
136. The plan of Capernaum's Insula 2 is found in Corbo, *Cafarnao I*, Tav. XIII. This plan and its scale were scanned into AutoCAD and closely measured using this program. "Internal surface area" in this article consistently means the total area inside the external walls of a given house or room. The plan of the Patrician House is found in Meyers, Strange, and Meyers, *Excavations at Ancient Meiron*, 53, fig. 3.16. This was measured using AutoCAD in the same way as was Corbo's diagram of Insula 2.
137. Horsley, *Archaeology, Society, and History in Galilee*, 103, 114–17.

Triple Courtyard House is 203 m² with its attached shop, and 168 m² without its attached shop (see table 1). If, moreover, the staircases found on both the northern and southern sides of one of the Triple Courtyard House's courtyards (see figs. 2, 3, and 10) indicate that the house also contained some second-story rooms, then the Capernaum house was even more comparatively spacious. At any rate, even if the walls could not sustain a second story, and even if we do not take into account the attached shop, this house still offered more living space than did the Patrician House (see table 1). Even the smaller Northeastern House in Capernaum, at 121 m², was almost as spacious as the Patrician House (see table 1).

TABLE 1. INTERNAL SURFACE AREAS OF THE FULLY EXCAVATED HOUSES AT CAPERNAUM VERSUS MERON

Triple Courtyard House	Northeastern House	Patrician House
Insula 2 of Capernaum	Insula 2 of Capernaum	Insula MII of Meron
(3rd–5th centuries C.E.)	(3rd–6th centuries C.E.)	(3rd–4th centuries C.E.)
168 m² (without attached shop)	102 m² (without attached shop)	79 m² (ground floor only)
203 m² (with attached shop)	121 m² (with attached shop/room)	130 m² (with second story)

Figure 10 offers a comparative presentation of reconstructions of the Capernaum Triple Courtyard House and of the Meiron Patrician House. The reconstruction of the Capernaum house presented here is quite similar to that of Yizhar Hirschfeld,[138] with an important exception. Hirschfeld's identification of one of the house's rooms as a "stable" is problematic, because the Triple Courtyard House had only one main entrance from the street to its south, which was not suitable for bringing in livestock.[139] (The attached shop had no entrance to the house.) Hence, it appears that this Capernaum house was devoted to human habitation only.

---

138. Hirschfeld, *Palestinian Dwelling*, 68–69. Hirschfeld does not adequately explain why he objects to this house being called the Triple Courtyard House by the excavators, a designation retained here. He insists that there is only "one inner courtyard" but does not identify in his plan of the house the function of the open areas that Corbo designates as the other two courtyards.

139. This observation I owe to the insightful analysis of George Yanchula.

When one consults table 1 and figure 10, it should be clear that it really is not justifiable to assert that the Meiron house's inhabitants were "modestly wealthy," while those of the Capernaum house were subsistence-level poor, whatever might be the relatively modest differences in the quality of the ashlar construction of their main entrances. Nor do the finds associated with the Capernaum houses justify such an assertion. The large quantity of late Roman and Byzantine imported fine wares (see fig. 6) found throughout Insula 2, and thus also owned by the inhabitants of the Triple Courtyard House, also surely speaks to their modest wealth.

It should also be patent from table 1 and figures 2, 3, and 10 that the Triple Courtyard House does not match Crossan and Reed's description of Capernaum's houses as consisting of "a series of rooms clustered around a single courtyard belonging to an extended family."[140] Even less sustainable are the claims of Freyne and Charlesworth that Capernaum's houses usually consisted of "a single room opening onto a courtyard that was shared by several different family units," and that "often the family lived in one room and perhaps in one large bed."[141] While it is of course not *impossible* that each of the various rooms of the Triple Courtyard House provided quarters for a complete nuclear family, the standing remains and recovered finds scarcely demand such a conclusion. Above all, on what basis could one conclude that the entire Meiron Patrician House was the home of nothing more than a nuclear family, while the Capernaum Triple Courtyard House was the home of multiple families, perhaps members of an extended family clan, all of whom shared its three courtyards in common? This is surely to read far more into the archaeological evidence than its limitations allow.

While it is not possible here to argue conclusively that the inhabitants of the Capernaum Triple Courtyard House were as well-to-do as those of the Meiron Patrician House, nor would it be possible to argue conclusively that they were not. Nevertheless, I would submit that carefully measured comparative house sizes, based on the archaeological plans of the final reports, offer a far more objective measure of comparative wealth than do the rather impressionistic assessments that have too often been asserted.

Similarly impressionistic is the assessment of Taylor, followed unquestioningly by Horsley, that the modern boundary line between the Fran-

---

140. Crossan and Reed, *Excavating Jesus*, 82.
141. Freyne, "Archaeology and the Historical Jesus," 78; Charlesworth, "Jesus Research and Archaeology," 18.

ciscan and Greek Orthodox sides of the site (see fig. 1) corresponds to an ancient socioeconomic demarcation in the village. "It is clear from the remains," Taylor declares, "that the lower classes lived in the west and the more affluent in the east."[142] This is actually not at all clear, however, at this stage of the publication of the Roman and Byzantine remains and finds from the site.

There is as yet no full report on the Roman and Byzantine strata of the Greek Orthodox side of the site, and so one must rely only on the brief preliminary archaeological report of John C. H. Laughlin, with its small scaled diagram.[143] Measurements of the various private and public structures in this diagram indicate that most of them compare unfavorably in size to the Triple Courtyard House (see table 2). For instance, the internal surface area of the "domestic structure" (fifth to sixth centuries C.E.) in Laughlin's plan is 74 m². It does seem to have had sturdier walls than its western counterpart, and so probably contained a second story, thereby offering its inhabitants 148 m² of space. But this is still significantly less space than the 203 m² enjoyed by the occupants of the Triple Courtyard House. Even one of the "public buildings" (second to sixth centuries C.E.) on the Greek Orthodox side has a ground plan with an internal surface area of only about 111 m².

TABLE 2. COMPARATIVE INTERNAL SURFACE AREAS OF BUILDINGS ON THE FRANCISCAN SIDE VERSUS THE GREEK ORTHODOX SIDE OF THE CAPERNAUM SITE

Triple Courtyard House	"Public Building"	"Domestic Structure"
Franciscan side of Capernaum	Orthodox side of Capernaum	Orthodox side of Capernaum
(3rd–5th centuries C.E.)	(2nd–6th centuries C.E.)	(5th–6th centuries C.E.)
168 m² (without attached shop)	111 m²	74 m² (ground floor only)
203 m² (with attached shop)		148 m² (with second story)

---

142. Taylor, *Christians and the Holy Places*, 277; compare with Horsley, *Archaeology, History and Society in Galilee*, 115–16.

143. Laughlin, "Capernaum," 57.

All of this, one might still object, tells us little about Capernaum's houses in Jesus' time. But this really is not true because it is possible to trace trends in the development of the continuously occupied houses of Insula 2 over time. Let us begin by going forward in time, which is the easier task, then take on the somewhat more challenging task of going backward in time.

Moving forward in time, it is interesting to note that the houses of Insula 2 reached their smallest dimensions in approximately 450 C.E., as is shown in figure 11. At around this time, the insula underwent a major reconfiguration, which introduced a fourth house into it, substantially reducing the sizes of all but the Northeastern House.[144] The new house took over the southern part of the Western House's (later) subdivided courtyard, as well as the double courtyard of the Triple Courtyard House, which now had only one courtyard and so could no longer be designated a Triple Courtyard House. Perhaps this occurred on account of increased population pressure as the village grew to its apex during the Byzantine period. In short, it appears that the general tendency of the houses of this insula was actually to get progressively smaller over time.

Indeed, moving backwards in time through Insula 2 also supports this argument that the general trend of its houses was to become increasingly smaller. The Western House, which could not be fully excavated on account of the modern pathway for tourists leading up to the synagogue, seems at one time to have been the most spacious house of the insula. In the early Roman period, it contained a large courtyard, which was only later subdivided into other rooms and courtyards (the walls of this courtyard are represented in dark gray in figs. 2 and 3). The courtyard's internal surface area was 97 m². There was another courtyard and an entrance corridor attached to its north, as well as rooms along its western side, although the modern pathway for tourists has made it difficult to determine the precise plan of these rooms (see figs. 2 and 3). The set of early Roman glassware (see fig. 7) is likely to have belonged to the inhabitants of this early Roman Western House, with its large courtyard. This is because the set was found along a wall of one of the rooms excavated directly to the west of the modern pathway (represented in dark gray in figs. 2 and 3).

In other words, the Triple Courtyard House was not the largest private house that ever existed in Insula 2. The incompletely excavated Western

---

144. For Corbo's dating of this reconfiguration to ca 450 C.E., see *Cafarnao I*, 14.

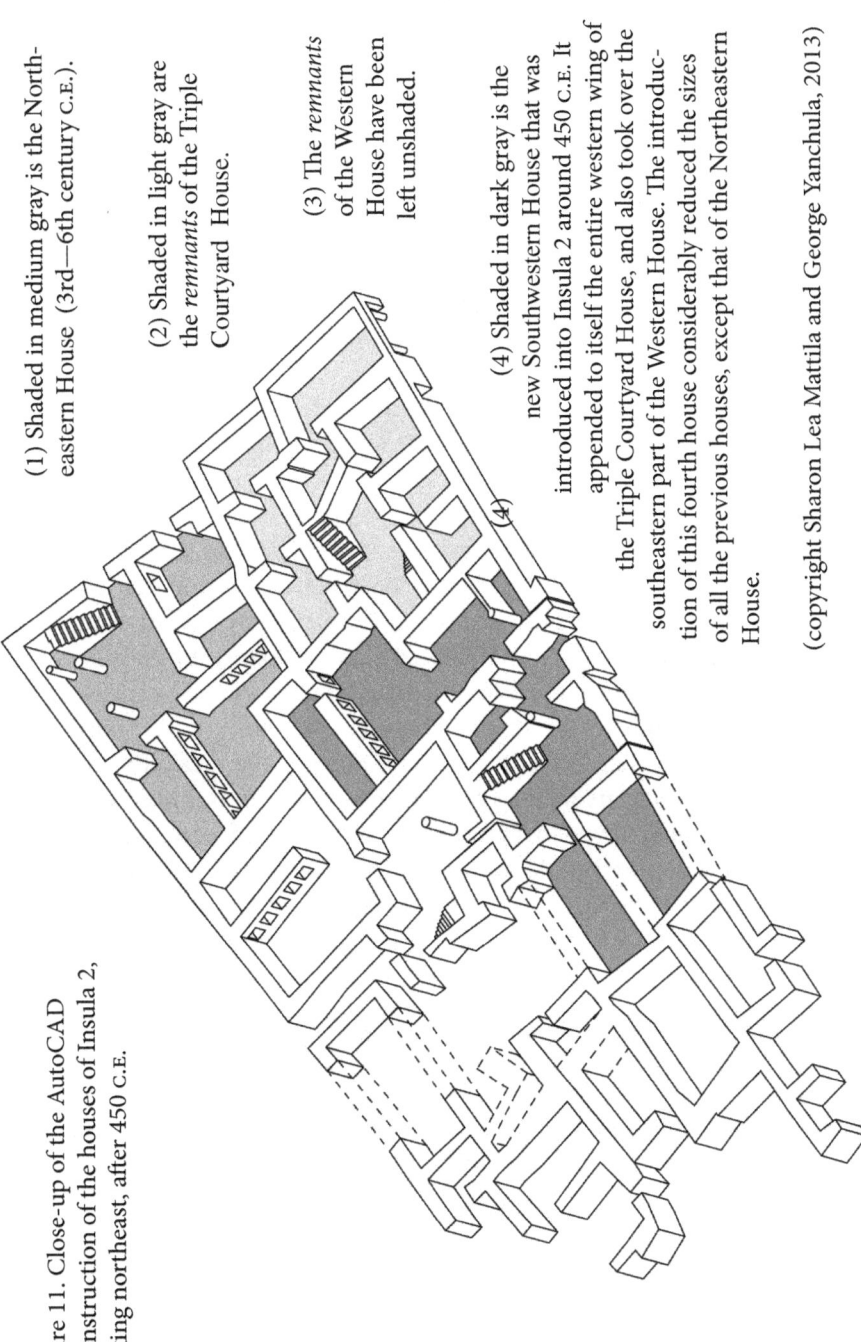

Figure 11. Close-up of the AutoCAD reconstruction of the houses of Insula 2, looking northeast, after 450 C.E.

(1) Shaded in medium gray is the Northeastern House (3rd–6th century C.E.).

(2) Shaded in light gray are the *remnants* of the Triple Courtyard House.

(3) The *remnants* of the Western House have been left unshaded.

(4) Shaded in dark gray is the new Southwestern House that was introduced into Insula 2 around 450 C.E. It appended to itself the entire western wing of the Triple Courtyard House, and also took over the southeastern part of the Western House. The introduction of this fourth house considerably reduced the sizes of all the previous houses, except that of the Northeastern House.

(copyright Sharon Lea Mattila and George Yanchula, 2013)

House, where the set of early Roman glassware was found, was probably the largest in the insula. This was especially the case in the early Roman period, before the house's spacious courtyard was subdivided. In the early Roman period, this courtyard's internal surface area of 97 m² was in itself larger than the entire ground floor plan of the later Meiron Patrician House, at only 79 m²![145]

Argument 4. Are the Walls of Insula 2's Houses an Indication of Their Subsistence-Level Poverty?

Finally, the fact that the houses of Insula 2 were constructed out of undressed local basalt stone cannot be taken as an unambiguous indication of their subsistence-level poverty. It goes without saying that high quality masonry and the presence of frescoes and fine mosaics are indications of wealth, whatever the size of a structure. But it is not conversely a given that poorer quality local materials and construction techniques used in the erection of walls indicates the subsistence-level poverty of their occupants. The distinct possibility needs to be kept in mind that the undressed basalt stone walls and floors of the domestic structures excavated by the Franciscans at Capernaum are but the bare bones or skeletons of the houses that once existed, whether in the Byzantine or in the earlier periods.

On this point, archaeological evidence from the farming village of Karanis in Roman Egypt—where the dry climate has preserved a good deal more than the more humid climate of the Galilee has allowed—is quite suggestive. By bringing in this comparative evidence, it is not my intention to imply that it is immediately or directly applicable to Capernaum. Nevertheless, the evidence from Karanis is worth considering, because it demonstrates how houses made using relatively humble construction

---

145. It would be interesting to compare the implied size of Insula 2's Western House in the early Roman period, with its large courtyard, to the sizes of courtyard houses dating to the same period that have been excavated at Jotapata and Khirbet Qana. Unfortunately, this is not yet possible, because only preliminary reports have thus far been published on these sites (see the well documented survey, based on the preliminary reports, in Jensen, *Herod Antipas in Galilee*, 163–69). Richardson has noted that archaeologists of the region "are gradually developing a three-item typology" of "differentiated neighborhoods": "terrace housing without courtyards, side courtyard houses, and central courtyard houses" ("Khirbet Qana," 133–35). Unfortunately, insufficient information survives from the early Roman period at Capernaum either to confirm or disaffirm the existence of such differentiated neighborhoods there.

techniques and local materials were, and therefore could, be fleshed out in a village of the eastern Roman Empire.

Karanis was founded in the third century B.C.E. under King Ptolemy II and flourished in the Roman period until it began to experience a decline in the fourth century C.E.[146] Like Capernaum's houses, those of Karanis were also made out of local materials using local techniques, having consisted mostly of mud brick (see fig. 12a), with some wood and stone also used.[147]

Interestingly, mudbrick houses were apparently also once common, according to Hirschfeld, in the lower-lying areas (valleys and foothills) of Roman Palestine. Because the climate is not as dry as Egypt, however, the mud brick in these regions of Palestine was not preserved, unlike the local stone of the houses of the Judean and Galilean hill country.[148] Indeed, the Mishnah confirms these variations in custom with respect to the use of local materials in different parts of ancient Palestine: "In the place where the custom is to build of unshaped stones, or of hewn stones, or of half-bricks, or of whole bricks, so they should build. Everything should follow local custom" (m. B. Bat. 1:1).[149] The early rabbinic sages do not imply that such variations in local construction techniques automatically corresponded to differences in wealth or status.

Not only was the mudbrick at Karanis preserved by the dry climate of Egypt; so were many other perishable items that are highly suggestive with regard to how the bare bones of the buildings at Capernaum might also once have been fleshed out. For instance, it is significant that at Karanis lime plaster was to be found only in the public buildings.[150] Mud plaster,

---

146. Andrea M. Berlin, "The Rural Economy," in *Karanis: An Egyptian Town in Roman Times* (ed. Elaine K. Gazda; Ann Arbor: University of Michigan Press, 1983), 8–18, especially 8–9.

147. Elaine K. Gazda and Jacqueline Royer, "Domestic Life," in Gazda, *Karanis*, 19–31; Elinor M. Husselman, *Karanis: Excavations of the University of Michigan in Egypt 1928–1935: Topography and Architecture* (Ann Arbor: University of Michigan Press, 1979), 33–35.

148. Hirschfeld, *Palestinian Dwelling*, 26.

149. The translation of the Hebrew is mine, in consultation with those of Herbert Danby (*The Mishnah, Translated from the Hebrew with Introduction and Brief Explanatory Notes* [Oxford: Oxford University Press, 1933]) and of Shmuel Himelstein (*The Mishnah. Seder Nizikin Vol. 2. Bava Batra* [ed. Rabbi A. H. Rabinowitz and Rabbi Bernard Susser; Jerusalem: Eliner Library, 1988]).

150. Arthur E. R. Boak, *Karanis: The Temples, Coin Hoards, Botanical and Zoö-*

Figure 12. Photographs from the Karanis Excavations. From Arthur E. R. Boak and Enoch E. Peterson, *Karanis: Topographical and Architectural Report of Excavations during the Seasons 1924–28* (Ann Arbor: University of Michigan Press, 1931), plate IV, fig. 7; plate X, fig. 20; plate XIX, fig. 38; plate XXIV, fig. 48.

Figure 12a (above) shows the mudbrick wall construction of the Karanis houses, with remnants of the thick mud plaster that once covered them. Figure 12d (below) shows a Karanis roof construction of wood and reeds with thick layers of mud plaster.

Figure 12b (above) shows a niche with elaborately worked mud plaster, found in an interior wall of a house. Figure 12c (below) shows a wall painting, executed on the mud plaster of the interior wall of a house, against the background of a thin lime whitewash.

however, was thickly applied to the exterior walls of the private houses and was also applied to their interior walls (see the remnants of this plaster in the photographs of fig. 12).[151] Indeed, inside the houses it could sometimes be quite elaborately molded into fine decorative frames for niches (see fig. 12b).

This is not to imply, of course, that the same type of ornamental mud plaster niches existed at Capernaum, especially since at Karanis these niches probably housed pagan deities. What the Karanis evidence does show, however, is that plaster without lime content could at the very least provide smooth and finished looking surfaces. Such plaster would not have survived the Capernaum climate to be detectable at excavations today, but was probably applied to the walls at least for purposes of bonding and finishing.

Likewise, the evidence for roof construction at Karanis shows that roofs supported by wooden beams and a bed of reeds were also not necessarily rustic looking, but could be quite smooth because they were coated with layers of mud plaster (see fig. 12d). Even the ceilings at Karanis were often plastered.[152] The construction technique for such roofs in Palestine, as Hirschfeld describes it,[153] seems quite similar to how the roofs were constructed at Karanis.

What is more, at Karanis the accidents of preservation have shown that many people who occupied its mudbrick houses took pride in the decoration and furnishing of the interiors of their homes. Both thin white lime washes and black washes (of uncertain chemical composition) were applied over the mud plaster, and the lower parts of walls could be decorated differently from their upper parts. Walls were sometimes adorned with strips of wood, used purely for decoration, and wood was also used extensively for windows, doorways, and cupboards, some of which were finely crafted. There are even remnants of wall paintings on the mud plaster (see fig. 12c), albeit not as finely executed as those found in urban contexts. The floors were also coated with mud plaster, and were in addition

---

logical Reports, Seasons 1924–31 (Ann Arbor: University of Michigan Press, 1933), 1–56; Arthur E. Boak and Enoch E. Peterson, *Karanis: Topographical and Architectural Report of Excavations during the Seasons 1924–28* (Ann Arbor: University of Michigan Press, 1931), 29.

151. Boak and Peterson, *Karanis*, 1–69.
152. Ibid.
153. Hirschfeld, *Palestinian Dwelling*, 237–39.

covered by mats or carpets, and possibly cushions. Mats were found in virtually every dwelling of the village.[154]

It is of course impossible to be certain that the same attention to interior décor once fleshed out the walls of Capernaum's houses. The far more durable remnants of glass, imported pottery, and other luxury items found at Capernaum, however, do suggest that throughout the centuries more perishable materials may once have graced their walls and floors as well. At Karanis, of course, more durable luxury items were also found among the more perishable ones. These include, it is interesting to note, African Red Slip Ware, one of the imported fine wares found commonly at Capernaum, in contexts dating to the same period (mostly the fourth and fifth centuries C.E.).[155]

Finally, it is interesting to note that, although the sizes of the Karanis houses varied considerably, the estimated median ground plan of the houses dating from the first century C.E. to the third century C.E. is approximately 70 m^2.[156] This is somewhat smaller than the ground floor area of the Patrician House at Meiron. Because many of the Karanis houses had basements as well as an upper story, however, the median-sized house there may have offered somewhat more space to its inhabitants than either the two-storied Meiron Patrician House or the single-storied Capernaum Triple Courtyard House. Nevertheless, it remains suggestive that the median Karanis house was comparable in size to the Meiron and Capernaum houses.

Once again, I do not at all mean to argue that one can apply the evidence from Karanis directly to Capernaum. What the Karanis evidence does reveal, however, are various ways in which village houses, with walls constructed out of rather humble local materials, were and therefore could be fleshed out in a rural region of the Roman Empire. Tastes and decorative styles would not have been the same in the Galilee as in Egypt, so one

---

154. Boak and Peterson, *Karanis*, 1-69; Husselman, *Karanis*, 36, plates 21a, 22b, 23, 24 a, b, 25; Gazda and Royer, *Karanis*, 19-31.

155. Barbara Johnson, *Pottery from Karanis: Excavations of the University of Michigan* (Ann Arbor: University of Michigan Press, 1981), 9-10, 46-50, plates 33-40; compare with Loffreda, *Cafarnao II*, 65-87, 166-85.

156. Richard Alston, "Houses and Households in Roman Egypt," in Laurence and Wallace-Hadrill, *Domestic Space in the Roman World*, 25-39, especially 27-28. Alston includes in his analysis the C- and B-level houses, which date from the mid-first century C.E. to the end of the third century C.E. (Husselman, *Karanis*, 7-31).

must be careful not to assume that the skeletons of the Capernaum houses were fleshed out in precisely the same way. But the Karanis evidence does alert us to keep our historical imaginations alive to the distinct possibility that the walls that stand today at the Capernaum site are indeed only the stripped bones of the houses that once were.

Summary of Arguments

Let us now briefly summarize the arguments presented here. First, a significant number of luxury items were unearthed from Hellenistic and early Roman contexts at Capernaum. These include an impressive set of early Roman fine glassware (see fig. 7); stamped handles from late Hellenistic amphorae imported all the way from Rhodes; and a surprising quantity (given the village's modest size) of Hellenistic table wares that had to travel considerable distances to arrive at the site, including elegant Eastern *Terra Sigillata* A (see fig. 8 for some examples from Gamla). None of these items were likely to have been owned by the subsistence-level poor.

Second, there is no good reason to suppose that the arrival of Byzantine fine wares (see fig. 6) at Capernaum is an indication of a sudden increase in the village's prosperity. The smaller quantity of imported stamped amphorae and ETSA versus the larger quantity of imported Byzantine fine wares at Capernaum must be understood within the context of a major shift in trade patterns related to religious, political, and demographic changes that occurred in the overall region of Palestine in the intervening centuries between the periods in question. This shift from deliberately more introverted to more open does not at all necessarily correspond with an increase or decrease in the purchasing power of the region's individual Jewish inhabitants. Even in the Byzantine period, it is questionable automatically to associate the appearance of imported fine wares at a site with an increase in its prosperity, as the *negative* correlation between their arrival at Meiron and the village's fortunes impressively shows.

Third, at no point in their history of occupation did the houses of Insula 2 match the descriptions of Capernaum's houses found in the discussions of Crossan and Reed, of Freyne, or of Charlesworth (see figs. 2, 3, 10, and 11). The best preserved and fully excavated houses of the insula, especially the Triple Courtyard House, compared favorably in size to the roughly contemporaneous Patrician House that has been fully excavated at Meiron (see table 1 and fig. 10). There is no good reason to conclude that the Meiron house was that of "modestly wealthy" individuals, while the Capernaum houses belonged to the subsistence-level poor. The houses of Insula 2 also compared favorably to the private and even the public structures unearthed on the Greek Orthodox side of the site (see table 2), rendering questionable the notion that the poorer classes lived in the west.

What is more, as one moves forward and backward in time through the insula, its houses seem to have become progressively smaller (with the exception of the North Eastern House), reaching their smallest dimensions around 450 C.E. (see fig. 11). Yet even the Byzantine villagers in their substantially smaller houses were not subsistence-level poor. They apparently continued to purchase imported fine wares quite regularly.[157] There is scarcely any reason to suppose that the early Roman inhabitants of what was once the largest house in the insula—the Western House, with a courtyard significantly larger than the entire ground floor plan of the later Meron Patrician House—were poorer than their Byzantine counterparts in their smaller houses! This is especially the case when one recalls that these early Roman inhabitants probably possessed the collection of glassware (see fig. 7) found against one of the Western House's walls (as shown in figs. 2 and 3).

Finally, the undressed basalt stone walls of Capernaum's houses are quite possibly merely the bare bones of the homes that once were. They do not unambiguously indicate that their inhabitants were ever subsistence-level poor. The evidence from Egyptian Karanis (see the photographs in fig. 12) shows how villagers living in houses constructed out of humble local materials could and did take pride in decorating their homes with mud plaster and other perishable items that would not have survived the climate of Capernaum. Hence, it is likely that at least some of the villagers in the Capernaum of Jesus' time—fishers and farmers though many of them probably were—enjoyed wealth beyond subsistence.

Bibliography

Adan-Bayewitz, David. *Common Pottery in Roman Galilee: A Study of Local Trade*. Ramat-Gan, Israel: Bar Ilan University Press, 1993.

Adan-Bayewitz, David, and Mordechai Aviam. "Iotapata, Josephus, and the Siege of 67: Preliminary Report on the 1992–94 Seasons." *Journal of Roman Archaeology* 10 (1997): 131–65.

---

157. Loffreda, *Cafarnao II*, 125–29.

Adan-Bayewitz, David, and Isadore Perlman. "The Local Trade of Sepphoris in the Roman Period." *IEJ* 40 (1990): 153–72.
Alston, Richard. "Houses and Households in Roman Egypt." Pages 25–39 in *Domestic Space in the Roman World: Pompeii and Beyond*. Edited by Ray Laurence and Andrew Wallace-Hadrill. Portsmouth, R.I.: Journal of Roman Archaeology, 1997.
Ariel, Donald T., and Aryeh Strikovsky. "Appendix." Pages 25–29 in *Imported Stamped Amphorae Handles, Coins, Worked Bone and Ivory, and Glass*. Vol. 2 of *Excavations at the City of David Directed by Yigal Shiloh 1978–1985*. Edited by Donald T. Ariel. Jerusalem: The Hebrew University of Jerusalem, 1990.
Aviam, Mordechai. "The Beginning of Mass Production of Olive Oil in the Galilee." Pages 51–60 in idem, *Jews, Pagans and Christians in the Galilee*. Rochester, N.Y.: University of Rochester Press, 2004.
———. "Distribution Maps of Archaeological Data from the Galilee: An Attempt to Establish Zones Indicative of Ethnicity and Religious Affiliation." Pages 115–32 in *Religion, Ethnicity, and Identity in Ancient Galilee: A Region in Transition*. Edited by Jürgen Zangenberg, Harold W. Attridge, and Dale B. Martin. Tübingen: Mohr Siebeck, 2007.
———. "First Century Jewish Galilee: An Archaeological Perspective." Pages 7–27 in *Religion and Society in Roman Palestine: Old Questions, New Approaches*. Edited by Douglas R. Edwards. New York : Routledge, 2004.
Avigad, Nahman. *Discovering Jerusalem*. Nashville: Thomas Nelson, 1983.
Bar-Nathan, Rachel. *The Pottery*. Vol. 3 of *Hasmonean and Herodian Palaces at Jericho: Final Reports of the 1973–1987 Excavations*. Jerusalem: Israel Exploration Society, 2002.
Berlin, Andrea M. *Gamla I: The Pottery of the Second Temple Period*. IAA Reports 29. Jerusalem: Israel Antiquities Authority, 2006.
———. "Romanization and Anti-Romanization in Pre-Revolt Galilee." Pages 57–73 in *The First Jewish Revolt: Archaeology, History and Ideology*. Edited by Andrea M. Berlin and J. Andrew Overman. London: Routledge, 2002.
———. "The Rural Economy." Pages 8–18 in *Karanis: An Egyptian Town in Roman Times*. Edited by Elaine K. Gazda. Ann Arbor: University of Michigan Press, 1983.
Bloedhorn, Hanswulf. "The Capitals of the Synagogue of Capernaum: Their Chronological and Stylistic Classification with Regard to the Development of Capitals in the Decapolis and in Palestine." Pages

49–54 in *Ancient Synagogues in Israel, Third-Seventh Century C.E.* Edited by Rachel Achlili. Oxford: Oxford University Press, 1989.

Boak, Arthur E. R. *Karanis: The Temples, Coin Hoards, Botanical and Zoölogical Reports, Seasons 1924–31.* Ann Arbor: University of Michigan Press, 1933.

Boak, Arthur E. R., and Enoch E. Peterson. *Karanis: Topographical and Architectural Report of Excavations during the Seasons 1924–28.* Ann Arbor: University of Michigan Press, 1931.

Bösen, Willibald. *Galiläa: Lebensraum und Wirkungsfeld Jesu.* Vienna: Herder, 1998.

Chancey, Mark A. *Greco-Roman Culture and the Galilee of Jesus.* Cambridge: Cambridge University Press, 2005.

———. *The Myth of a Gentile Galilee.* Cambridge: Cambridge University Press, 2002.

Charlesworth, James H. "Jesus Research and Archaeology: A New Perspective." Pages 11–63 in *Jesus and Archaeology.* Edited by James H. Charlesworth. Grand Rapids: Eerdmans, 2006.

Corbo, Virgilio. *Cafarnao I: Gli edifici della città.* Jerusalem: Franciscan Printing Press, 1975.

———. "The Church of the House of St. Peter at Capernaum." Pages 71–76 in *Ancient Churches Revealed.* Edited by Yoram Tsafrir. Jerusalem: Israel Exploration Society, 1993.

———. *The House of St. Peter at Capharnaum.* Translated by Sylvester Saller. Jerusalem: Franciscan Printing Press, 1969.

———. "Resti della sinagoga del primo secolo a Cafarnao." Pages 313–57 in *Studia Hierosolymitana III.* Edited by Giovanni Claudio Bottini. Jerusalem: Franciscan Printing Press, 1982.

Corbo, Virgilio, and Stanislao Loffreda. "Resti del bronzo medio a Cafarnao." *LA* 35 (1985): 375–90.

Crossan, John Dominic. *The Birth of Christianity: Discovering What Happened in the Years Immediately after the Execution of Jesus.* San Francisco: HarperSanFrancisco, 1998.

Crossan, John Dominic, and Jonathan L. Reed. *Excavating Jesus: Beneath the Stones, Behind the Texts.* San Francisco: Harper, 2001.

Danby, Herbert. *The Mishnah, Translated from the Hebrew with Introduction and Brief Explanatory Notes.* Oxford: Oxford University Press, 1933.

Edwards, Douglas R. "Identity and Social Location in Roman Galilean Villages." Pages 357–74 in *Religion, Ethnicity, and Identity in Ancient*

Galilee: A Region in Transition. Edited by Jürgen Zangenberg, Harold W. Attridge, and Dale B. Martin. Tübingen: Mohr Siebeck, 2007.

Eschebach, Hans. "Erläuterungen zum Plan von Pompeji." Pages 331–38 in *Neue Forschungen in Pompeji und den anderen vom Vesuvausbruch 79 n. Chr. vershütteten Städten*. Edited by Bernard Andreae and Helmut Kyrieleis. Recklinghausen: Verlag Aurel Bongers Recklinghausen, 1975.

Foerster, Gideon. "Notes on Recent Excavations at Capernaum (Review Article)." *IEJ* 21 (1971): 207–11.

Foss, Pedar W. "Watchful Lares: Roman Household Organization and the Rituals of Cooking and Eating." Pages 197–218 in *Domestic Space in the Roman World: Pompeii and Beyond*. Edited by Ray Laurence and Andrew Wallace-Hadrill. Portsmouth, R.I.: Journal of Roman Archaeology, 1997.

Frankel, Rafael, Nimrod Getzov, Mordechai Aviam, and Avi Degani. *Settlement Dynamics and Regional Diversity in Ancient Upper Galilee: Archaeological Survey of Upper Galilee*. Jerusalem: Israel Antiquities Authority, 2001.

Freyne, Seán. "Archaeology and the Historical Jesus." Pages 64–83 in *Jesus and Archaeology*. Edited by James H. Charlesworth. Grand Rapids: Eerdmans, 2006.

Gazda, Elaine K., and Jacqueline Royer. "Domestic Life." Pages 19–31 in *Karanis: An Egyptian Town in Roman Times*. Edited by Elaine K. Gazda. Ann Arbor: University of Michigan Press, 1983.

Goodblatt, David. "The Political and Social History of the Jewish Community in the Land of Israel, c. 235–638." Pages 404–30 in *The Late Roman–Rabbinic Period*. Vol. 4 of *The Cambridge History of Judaism*. Edited by Steven T. Katz. Cambridge: Cambridge University Press, 2006.

Groh, Dennis. "The Finewares from the Patrician and Lintel Houses." Pages 129–38 in *Excavations at Ancient Meiron, Upper Galilee, Israel 1971–72, 1974–75, 1977*. Edited by Eric M. Meyers, James F. Strange, and Carol L. Meyers. Cambridge: American Schools of Oriental Research, 1981.

Gutman, Shemaryahu. "Gamala." *NEAEHL* 2:459–63.

Harland, Philip A. "The Economy of First-Century Palestine: State of the Scholarly Discussion." Pages 511–27 in *Handbook of Early Christianity*. Edited by Anthony J. Blasi, Jean Duhaime, and Paul-André Turcotte. Oxford: AltaMira, 2002.

Hayes, Christine E. *Gentile Impurities and Jewish Identities: Intermarriage and Conversion from the Bible to the Talmud*. Oxford: Oxford University Press, 2002.

Herbert, Sharon C. "Introduction." Pages 1–25 in *Tel Anafa I, i: Final Report on Ten Years of Excavation at a Hellenistic and Roman Settlement in Northern Israel*. Edited by Sharon C. Herbert. Ann Arbor, Mich.: Kelsey Museum, 1994.

———. "Occupational History and Stratigraphy." Pages 26–182 in *Tel Anafa I, i: Final Report on Ten Years of Excavation at a Hellenistic and Roman Settlement in Northern Israel*. Edited by Sharon C. Herbert. Ann Arbor, Mich.: Kelsey Museum, 1994.

Hirschfeld, Yizhar. *The Palestinian Dwelling in the Roman-Byzantine Periods*. Jerusalem: Israel Exploration Society, 1995.

Horsley, Richard A. *Archaeology, History, and Society in Galilee: The Social Context of Jesus and the Rabbis*. Valley Forge, Pa.: Trinity Press International, 1996.

Husselman, Elinor M. *Karanis: Excavations of the University of Michigan in Egypt 1928–1935: Topography and Architecture*. Ann Arbor: University of Michigan Press, 1979.

Jensen, Morten Hørning. *Herod Antipas in Galilee: The Literary and Archaeological Sources on the Reign of Herod Antipas and Its Socioeconomic Impact on Galilee*. Tübingen: Mohr Siebeck, 2006.

Johnson, Barbara. *Pottery from Karanis: Excavations of the University of Michigan*. Ann Arbor: University of Michigan Press, 1981.

Kazen, Thomas. *Issues of Impurity in Early Judaism*. Winona Lake, Ind.: Eisenbrauns, 2010.

———. *Jesus and Purity Halakah: Was Jesus Indifferent to Impurity?* Rev. ed. Winona Lake, Ind.: Eisenbrauns, 2010.

Kim, H. S. "Small Change and the Moneyed Economy." Pages 44–51 in *Money, Labour and Land: Approaches to the Economies of Ancient Greece*. Edited by Paul Cartledge, Edward E. Cohen, and Lin Foxhall. London: Routledge, 2002.

Kingsley, Sean A. "The Economic Impact of the Palestinian Wine Trade in Late Antiquity." Pages 44–68 in *Economy and Exchange in the East Mediterranean during Late Antiquity*. Edited by Sean A. Kingsley and Michael Decker. Oxford: Oxbow, 2001.

Klawans, Jonathan. *Impurity and Sin in Ancient Judaism*. Oxford: Oxford University Press, 2000.

———. "Notions of Gentile Impurity in Ancient Judaism." *AJS Review* 20 (1995): 285–312.

Lapin, Hayim. "The Origins and Development of the Rabbinic Movement in the Land of Israel." Pages 204–29 in *The Late Roman-Rabbinic Period*. Vol. 4 of *The Cambridge History of Judaism*. Edited by Steven T. Katz. Cambridge: Cambridge University Press, 2006.

Laughlin, John C. H. "Capernaum: From Jesus' Time and After." *BAR* 19.5 (1993): 55–61, 90.

Levine, Lee I. "Jewish Archaeology in Late Antiquity: Art, Architecture, and Inscriptions." Pages 519–555 in *The Late Roman-Rabbinic Period*. Vol. 4 of *The Cambridge History of Judaism*. Edited by Steven T. Katz. Cambridge: Cambridge University Press, 2006.

Loffreda, Stanislao. *Cafarnao II: La Ceramica*. Jerusalem: Franciscan Printing Press, 1974.

———. "Capernaum." *NEAEHL* 1:291–95.

———. "Ceramica ellenistico-romana nel sottosuolo della sinagoga di Cafarnao." Pages 273–312 in *Studia Hierosolymitana III*. Edited by Giovanni Claudio Bottini. Jerusalem: Franciscan Printing Press, 1982.

———. "Coins from the Synagogue of Capharnaum." *LA* 47 (1997): 223–44.

———. *Holy Land Pottery at the Time of Jesus: Early Roman Period, 63 BC–70 AD*. Jerusalem: Franciscan Printing Press, 2002.

———. *Recovering Capharnaum*. Jerusalem: Edizioni Custodia Terra Santa, 1985.

———. "Vasi in vetro e in argilla trovati a Cafarnao nel 1984: Rapporto preliminare." *LA* 34 (1984): 385–408.

Magen, Yitzhak. "The Land of Benjamin in the Second Temple Period." Pages 1–28 in *The Land of Benjamin*. Edited by Yitzhak Magen, Donald T. Ariel, Gabriela Bijovsky, Yoav Tzionit, and Orna Sirkis. Jerusalem: Israel Antiquities Authority, 2004.

———. *The Stone Vessel Industry in the Second Temple Period: Excavations at Hizma and the Jerusalem Temple Mount*. Jerusalem: Israel Exploration Society, 2002.

Magness, Jodi. *Stone and Dung, Oil and Spit: Jewish Daily Life in the Time of Jesus*. Grand Rapids: Eerdmans, 2011.

Ma'oz, Zvi Uri. "The Synagogue at Capernaum: A Radical Solution." Pages 137–48 in vol. 2 of *The Roman and Byzantine Near East: Some Recent Archaeological Research*. Edited by John H. Humphry. Portsmouth, R.I.: Journal of Roman Archaeology, 1999.

Mattila, Sharon Lea. "Jesus and the 'Middle Peasants': Problematizing a Social-Scientific Concept." *CBQ* 72 (2010): 291–313.

Meier, John P. *Law and Love*. Vol. 4 of *A Marginal Jew: Rethinking the Historical Jesus*. New Haven: Yale University Press, 2009.

Meyers, Eric M. "Early Judaism and Christianity in the Light of Archaeology." *BA* (1988): 69–79.

———. "Galilean Regionalism: A Reappraisal." Pages 115–31 in *Studies in Judaism and Its Greco-Roman Context*. Vol. 5 of *Approaches to Ancient Judaism*. Edited by William Scott Green. Chico, Calif.: Scholars Press, 1985.

———. "Jesus and His Galilean Context. Pages 57–66 in *Archaeology and the Galilee: Texts and Contexts in the Greco-Roman and Byzantine Periods*. Edited by Douglas R. Edwards and C. Thomas McCollough. Atlanta: Scholars Press, 1997.

———. "Jewish Art and Architecture in the Land of Israel, 70–c. 235." Pages 174–90 in *The Late Roman–Rabbinic Period*. Vol. 4 of *The Cambridge History of Judaism*. Edited by Steven T. Katz. Cambridge: Cambridge University Press, 2006.

Meyers, Eric M., and James F. Strange. *Archaeology, the Rabbis, and Early Christianity*. Nashville: Abingdon, 1981.

Meyers, Eric M., James F. Strange, and Dennis E. Groh. "The Meiron Excavations Project: Archaeological Survey in Galilee and Golan, 1976." *BASOR* 230 (1978): 1–24.

Meyers, Eric M., James F. Strange, and Carol L. Meyers, eds. *Excavations at Ancient Meiron, Upper Galilee, Israel 1971-72, 1974-75, 1977*. Cambridge: American Schools of Oriental Research, 1981.

Mizzi, Dennis J. "The Glass from Khirbet Qumran: What Does It Tell Us about the Qumran Community?" Pages 99–198 in *The Dead Sea Scrolls: Texts and Contexts*. Edited by Charlotte Hempel. Leiden: Brill, 2010.

Nagy, Rebecca Martin, ed. *Sepphoris in Galilee: Crosscurrents of Culture*. Winona Lake, Ind.: Eisenbrauns, 1996.

Netzer, Ehud, ed. *Hasmonean and Herodian Palaces at Jericho: Final Reports of the 1973–1987 Excavations*. 3 vols. Jerusalem: Israel Exploration Society, 2001.

Olyan, Saul M. "Purity Ideology in Ezra-Nehemiah as a Tool to Reconstitute the Community." *JSJ* 35 (2004): 1–16.

Pirson, Felix. "Rented Accommodation at Pompeii: The Evidence of the Insula Arriana Polliana VI.6." Pages 165–81 in *Domestic Space in the Roman World: Pompeii and Beyond.* Edited by Ray Laurence and Andrew Wallace-Hadrill. Portsmouth, RI: Journal of Roman Archaeology, 1997.

Poirier, John C. "Purity beyond the Temple in the Second Temple Era." *JBL* 122 (2003): 247–65.

Rabinowitz, A. H., and Bernard Susser, eds. *The Mishnah. Seder Nizikin Vol. 2. Bava Batra.* Translated by Shmuel Himelstein. Jerusalem: Eliner Library, 1988.

Raynor, Joyce, and Yaakov Meshorer. *The Coins of Ancient Meiron.* Meiron Excavation Project Series 4. Winona Lake, Ind.: Eisenbrauns, 1988.

Reed, Jonathan L. *Archaeology and the Galilean Jesus: A Re-examination of the Evidence.* Harrisburg, Pa.: Trinity Press International, 2000.

———. "Population Numbers, Urbanization, and Economics: Galilean Archaeology and the Historical Jesus." Pages 203–19 in *Society of Biblical Literature 1994 Seminar Papers.* Atlanta: Scholars Press, 1994.

———. "Stone Vessels and Gospel Texts: Purity and Socio-Economics in John 2." Pages 381–401 in *Zeichen aus Text und Stein: Studien auf dem Weg zu einer Archäologie des Neuen Testaments.* Edited by Stefan Alkier and Jürgen Zangenburg. Tübingen: Francke, 2003.

Richardson, Peter. "First-Century Houses and Q's Setting." Pages 63–83 in *Christology, Controversy and Community: New Testament Essays in Honour of David R. Catchpole.* Edited by David G. Horrell and Christopher M. Tuckett. Leiden: Brill, 2000.

———. "Khirbet Qana (and Other Villages) as a Context for Jesus." Pages 120–44 in *Jesus and Archaeology.* Edited by James H. Charlesworth. Grand Rapids: Eerdmans, 2006.

———. "Towards a Typology of Levantine/Palestinian Houses." *JSNT* 27 (2004): 47–68.

———. "What Has Cana To Do with Capernaum?" *NTS* 48 (2002): 314–31.

Rosenthal-Heginbottom, Renate. "Chapter 6 (b): Hellenistic and Roman Fine Ware and Lamps from Area A." Pages 192–223 in *The Finds from Areas A, W and X-2: Final Report.* Vol. 2 of *Jewish Quarter Excavations in the Old City of Jerusalem Conducted by Nahman Avigad, 1969–1982.* Edited by Hillel Geva. Jerusalem: Israel Exploration Society, 2003.

Rousseau, John J., and Rami Arav. *Jesus and His World: An Archaeological and Cultural Dictionary.* Minneapolis: Fortress, 1995.

Safrai, Ze'ev. *The Economy of Roman Palestine.* London: Routledge, 1994.

Slane, Kathleen Warner. "The Fine Wares." Pages 249–406 in *Tel Anafa II, i: The Hellenistic and Roman Pottery*. Edited by Sharon C. Herbert. Ann Arbor, Mich.: Kelsey Museum, 1997.

Strange, James F. "First Century Galilee from Archaeology and from the Texts." Pages 39–48 in *Archaeology and the Galilee: Texts and Contexts in the Graeco-Roman and Byzantine Periods*. Edited by Douglas R. Edwards and C. Thomas McCollough. Atlanta: Scholars, 1997.

———. "Review: The Capernaum and Herodium Publications." *BASOR* 226 (1977): 65–73.

———. "Review: The Capernaum and Herodium Publications, Part 2." *BASOR* 233 (1979): 63–69.

Strange, James F., and Hershel Shanks. "Has the House Where Jesus Stayed in Capernaum Been Found?" *BAR* 8.6 (1982): 26–37.

———. "Synagogue Where Jesus Preached Found at Capernaum." *BAR* 9.6 (1983): 24–31.

Syon, Danny. "Gamla: Portrait of a Rebellion." *BAR* 18.1 (1992): 20–37.

Taylor, Joan E. *Christians and the Holy Places: The Myth of Jewish-Christian Origins*. Oxford: Clarendon, 1993.

Tsafrir, Yoram. "The Synagogues at Capernaum and Meroth and the Dating of the Galilean Synagogue." Pages 151–61 in *The Roman and Byzantine Near East: Some Recent Archaeological Research*. Edited by John H. Humphrey. Ann Arbor, Mich.: Journal of Roman Archaeology, 1995.

Tzaferis, Vassilios. "Capernaum: Excavations in the Area of the Greek Orthodox Church." *NEAEHL* 1:295–96.

———. *Excavations at Capernaum, Volume I: 1978–1982*. Winona Lake, Ind.: Eisenbrauns, 1989.

Wallace-Hadrill, Andrew. *Houses and Society in Pompeii and Herculaneum*. Princeton: Princeton University Press, 1994.

Weiss, Zeev, and Ehud Netzer. "Sepphoris during the Byzantine Period." Pages 81–89 in *Sepphoris in Galilee: Crosscurrents of Culture*. Edited by Rebecca Martin Nagy. Winona Lake, Ind.: Eisenbrauns, 1996.

Xenophontos, Costas, Carolyn Elliott, and John G. Malpas. "Major and Trace-Element Geochemistry Used in Tracing the Provenance of Late Bronze Age and Roman Basalt Artefacts from Cyprus." *Levant* 20 (1988): 169–83.

4
Execrating? or Execrable Peasants!

Douglas E. Oakman

> Well, ours is not a maritime country; neither commerce nor the intercourse which it promotes with the outside world has any attraction for us. Our cities are built inland, remote from the sea; and we devote ourselves to the cultivation of the productive country with which we are blessed. (Josephus, *C. Ap.* 1.60)

> Herod was a shrewd businessman, who took advantage of many commercial enterprises, both domestically and internationally.[1]

My response to Mordechai Aviam's excellent survey in this volume will be to offer selective ruminations about peasants and political economy in first-century Galilee, including definitions and models drawn from peasant or agrarian theorists, along with some observations or questions about the archaeological data, especially money, in the light of these models.[2]

What Is a "Peasant"?

The word "peasant" has been securely attested in the English language since the fifteenth century.[3] Karl Marx, Werner Sombart, and Max Weber wrote early scientific works on the social life and values of the German

---

1. Shimon Dar, "The Agrarian Economy in the Herodian Period," in *The World of the Herods* (ed. Nikos Kokkinos; Stuttgart: Steiner, 2007), 305–6.
2. David Christian, *Maps of Time: An Introduction to Big History* (Berkeley: University of California Press, 2004), provides the largest framework and plausibility for the following response, especially his chapters on agrarian civilizations.
3. Borrowed from French, according to *The Compact Edition of the Oxford English Dictionary* (2 vols.; Glasgow: Oxford University Press, 1971), 2:594.

peasantry.[4] Others were producing more anecdotal and impressionistic studies of peasants.[5] For instance, Elihu Grant wrote on *The Peasantry of Palestine* in 1907.[6] Gustav Dalman's *Arbeit und Sitte in Palästina* appeared from 1928 to 1942.[7] Dalman cataloged the details of everyday Arab peasant life. In the 1930 collection of Sorokin, Zimmerman, and Galpin, the three-volume *A Systematic Source Book in Rural Sociology*, the terms "peasant" and "farmer" still are used rather interchangeably. Mintz points to Robert Redfield's *Tepoztlán* (1930) as an early study by an anthropologist.[8] The study of the history and anthropology of peasantry took firm shape and flourished after World War II, reaching perhaps an apogee with the work of Eric Wolf and James C. Scott in the 1980s and 1990s. Impetus for study came not only from historical and ethnographic interests but also from postcolonial and development policy issues.[9] Traditional peasantries have been disappearing for some time now under the impact of global markets and urbanization.[10] Recently postmodern trends and the turn to the emic

---

4. Karl Marx, "The Eighteenth Brumaire of Louis Bonaparte," excerpt in *Peasants and Peasant Societies: Selected Readings* (ed. Teodor Shanin; Harmondsworth: Penguin, 1971), 229–37; Werner Sombart, *Der moderne Kapitalismus*, 3rd edition, excerpted in Pitirim Aleksandrovich Sorokin, Carle C. Zimmerman, and Charles Josiah Galpin, *A Systematic Source Book in Rural Sociology* (3 vols.; New York: Russell & Russell, 1930–1932), 1:170–84; Max Weber, *Economy and Society* (ed. Günther Roth and Claus Wittich; 2 vols.; Berkeley: University of California Press, 1978), e.g., 1:90 or 1:468.

5. George Foster, "What Is a Peasant?" in *Peasant Society: A Reader* (ed. Jack M. Potter, May N. Diaz, and George M. Foster; The Little, Brown Series in Anthropology; Boston: Little, Brown, 1967), 2–14.

6. Elihu Grant, *The Peasantry of Palestine: the Life, Manners and Customs of the Village* (Boston: Pilgrim, 1907).

7. Gustaf Dalman, *Arbeit und Sitte in Palästina* (7 vols.; Gütersloh: Bertelsmann, 1928–1942).

8. Sidney W. Mintz, "A Note on the Definition of Peasantries," *Journal of Peasant Studies* 1 (1973): 92.

9. The readings in Shanin, *Peasants and Peasant Societies*, provide a sense of the rise of peasant studies; Robert Redfield, *The Little Community and Peasant Society and Culture* (Chicago: University of Chicago Press, 1960), 15–39, gives a brief history of anthropological recognition of peasants.

10. Stuart Plattner, ed., *Economic Anthropology* (Stanford, Calif.: Stanford University Press, 1989); Henry Bernstein and Terence J. Byres, "From Peasant Studies to Agrarian Change," *Journal of Agrarian Change* 1 (2001): 1–56; Christian writes, "In the late agrarian era, most households lived in the countryside and engaged in small-scale farming. Today, small farming has vanished in many regions and is declining where

subject in social sciences have brought the term "peasant" into doubt as a general category (see below "Accursed Peasants").

The ancients certainly had words for agricultural types that we could better understand through the literature on peasants: the Latin *rusticus* or *agricola*, the Greek γεωργός or ἄγροικος, the Semitic 'kr, and so on. Rural types are often praised by Roman writers as those most to be honored. These agrarian viewpoints, for the most part, represented the ideals and prejudices of elite "gentlemen farmers." For instance, Cato writes, "And when [our ancestors] would praise a worthy their praise took this form: 'good husbandman,' 'good farmer'" (M. Porcius Cato, *De Agri Cultura* 2). Varro likewise comments:

> And not only is the tilling of the fields more ancient—it is more noble. It was therefore not without reason that our ancestors tried to entice their citizens back from the city to the country; for in time of peace they were fed by the country Romans, and in time of war aided by them. (M. Terentius Varro, *Rerum Rusticarum* 3.1.4)

There was also the snobbish view of the peasant as a rube. Theophrastus says of the ἄγροικος:

> He will sit down with his cloak above his knee, and thus expose too much of himself. Most things this man sees in the streets strike him not at all, but let him espy an ox or an ass or a billy-goat, and he will stand and contemplate him. He is apt also to take from the larder as he eats, and to drink his wine over-strong; to make secret love to the bake-wench, and then help her grind the day's corn for the whole household and himself with it.... When he receives money he tests it and finds it wanting; it looks, says he, too much like lead; and changes it for other. And if he has lent his plough, or a basket, or a sickle, or a sack, he will remember it as he lies awake one night and rise and go out to seek it. (Theophrastus, *Characters* 4.4–11)

Perhaps a more realistic view of the peasant comes from Jesus ben Sirach in the early second century B.C.E.:

---

it still survives" (*Maps of Time*, 348). So, I note in my *Jesus and the Peasants* (Eugene, Ore.: Cascade, 2008), 1–2, that urbanization since 1900 has left most scholars with little feel for or experience of the lives and realities of peasants.

The wisdom of the scribe depends on the opportunity of leisure; and he who has little business may become wise. How can he become wise who handles the plow, and who glories in the shaft of a goad, who drives oxen and is occupied with their work, and whose talk is about bulls? He sets his heart on plowing furrows, and he is careful about fodder for the heifers. (38:24–26, RSV)

Sirach also gives a sense of limited labor specialization in Hellenistic period Judea, naming craftsmen (especially the makers of signets), the smith, and the potter. Again, this is a depiction of villagers, village life, proletarian and rural labor from the vantage point of elites.[11]

Josephus, as is well known, gives us every expectation of having to deal with conditions and arrangements of agrarian production:

For the land [of the two Galilees] is everywhere so rich in soil and pasturage and produces such variety of trees, that even the most indolent are tempted by these facilities to devote themselves to agriculture. In fact, every inch of the soil has been cultivated by the inhabitants; there is not a parcel of waste land. (Josephus, *J.W.* 3.42–43.)

Of course, use of "farmer" versus "peasant" could be seen as merely a semantic issue. But this is not the best approach from the standpoint of the comparative social sciences. There have been good reasons to identify under the term "peasant" a general agricultural phenomenon through much of world history.[12] One of these reasons has been the synthetic and compara-

---

11. Joachim Jeremias, *Jerusalem in the Time of Jesus* (trans. F. H. Cave and C. H. Cave; Philadelphia: Fortress, 1969), 4–27, gives some idea of urban division of labor at the time of Jesus. By the Middle Roman period, the list could include at least "forty kinds of craftsmen": "Tailors, shoemakers, builders, masons, carpenters, millers, bakers, tanners, spice-merchants, apothecaries, cattlemen butchers, slaughterers, dairymen, cheesemakers, physicians and bloodletters, barbers, hairdressers, laundrymen, jewellers, smiths, weavers, dryers, embroiderers, workers in gold brocade, carpet makers, matting makers, well-diggers, fishermen, bee-keepers, potters and platemakers (who were also pottery dealers), pitcher makers, coopers, pitch-refiners and glaze-makers, makers of glass and glassware, armourers, copyists, painters and engravers" (Joseph Klausner, *Jesus of Nazareth: His Life, Times, and Teaching* [trans. Herbert Danby; New York: Macmillan, 1925], 177).

12. Michael Kearney, "Peasantry," in *International Encyclopedia of the Social Sciences* (2nd ed.; ed. William A. Darity Jr.; 9 vols.; Detroit: Thomson Gale, 2008), 6:195–96; C. von Dietze, "Peasantry," in *Encyclopaedia of the Social Sciences* (ed. Edwin R. A.

tive work of macrosociology—for instance, exemplified in the early twentieth-century work of Weber, then in the 1950s and 1960s in the work of Gideon Sjøberg, Karl Wittfogel, and Gerhard Lenski, and then in the 1980s by the work of John Kautsky.[13] Further, the historically and ethnographically informed works of Barrington Moore, Robert Redfield, George Foster, Teodore Shanin, Eric Hobsbawm, Eric Wolf, and James Scott have provided us with a very persuasive set of studies on the variations on a theme we call "peasantry."[14] In addition, postwar work of Karl Polanyi was especially important for characterizing premodern economics as "substantive" and embedded within noneconomic social and political concerns.[15]

Seligman and Alvin Johnson; 15 vols.; New York: Macmillan, 1930–1935), 12:48–53; see Robartus J. Van der Spek, "The Hellenistic Near East," in *The Cambridge Economic History of the Greco-Roman World* (ed. Walter Scheidel, Ian Morris, and Richard Saller; Cambridge: Cambridge University Press, 2007), 414. Van der Spek makes it clear that subordinate rural labor was typical in the eastern Mediterranean world.

13. Weber, *Economy and Society*; Karl A. Wittfogel, *Oriental Despotism* (New Haven: Yale University Press, 1957); Gideon Sjøberg, *The Preindustrial City: Past and Present* (New York: Free Press, 1960); Gerhard E. Lenski, *Power and Privilege: A Theory of Social Stratification* (2nd ed.; Chapel Hill: University of North Carolina Press, 1984); John H. Kautsky, *The Politics of Aristocratic Empires* (Chapel Hill: University of North Carolina Press, 1982).

14. Barrington Moore, *Social Origins of Dictatorship and Democracy: Lord and Peasant in the Making of the Modern World* (Boston: Beacon, 1966); Robert Redfield, *The Little Community*; George Foster, "Peasant Society and the Image of Limited Good," in Potter, Diaz, and Foster, *Peasant Society*, 300–323; Teodor Shanin, *Peasants and Peasant Societies*; Eric J. Hobsbawm, *Primitive Rebels: Studies in Archaic Forms of Social Movements in the 19th and 20th Centuries* (New York: Norton, 1959); idem, "Peasants and Politics," *Journal of Peasant Studies* 1 (1973): 3–23; Eric R. Wolf, *Peasants* (Foundations of Modern Anthropology; Englewood-Cliffs, N.J.: Prentice-Hall, 1966); James C. Scott, *The Moral Economy of the Peasant: Rebellion and Subsistence in Southeast Asia* (New Haven: Yale University Press, 1976). James C. Scott writes to me (private communication) that he still considers Wolf's *Peasants* one of the best synthetic treatments.

15. Karl Polanyi, Conrad M. Arensberg, and Harry W. Pearson, *Trade and Market in the Early Empires: Economies in History and Theory* (Glencoe, Ill.: Free Press, 1957); Karl Polanyi, *The Livelihood of Man* (ed. Harry W. Pearson; Studies in Social Discontinuity; New York: Academic Press, 1977). The critique of Polanyi by Douglass C. North, *Structure and Change in Economic History* (New York: Norton, 1981), 106, represents the formalist position. However, the formalist critique fails to appreciate that rational choice theory or maximization of self interest does not encompass all human economic motivations.

Marx proposed the cultural and social isolation of peasants:

> The small-holding peasants [of France] form a vast mass, the members of which live in similar conditions but without entering into manifold relations with one another. Their mode of production isolates them from one another instead of bringing them into mutual intercourse.[16]

Chayanov emphasized in his theory that the family was the economic producing and consuming unit, while Wolf stressed that the peasant had to balance subsistence concerns with outside demands. Raymond Firth (1950) argued that the word "peasant" includes "other small-scale producers, such as fishermen and rural craftsmen, pointing out that 'they are of the same social class as the agriculturalists, and often members of the same families.'"[17] Here are some other representative definitions from significant peasant theorists:

> Barrington Moore (1966): A previous history of subordination to a landed upper class recognized and enforced in the laws, which, however, need not always prohibit movement out of this class, sharp cultural distinctions, and a considerable degree of *de facto* possession of the land, constitute the main distinguishing features of a peasantry.[18]

> George Foster (1967): "prepeasants [in ANE] were turned into peasants with the appearance of the first towns or incipient cities ... in which political and usually religious control began to be exercised over the hinterland."[19]

> James Scott (1976): "the distinctive economic behavior of the subsistence-oriented peasant family results from the fact that, unlike a capitalist enterprise, it is a unit of consumption as well as a unit of production."[20]

> John Kautsky (1982): "I have sought to confine use of the term 'peasants' to agriculturalists exploited by aristocrats.... There can be no aristocrat without peasants and no peasants without aristocrat." Regarding "The Aristocracy in the Economy," he adds, "exploitation is, indeed, the princi-

---

16. Quoted in Teodor Shanin, *Peasants and Peasant Societies*, 230.
17. Quoted in Foster, "What Is a Peasant," 4.
18. Moore, *Social Origins of Dictatorship and Democracy*, 111.
19. Foster, "What Is a Peasant," 7.
20. Scott, *Moral Economy of the Peasant*, 13.

pal and only necessary link between the peasants' societies in their villages and the society of the aristocracy, regardless of who 'owns' the land."[21]

"Peasant" as a Model for Agrarian Rural Labor

Table 1 provides contrasting ideal types to define some of the salient differences between premodern peasants and modern farmers.

TABLE 1: IDEAL TYPE DEFINITIONS OF PREMODERN "PEASANT" AND MODERN "FARMER"

Peasant	Farmer, "agricultural entrepreneur"
Technology: iron plows and tools, human and animal energies, village cooperation	**Technology**: steel plows and tools, machinery, petrochemicals, farm cooperatives
Strong familism: Rigid family codes and hierarchy, mistrust of outsiders, strict gender roles	**Weaker familism**: Family codes upheld in the face of cultural change, works with outsiders for business purposes under terms of limited trust, gender roles more open
Politics: The state is always an enemy to the subsistence margin; little-to-no participation in politics, localism, payment (or evasion) of taxes and dues	**Politics**: Some participation for the sake of promoting rural interests (cf. Jefferson: farming as basis for democracy), broader horizons, government liens upon profits
Family production: Self-sufficiency, subsistence, production for consumption	**Family production**: Market orientation, production for sale, buying of food
Economic exchange: Household economy; generalized reciprocity within the family, balanced reciprocity with villagers or other villages, negative reciprocity with strangers or agents of the elites	**Economic exchange**: Market-orientation; generalized reciprocity within the family, universalizing of balanced reciprocity; local cooperatives, appeals to the courts

---

21. Kautsky, *The Politics of Aristocratic Empires*, 271; on aristocrats and the economy, 103.

Culture: Traditional, no education, very limited literacy (if any)	**Culture**: Traditional, some education and literacy, openness to technological innovation, modern scientific farming requires a high degree of technical knowledge
Traditional religion: Local (little) traditions; great tradition cared for by distant priests (cf. M. Weber, *Economy and Society*: religion of peasants is magic)	**Traditional religion**: More integrated into great traditions (cf. H. R. Niebuhr, *Social Sources of Denominationalism*)

Further, table 2 contrasts typical peasant values and attitudes with those of modern farmers.

TABLE 2: PEASANT VALUES AND ECONOMIC ORIENTATION IN CONTRAST TO MODERN FARMER

Peasant household embedded in imperial politics	Farming embedded in modern economy
Production for consumption, self-sufficiency the ideal, but some labor specialization in the village, limited exchange between villages and towns	Production for market profit, production and consumption separated, modern farmer depends on a range of labor specializations
Peasant subsistence "mortgaged" by requisitions by outsiders	Taxation on profits
Local markets are in kind or simple products that peasant household cannot make for itself; markets require permission to enter; distinguish local markets from translocal or long-distance commerce	Land, labor, capital markets open to those with capital
Money: limited economic utility for most; money barter with copper tokens, silver needed for tax payments, distribution dependent on political forces and patronage	Money: generalized economic utility, "everything" is for sale for money

Debt: peasants are inevitably in debt, which usually expresses relations of long-term political indenture, extensive tenancy likely in early Roman Palestine	Debt: the farm can be foreclosed on, but some debt can periodically be assumed in order to invest in the operation or increase productivity (heavy machinery)
Politics structured through patronage, patrons control real wealth, elites control markets, banks, commerce	Politics structured through democratic systems

These tabular models are my own, representing the opposite ends of a spectrum of agrarian possibilities. They are constructed to highlight a significant issue in the discussion of the papers in this volume—the characteristics and situation of the typical first-century Galilean peasant family (household economy) embedded within Roman political-economy (involving imperial patronage politics and commercial interests). Max Weber would never allow us to say that peasant villagers in Roman Galilee were in every respect like the ideal types in the lefthand columns. The models are not reality. But they help us to think about the social dynamics in Roman Galilee in significant ways.

Peasants in Early Roman Galilee

Why should we think that rural cultivators in first-century Galilee were peasants? Here are several reasons. Rural families were the basic producing units. Considerations of technology and comparative social typology suggest that agriculture in early first-century Palestine was low-yield, based as it was upon the animal-drawn iron plow and iron hand implements (hoe, scythe, etc.). Helmuth Schneider concurs:

> In ancient agriculture, certainly, much of the work hardly changed over long periods of time: for example, ploughing with a pair of oxen, hoeing of the ground to eliminate weeds, harvesting the grain with a simple sickle, winnowing, or harvesting olives with long sticks. ... Under the conditions of ancient technology, human muscle power remained one of the most important energy sources. Agricultural work in particular was highly physical work, done with simple tools such as hoe, sickle, or scythe.[22]

---

22. Helmuth Schneider, "Technology," in Scheidel, Morris, and Saller, *Cambridge*

Archaeological surveys of Galilee also show varying agricultural plot sizes, but with the majority of the populace farming very small plots. Some time ago, David Fiensy and I respectively tried to estimate the size of a first-century subsistence plot. My result came to 0.6 ha (1.5 acre) per adult.[23] Joel M. Halpern has shown for mid-twentieth-century Serbian peasants, 5 ha (12.4 acres) was the threshold between "pure agriculturalist" families and "mixed agriculturalist" families.[24] Smaller plots on average would imply many families on the subsistence margin.

Lenski would classify large portions of the Roman east as fitting the macrosocietal type of the "advanced agrarian society," in which peasants and (iron) hand tools were the foundation of agricultural production. Proximity to the Mediterranean led to interconnections between agrarian society and maritime society, and commercial opportunities for elites.[25]

We could think of Herodian Palestine as a whole as a "peasant society." Daniel Thorner once proposed that such societies had these major structural features:

(1) "One half or more of the total production must be agricultural";
(2) "More than half the working population must be engaged in agriculture";
(3) Within a territorial state, having an administration with "at least five thousand officers, minor officials, flunkeys, and underlings";

Economic History of the Greco-Roman World, 149, 150. Based upon work of M. Jones, Kevin Greene, "Agriculture in the Roman Empire," in idem, *The Archaeology of the Roman Economy* (Berkeley: University of California Press, 1986), 75, gives a sense of the slow rate of technological innovation in agricultural tools. Further information on the simple agricultural technology of antiquity can be found in K. D. White, *Greek and Roman Technology* (Ithaca, N.Y.: Cornell University Press, 1984), 58–72.

23. Douglas E. Oakman, *Jesus and the Economic Questions of His Day* (Studies in the Bible and Early Christianity 8; Lewiston, N.Y.: Mellen, 1986), 62; David A. Fiensy, *The Social History of Palestine in the Herodian Period: The Land Is Mine* (Studies in the Bible and Early Christianity 20; Lewiston, N.Y.: Mellen, 1991), 93–94.

24. Joel M. Halpern, *A Serbian Village: Social and Cultural Change in a Yugoslav Community* (rev. ed.; New York: Harper Colophon Books, 1967), 73, 75.

25. "Agrarian society" and "maritime society," Gerhard E. Lenski, *Power and Privilege: A Theory of Social Stratification*, 191; "advanced agrarian society" denotes the move from bronze to iron implements, Gerhard E. Lenski and Jean Lenski, *Human Societies: An Introduction to Macrosociology* (5th ed.; New York: McGraw-Hill, 1987), 219.

(4) With towns and a break between town and country that is "simultaneously political, economic, social, and cultural"; total urban population is at least 500,000 or, alternatively, "at least 5 per cent of the entire population ... reside in towns";
(5) agrarian production is accomplished by family household units.[26]

By Thorner's yardsticks, Roman Galilee would have most if not all of the salient features. Conditions 1, 2, and 5 are met (Josephus, *C. Ap.* 1.60). Population estimates for early Roman Palestine are available, with 500,000 being a credible figure. Five percent of this gives 25,000 elites and their retainers—not difficult to imagine. Consider that this is at the right order of magnitude if populations of Jerusalem (25,000), Sepphoris and Tiberias (5,000 to 10,000 each), and all other urban and town areas are added together. Current estimates of the populations for Galilee and Galilean cities would also indicate that the 5 percent threshold is crossed within that region.[27] Finally, there is certainly a political, economic, and cultural break between the Herodian regime and the village Galilean/Judean cultivators.

It should not be forgotten that peasants always exist within political, city, or commercial systems that put varying degrees of stress on traditional peasant subsistence concerns. A period of increased commercialization and urbanization, such as we see in early Roman Palestine, would involve such stress. The final model, "A Dynamic Model of the Causes of Agrarian Conflict," shows how the economic development efforts of

---

26. Daniel Thorner, "Peasantry," in *International Encyclopedia of the Social Sciences* (ed. David L. Sills; 17 vols.; New York: Macmillan, 1968), 11:508.

27. Gildas Hamel, *Poverty and Charity in Roman Palestine, First Three Centuries C.E.* (Near Eastern Studies 23; Berkeley: University of California Press, 1990), 139, sees a possible population range for Roman Palestine between 250,000 and 1,000,000. Jonathan L. Reed, *Archaeology and the Galilean Jesus: A Re-examination of the Evidence* (Harrisburg, Pa.: Trinity Press International, 2000), 89, estimates the populations of Sepphoris and Tiberias as between 8,000 and 12,000. David Fiensy, *Jesus the Galilean: Soundings in a First Century Life* (Piscataway, N.J.: Gorgias, 2007), 40, gives a population figure of 175,000 for Galilee but only 3,500 elites in both Sepphoris and Tiberias. Still, with retainers and town populations included, this estimate of Galilean urban population would likely cross the 5 percent threshold. See further note 50 on settlement populations and orders of magnitude.

Judean and Galilean elites, with interest in translocal or Mediterranean commerce, would negatively impact peasant attitudes and values.[28]

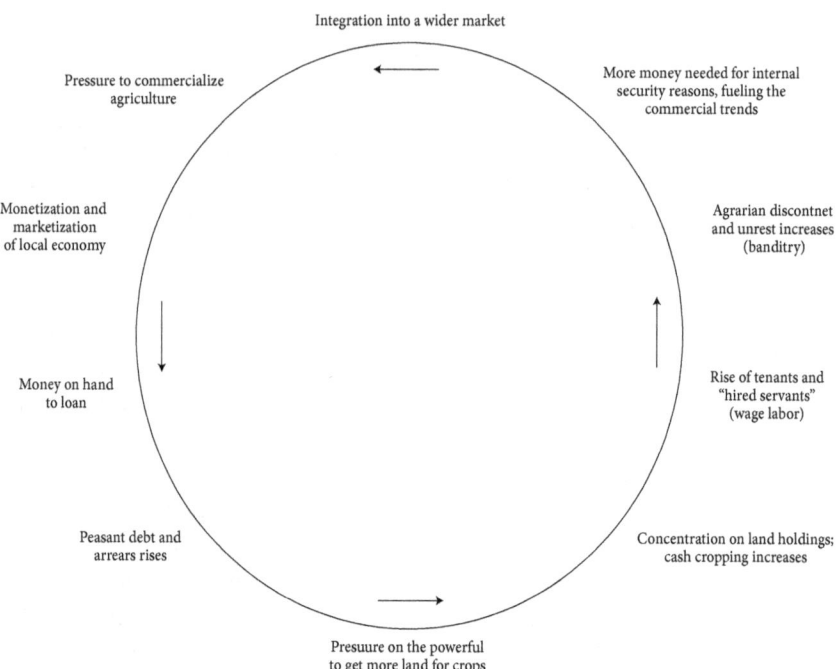

These models and considerations indicate that at least four important interpretive dimensions should be considered for nonelite Roman Galilee: (1) the relative extent of "pure agriculturalists" (subsistence agriculture), "mixed agriculturalists" (agriculture plus wage labor), and landless workers or rural proletariat; (2) taxation and the political impact of patronage politics; (3) the degree to which and the ways in which agrarian sectors of Galilee were drawn into Mediterranean commerce, and (4) the influence of peasant culture and values in the lives of the nonelite landless or rural proletariate (like Jesus or the fishers of the lake).

---

28. Model derived from comments of Henry Landsberger, taken from K. C. Hanson and Douglas E. Oakman, *Palestine in the Time of Jesus: Social Structures and Social Conflicts* (Minneapolis: Fortress, 2008), 168.

The entire situation of Galilean agriculturalists and nonelites, shaped in the first place by subsistence concerns and political realities, is best elucidated by theory informed by comparative study of peasants and agrarian societies. Interpretations without models informed by comparative social science will miss crucial social dynamics.[29] Interpretations without models will have a basis in uncertain social categories, or will simply be anachronistic. The regularity of premodern patterns of elite organization of political economy based upon the labor of subsistence-oriented rural persons would urge against reading Galilee too much in terms of postcapitalist or postindustrial modernization. Ancient commerce and economic development served the interests of elites and their storehouses. Participation at the village level was more in terms of labor exploitation, mortgages on subsistence, and distortion of traditional/local/peasant values. David Christian borrows the term of William H. McNeill for this relationship: parasitism. The broad lines of "agrarian civilizations," Christian claims, are founded upon a multitude of primary producers and relatively small number of elite tribute-takers. Perspectives of "Big History" would argue in favor of the main definitions and historical findings of peasant studies.[30] Closer to the first-century Galilean soil, we have clear evidence in the early Jesus traditions, such as the parables (Talents/Minas, Unjust Steward) and some of the red-letter Q material (Lord's Prayer, pericope addressing anxiety about food and clothing, saying about God and Mammon), that subsistence and debt concerns were wrapped up with the Jesus movement. Social tensions also account for the appearance of Judah of Gamla. And there are very good indications that agrarian problems played a prominent role in the genesis of the Judean-Roman War; if Galilee is socially articulated to Judea as the archaeologists say, then such agrarian problems were likely also entailed in Galilee.[31]

---

29. On the importance of explicit models, see Thomas F. Carney, *The Shape of the Past: Models and Antiquity* (Lawrence, Kans.: Coronado, 1975), 1–43; more recently, Neville Morley, *Approaching the Ancient World: Theories, Models and Concepts in Ancient History* (New York: Routledge, 2004), 1–31.

30. Christian, *Maps of Time*, 283–89; further, Christian writes, 389, "Though the Chinese countryside was highly commericalized in the eighteenth century, structures of ownership and control of the land limited the extent to which the majority of the population could be involved in commercial networks."

31. Martin Goodman, "The First Jewish Revolt: Social Conflict and the Problem of Debt," *JJS* 33 (1982): 417–27; Shimon Applebaum, "Josephus and the Economic

Accursed Peasants: The Current Critique

It is clear (from the discussion at the conference where these papers were first presented) that the category of "peasantry" has come into disrepute among some Galilean historians and archaeologists. Aviam completely rejects the use of "peasant" as an interpretive category. He would use biblical terms like איש עבד אדמה (*'š 'bd 'dmh*, Zech 13:5). Sharon Mattila spoke from the audience during the brief panel discussion to urge that the term "peasant" simply be dropped. She has just published a very thorough account of why she believes the term is no longer helpful.[32] Her main conclusions are that peasants are often significantly differentiated by socio-economic inequalities (not simply Marx's "potatoes in a sack"); also, rural cultivators have often utilized a "multiplicity of economic strategies" (not just subsistence agriculture).[33] The chapter of David Fiensy in this volume warns against reifying models or supplying missing data from models. Part of the concern in these critiques is that a social-science category replaces inferences solely from historical or archaeological data; part of the concern is that a social science category like "peasant" is too simplistic in accounting for first-century Galilean social dynamics.

Among social scientists, of course, the terminological critique or questionable status of generalizations about rural peoples is not entirely new.[34] Already in 1934, von Dietze could write,

> The term peasantry has undergone many changes in meaning in the past and is still subject to various interpretations. Common to all the shifting meanings, however, is a view of the peasant as a tiller of the soil to whom the land which he and his family work offers both a home and a living.[35]

Historical studies and ethnography show that "peasant" is not a simple category; nonetheless, social scientists continue to use the term. Part of

---

Causes of the Jewish War," in *Josephus, the Bible, and History* (ed. Louis H. Feldman and Gohei Hata; Detroit: Wayne State University Press, 1989), 237–64.

32. Sharon Lea Mattila, "Jesus and the 'Middle Peasants'? Problematizing a Social-Scientific Concept," *CBQ* 72 (2010): 291–313. Mattila's article gives an excellent history of some aspects of peasant studies and a focused critique of Richard A. Horsley.

33. Ibid., 301, 313.

34. Mintz, "A Note on the Definition of Peasantries," 91: "a persisting lack of consensus among scholars about the definition of the peasantry."

35. Von Dietze, "Peasantry," 48.

the reason for this is that the social sciences concern themselves by definition with the typical; part of the reason for this is that social dynamics are otherwise unintelligible. Marc Becker, for instance, makes the following helpful observations:

> It is difficult to establish a precise definition of the word "peasant" and, as Sidney Mintz noted in a 1973 essay in the *Journal of Peasant Studies*, this issue has invoked a lengthy debate. Issues of self-identity, created identity, and situational identity all complicate a definition. On one hand, some scholars favor tightly restrictive definitions that limit peasants to a nineteenth-century rural French population, while others have broadened the term to include virtually anyone involved in agriculture, from hunters and gatherers to small landholders, whatever the economic mode of production involved. Increasingly, many historians who study peasants in Latin America have largely eschewed issues of terminology in order to focus on deeper and more significant questions of power and the role that the peasantry played in nation building. Collapsing diverse economic modes of production into a simplistic catch-all category of "peasant," however, tends to hide certain forms of rural consciousness. Not only has the term become so commonly used that it can hardly be avoided, but also a more critical inquiry into what it means to be a "peasant" helps to understand rural protest movements.[36]

Despite critical doubts, *The Journal of Peasant Studies* is still being published after nearly forty years, yet the people known historically under the label "peasants" are becoming extinct. Christian quotes Eric Hobsbawm, "The most dramatic and far-reaching social change of the second half of [the twentieth century], and the one which cuts us off for ever from the world of the past, is the death of the peasantry."[37] Kearney remarks: "Until the mid-twentieth century, most of the world's population could be characterized as peasant, but since that time peasant

---

36. Marc Becker, "Peasant Identity, Worker Identity: Conflicting Modes of Rural Consciousness in Highland Ecuador," *Estudios Interdisciplinarios de América Latina y el Caribe* (University of Tel Aviv) 15 (2004): 118; also available online: http://www1.tau.ac.il/eial/index.php?option=com_content&task=blogsection&id=27&Itemid=192. In a private communication, Professor Becker has written to me, "[I see] all of the terminology I use as socially constructed and contradictory, but continue to use them with all of their vagueness anyway because of how they function as convenient shorthands for much more complicated concepts."

37. Eric Hobsbawm quoted in Christian, *Maps of Time*, 453.

communities have tended to become more complex, due largely to ever increasing rates of permanent and circular migration from agricultural communities to urban areas."[38] Bernstein and Byres note the difficulties of a "peasant essentialism" and provide a lengthy discussion of the reasons for a shift "From Peasant Studies to Agrarian Change." More recent studies of peasants thus move away from the traditional or historical to study rural peoples under the impact of modernization and globalism. This shift in the social situation of contemporary rural groups and in the focus of agrarian social sciences does not invalidate the use of comparative agrarian macrosociology or models inspired by peasant studies applied to the study of ancient rural social realities.

The concerns of Aviam, Mattila, and Fiensy can also be answered by several other considerations: First, "peasant" denotes a multidimensional concept, backed by a significant social-scientific literature, as both the models of this paper and Marc Becker's comments show. The term peasant and related model(s), in other words, provide an important index into both comparative social science literature and the agrarian realities on the first-century ground.[39] Particularly important, given that family is the basic institutional domain of Mediterranean societies, is the interpretive articulation family (peasant households)—politics (elite households and others)—economics/religion. What is noticeably missing from Aviam's interpretive account is the extension of family networks and patronage and the political structuring of socioeconomic relations as the basis for Hellenistic-Roman political economy. Economy and Religion are embedded in family and politics, not the other way around.[40] Although the term peasant is a shorthand conceptual model for a great variety of rural cultivator situations, it points to a complex of many typical features. Second, all of our interpretations of the past are "etic," and without the use of explicit, clearly (con)tested interpretive models—most fitting for understanding the politics, economics, and culture of agrarian societies—some other interpretive framework will be imposed. Third, all of us have to supply missing elements in the data, since historical and archaeological data are

---

38. Bernstein and Byres, "From Peasant Studies to Agrarian Change," 4–5, 7–8; Kearney, "Peasantry," 196.

39. The "indexical" value of a model has to do with its incisive isomorphic qualities, in terms of Carney's distinction between "homomorphic" (abstract) models and "isomorphic" (representational) models.

40. Hanson and Oakman, *Palestine in the Time of Jesus*, passim.

always incomplete. Further discoveries of texts and artifacts can correct previous interpretations, of course, but the main lines of social interpretation are best informed by comparative social-scientific models and theory.

In sum, it is not a matter of discarding a term or a whole body of social-scientific work, but utilizing it with care to best elucidate the agrarian conditions of early Roman Galilee, especially the familial-political-economic and religio-cultural dynamics of that time and place.

Peasants and Money, Markets, Commerce in Early Roman Galilee

The Hasmonean kingdom of Alexander Jannaeus, as the archeological accounts of Aviam and Berlin indicate, was an insular kingdom. Berlin shows that the Judean crown retained its simple cultural assemblages, eschewing the fancy imports from the Mediterranean.[41] Aviam's paper in this volume shows that Jannaeus developed Migdal as a fishing harbor on the Kinnereth Lake; Jannaeus must have viewed the lake as a royal monopoly.[42] Surely, the economic aims of Herod the Great, Herod Antipas, and Philip would have claimed no less. It is clear that Herod the Great abandoned Hasmonean isolationism and embraced commerce. This is dramatically signified by the building of Caesarea Maritima. But Dar also shows that Herod had economic interests in balsam plantations, copper mining, and tax farming in Nabatea, Syria, and Asia.[43]

Even if there is a rapidly developing commercial-type economy in first-century Galilee, it must be asked, *Cui bono*? Lenski clearly sees the Mediterranean littoral as a mixed-type, a combination of advanced agrarian society (with peasants) and commercial society (with sea-borne commerce and cities). The key articulation between the two is politics and

---

41. Andrea M. Berlin, "Between Large Forces: Palestine in the Hellenistic Period," *BA* 60 (1997): 25–26.

42. Michael Rostovtzeff lists fishing among the numerous tightly controlled concessions of Ptolemaic Egypt (*Social and Economic History of the Hellenistic World* [3 vols.; Oxford: Clarendon, 1941], 1:296–97): "[accounts show] how small a share went to the actual fishermen." Usual royal monopolies in the ancient world were hunting preserves, special forests, salt, mines, and the like; i.e., monopolies were political, not "economic" realities. See Paul C. Millett, "Monopolies," *OCD*, 994; see also K. C. Hanson, "The Galilean Fishing Economy and the Jesus Tradition," *BTB* 27 (1997): 99–111.

43. Shimon Dar, "The Agrarian Economy in the Herodian Period," 306.

patronage. Commerce does not automatically mean that all participate or benefit; it is important to clarify who controlled the commerce, and how product distribution in Galilee (ceramics, clothing) relates to imperial patronage and Galilean social stratification.

Ancient peasants preferred barter in kind. They knew money as a political reality with extremely limited economic utility; copper money or product had to be exchanged "up" to pay taxes or debts. This was always at a disadvantage to the villagers and even townspeople. Galilean peasants evaded taxes by hiding produce (in the underground tunnels) and if possible by deceiving the tax collectors.[44] Likewise, literacy worked against peasants in terms of debt contracts and records of tax arrears. Peasants and their villages were incorporated into the Roman patronage systems and territories of elite estates or cities. The towns played a crucial role in this articulation process. The elites owned or controlled all the major factors of production. If there were such entities as "'free' smallholding peasants" in the early Roman period, they were rapidly becoming a rarity.[45]

I have argued that the Roman monetary policy, at least by effect if not by intention, maintained by imperial client elites around the Mediterranean, was to "leverage" real goods through reserving silver for tax and debt payments and wide distribution of copper tokens. Gresham's Law ("bad money drives out the good") helps us to understand that bad copper money drives out the good silver money, and I add that it drives out the goods (to the imperial towns and cities). The Romans and their agents obviously exploited money through location of mints. The coin profiles of all archaeological sites show that copper coins were aplenty, but silver was preciously rare in situ.[46]

The Romans must have learned something about bimetallic money systems, and their convenience for handling agrarian debt and taxes, from

---

[44]. Aviam claims that we cannot be certain about the purpose and use of these underground chambers. See Mordechai Aviam, Zvi Gal, and Avraham Ronen, "Galilee," *NEAEHL* 2:454; Mordechai Aviam, *Jews, Pagans and Christians in the Galilee* (Rochester, N.Y.: University of Rochester Press, 2004), 123–32.

[45]. John S. Kloppenborg, "The Growth and Impact of Agricultural Tenancy in Jewish Palestine (III BCE—I CE)," *JESHO* 51 (2008): 33–66.

[46]. Douglas E. Oakman, "Batteries of Power: Coinage in the Judean Temple System," in *In Other Words: Essays on Social Science Methods and the New Testament in Honor of Jerome H. Neyrey* (ed. Anselm C. Hagedorn, Zeba A. Crook, and Eric Stewart; Sheffield: Sheffield Phoenix, 2007), 171–85.

the Hellenistic kingdoms. Rostovtzeff wrote the following in 1941 about Ptolemaic money policy:

> The copper coinage of [Ptolemy] Philadelphus was consequently another symbol and expression of the dualism which was established in Egypt by the Ptolemaic system of organization: old Egypt, the Egypt of the natives, with its heavy and clumsy old-fashioned copper, coexisted with the new Egypt, that of Alexandria and the Greeks, with its elegant and handy silver and magnificent gold. But to satisfy the requirements of the natives was not the only aim of Philadelphus in introducing the new bronze coinage. He foresaw that the new coins would drive silver and gold out of circulation, and that the coins made of these two metals would gradually come to be hoarded in the royal treasury and used by the king for his own purposes. And that, without doubt, was what happened, especially after his time.[47]

The detailed numismatic study of Danny Syon, "Tyre and Gamla" (used with his permission), provides some additional corroborations and support for these assertions.[48] Syon does note the operation of Gresham's Law in regard to the circulation of the less pure Eagle Tetradrachms in 60 to 66 C.E. However, he does not extend this principle in relation to the ubiquity of coppers and the rarity of silvers in the excavations. Coin hoards are another illustration of the operation of Gresham's Law.

The systematic coin counts done by Syon can tell us something about the distribution—I do not say circulation—of money in Galilee during our periods. We can take Gamla, Yodefat, and Qana to heart here. We know that Yodefat and Gamla were never rebuilt after 67 C.E. The coin counts for these uninhabited places for the 70 to 256 C.E. period are: Gamla 0; Yodefat 11; Qana, for comparison, 5. An uninhabited period, on average, will yield about ten coin-finds or less. Compare with this the Hasmonean period 125 to 63 B.C.E.: Gamla 1,255; Yodefat 409; Qana 16; and for the early Roman period 63 B.C.E. to 70 C.E.: Gamla 537; Yodefat 77; Qana 7. Qana's profile is consistent and unremarkable, almost no different from

---

47. Rostovtzeff, *Social and Economic History*, 1:400.
48. Danny Syon, "Tyre and Gamla: A Study in the Monetary Influence of Southern Phoenicia on Galilee and the Golan in the Hellenistic and Roman Periods" (Ph. D. diss., Hebrew University, 2004).

the uninhabited average. However, Yodefat and Gamla have noticeable volumes before destruction.[49]

What this shows, I believe, is the *political* (not the economic) importance of money. The profiles show accumulations at strong-points, towns which we might identify as the administrative-juridical-security nodes. Not surprisingly, the Romans had to take Yodefat and Gamla with force. By contrast, Qana was untouched by the war, unwalled, and apparently the domicile only for agrarian labor and some local gentry.[50]

There were periodic fairs and markets that peasants could enter; however, they entered only with permission and always at a disadvantage.[51] Conversely, peasant "cunning" typically looked for ways to deceive and cheat to an advantage. Trade in these occasional markets or the town αγοραι is not to be confused with translocal or long-distance commerce carried on by elites and their agents. "Banks" or tables were controlled by the elites of Roman Palestine. The tables were for loans at interest, based upon money on deposit or μαμωνᾶς (*mamōnas*) or money exchange (with disadvantageous fees). Archives in Jerusalem and Tiberias, what Josephus called the "sinews" of the city (*Vita* 38), maintained records about family lines and debts.[52]

---

49. Ibid., 196, 198, 200.
50. There are unadorned, rock-cut tombs at Qana, indicating a wealthier class there. Mattila calls Yodefat and Gamla villages ("Jesus and the 'Middle Peasants,'" 309–10). Interestingly, the typology of Galilean settlements could also use more critical discussion. In my view, these are towns with administrative roles in the political structures of Galilee. Therefore, one would expect to find painted-plaster houses and signs of wealth at each site. See my classification of settlements by rank-size distribution of population in *Jesus and the Peasants*, 46–52. Nazareth, with population of the order of magnitude 10^2, would represent a typical Galilean village. Yodefat, Capernaum, and Gamla, by contrast, were towns with important political-economic roles and populations of the order of magnitude 10^3. Cities (Jerusalem, Sepphoris, Tiberias) would be closer to the order of magnitude 10^4.
51. Neville Morley, "The Early Roman Empire: Distribution," in Scheidel, Morris, and Saller, *Cambridge Economic History of the Greco-Roman World*, 586.
52. Consider the controlling presence of the ἀγορανόμος. Dominic W. Rathbone says "Monetized exchange functioned, and grew across time, through credit arrangements" ("Roman Egypt," in Scheidel, Morris, and Saller, *Cambridge Economic History of the Greco-Roman World*, 715). "Credit arrangements" for peasants are the obverse of perennial debts. Rathbone mentions that private Egyptian banks played an important role in arrangements of ongoing "credit."

This picture is certainly not entirely that of the isolated peasant family of other times and places. But neither is it the modern farmer or democratic, free market system read back into the first century. The early Roman economy in Galilee is a political-economy, and in many senses, only a semi-economy. Economic development functions for the sake of the urban and imperial elites, but only in basic and limited senses at the village level or on the lake. Distributed money does not circulate so much as effect the political will of the elites in keeping the masses in debt and the goods flowing toward the cities and the sea coast.

I hope this response serves to explain why I believe Galilee holds plenty of evidence for execrable, first-century peasants and their landless or rural proletariat offspring within an economy that existed essentially for the benefit of Rome and its regional agents. My guess is that Jesus of Nazareth, Judas of Gamla, and Simon bar Giora might have sympathized with the remark of Calgacus in Tacitus's *Agricola*, "To plunder, butcher, steal, these things [the Romans] misname empire; they make a desolation and they call it peace."[53] Thanks to Mordechai Aviam and the panelists for the excellent stimulus and provocation to discuss these matters.[54]

Bibliography

Applebaum, Shimon. "Josephus and the Economic Causes of the Jewish War." Pages 237–64 in *Josephus, the Bible, and History*. Edited by Louis H. Feldman and Gohei Hata. Detroit: Wayne State University Press, 1989.

Aviam, Mordechai. *Jews, Pagans and Christians in the Galilee*. Rochester, N.Y.: University of Rochester Press, 2004.

Aviam, Mordechai, Zvi Gal, and Avraham Ronen. "Galilee." *NEAEHL* 2:449–58.

---

53. Cornelius Tacitus, *Agricola* 30: "Auferre trucidare rapere falsis nominibus imperium, atque ubi solitudinem faciunt, pacem appellant."

54. I wish to express my deep appreciation for Mordechai Aviam, my friend for nearly twenty years and one of my original guides in field archaeology at Yodefat in 1992. Few know the archaeological data for Galilee as well as Aviam, and I will not presume to contest his account of facts on the archaeological ground. I am also indebted to Professor David Gowler for his perceptive critique of this essay response. His questions and suggestions have helped in refining the text for publication. The essay's faults and limitations are, of course, mine alone.

Becker, Marc. "Peasant Identity, Worker Identity: Conflicting Modes of Rural Consciousness in Highland Ecuador." *Estudios Interdisciplinarios de América Latina y el Caribe (University of Tel Aviv)* 15 (2004): 115–39.

Berlin, Andrea M. "Between Large Forces: Palestine in the Hellenistic Period." *BA* 60 (1997): 2–51.

Bernstein, Henry, and Terence J. Byres. "From Peasant Studies to Agrarian Change." *Journal of Agrarian Change* 1 (2001): 1–56.

Carney, Thomas F. *The Shape of the Past: Models and Antiquity.* Lawrence, Kans.: Coronado, 1975.

Cato, Marcus Porcius. *Marcus Porcius Cato, On Agriculture; Marcus Terentius Varro, On Agriculture.* Translated by William Davis Hooper and Harrison Boyd Ash. Rev. ed. LCL. Cambridge: Harvard University Press, 1935.

Christian, David. *Maps of Time: An Introduction to Big History.* Berkeley: University of California Press, 2004.

Dalman, Gustaf. *Arbeit und Sitte in Palästina.* 7 vols. Gütersloh: Bertelsmann, 1928–1942.

Dar, Shimon. "The Agrarian Economy in the Herodian Period." Pages 305–11 in *The World of the Herods.* Edited by Nikos Kokkinos. Stuttgart: Steiner, 2007.

Fiensy, David A. *Jesus the Galilean: Soundings in a First Century Life.* Piscataway, N.J.: Gorgias, 2007.

———. *The Social History of Palestine in the Herodian Period: The Land Is Mine.* Studies in the Bible and Early Christianity 20. Lewiston, N.Y.: Mellen, 1991.

Foster, George. "Peasant Society and the Image of Limited Good." Pages 300–323 in *Peasant Society: A Reader.* Edited by Jack M. Potter, May N. Diaz, and George M. Foster. The Little, Brown Series in Anthropology. Boston: Little, Brown, 1967.

———. "What Is a Peasant?" Pages 2–14 in *Peasant Society: A Reader.* Edited by Jack M. Potter, May N. Diaz, and George M. Foster. The Little, Brown Series in Anthropology. Boston: Little, Brown, 1967.

Goodman, Martin. "The First Jewish Revolt: Social Conflict and the Problem of Debt." *JJS* 33 (1982): 417–27.

Grant, Elihu. *The Peasantry of Palestine: The Life, Manners and Customs of the Village.* Boston: Pilgrim, 1907.

Greene, Kevin. "Agriculture in the Roman Empire." Pages 67–97 in idem, *The Archaeology of the Roman Economy*. Berkeley: University of California Press, 1986.
Halpern, Joel M. *A Serbian Village: Social and Cultural Change in a Yugoslav Community*. Rev. ed. New York: Harper Colophon Books, 1967.
Hamel, Gildas. *Poverty and Charity in Roman Palestine, First Three Centuries C.E.* Near Eastern Studies 23. Berkeley: University of California Press, 1990.
Hanson, K. C. "The Galilean Fishing Economy and the Jesus Tradition." *BTB* 27 (1997): 99–111.
Hanson, K. C., and Douglas E. Oakman. *Palestine in the Time of Jesus: Social Structures and Social Conflicts*. Minneapolis: Fortress, 2008.
Hobsbawm, Eric J. "Peasants and Politics." *JPS* 1 (1973): 3–23.
———. *Primitive Rebels: Studies in Archaic Forms of Social Movements in the 19th and 20th Centuries*. New York: Norton, 1959.
Horsley, Richard A. *Galilee: History, Politics, People*. Valley Forge, Pa.: Trinity Press International, 1995.
Jeremias, Joachim. *Jerusalem in the Time of Jesus*. Translated by F. H. Cave and C. H. Cave. Philadelphia: Fortress, 1969.
Josephus. LCL. London: Heinemann; New York: Putnam, 1926–1981.
Kautsky, John H. *The Politics of Aristocratic Empires*. Chapel Hill: University of North Carolina Press, 1982.
Kearney, Michael. "Peasantry." Pages 195–96 in vol. 6 of *International Encyclopedia of the Social Sciences*. 2nd ed. Edited by William A. Darity Jr. 9 vols. Detroit: Thomson Gale, 2008.
Klausner, Joseph. *Jesus of Nazareth: His Life, Times, and Teaching*. Translated by Herbert Danby. New York: Macmillan, 1925.
Kloppenborg, John S. "The Growth and Impact of Agricultural Tenancy in Jewish Palestine (III BCE–I CE)." *JESHO* 51 (2008): 33–66.
Lenski, Gerhard E. *Power and Privilege: A Theory of Social Stratification*. 2nd ed. Chapel Hill: University of North Carolina Press, 1984.
Lenski, Gerhard E., and Jean Lenski. *Human Societies: An Introduction to Macrosociology*. 5th ed. New York: McGraw-Hill, 1987.
Mattila, Sharon Lea. "Jesus and the 'Middle Peasants?' Problematizing a Social-Scientific Concept." *CBQ* 72 (2010): 291–313.
Millett, Paul C. "Monopolies." Page 994 in *The Oxford Classical Dictionary*. Edited by Simon Hornblower and Antony Spawforth. Oxford: Oxford University Press, 1999.

Mintz, Sidney. "A Note on the Definition of Peasantries." *Journal of Peasant Studies* 1 (1973): 91–106.

Moore, Barrington. *Social Origins of Dictatorship and Democracy: Lord and Peasant in the Making of the Modern World*. Boston: Beacon, 1966.

Moreley, Neville. *Approaching the Ancient World: Theories, Models and Concepts in Ancient History*. New York: Routledge, 2004.

———. "The Early Roman Empire: Distribution." Pages 570–91 in *The Cambridge Economic History of the Greco-Roman World*. Edited by Walter Scheidel, Ian Morris, and Richard Saller. Cambridge: Cambridge University Press, 2007.

North, Douglass C. *Structure and Change in Economic History*. New York: Norton, 1981.

Oakman, Douglas E. "Batteries of Power: Coinage in the Judean Temple System." Pages 171–85 in *In Other Words: Essays on Social Science Methods and the New Testament in Honor of Jerome H. Neyrey*. Edited by Anselm C. Hagedorn, Zeba A. Crook, and Eric Stewart. Sheffield: Sheffield Phoenix, 2007.

———. *Jesus and the Economic Questions of His Day*. Studies in the Bible and Early Christianity 8. Lewiston, N.Y.: Mellen, 1986.

———. *Jesus and the Peasants*. Matrix: The Bible in Mediterranean Context. Eugene, Ore.: Cascade, 2008.

Plattner, Stuart, ed. *Economic Anthropology*. Stanford, Calif.: Stanford University Press, 1989.

Polanyi, Karl. *The Livelihood of Man*. Edited by Harry W. Pearson. Studies in Social Discontinuity. New York: Academic Press, 1977.

Polanyi, Karl, Conrad M. Arensberg, and Harry W. Pearson. *Trade and Market in the Early Empires: Economies in History and Theory*. Glencoe, Ill.: Free Press, 1957.

Rathbone, Dominic W. "Roman Egypt." Pages 698–719 in *The Cambridge Economic History of the Greco-Roman World*. Edited by Walter Scheidel, Ian Morris, and Richard Saller. Cambridge: Cambridge University Press, 2007.

Redfield, Robert. *The Little Community and Peasant Society and Culture*. Chicago: University of Chicago Press, 1960.

Reed, Jonathan L. *Archaeology and the Galilean Jesus: A Re-examination of the Evidence*. Harrisburg, Pa.: Trinity Press International, 2000.

Rostovtzeff, Michael. *Social and Economic History of the Hellenistic World*. 3 vols. Oxford: Clarendon, 1941.

Schneider, Helmuth. "Technology." Pages 144–71 in *The Cambridge Economic History of the Greco-Roman World*. Edited by Walter Scheidel, Ian Morris, and Richard Saller. Cambridge: Cambridge University Press, 2007.

Scott, James C. *The Moral Economy of the Peasant: Rebellion and Subsistence in Southeast Asia*. New Haven: Yale University Press, 1976.

Shanin, Teodor, ed. *Peasants and Peasant Societies: Selected Readings*. Harmondsworth: Penguin, 1971.

Sjøberg, Gideon. *The Preindustrial City: Past and Present*. New York: Free Press, 1960.

Sorokin, Pitirim Aleksandrovich, Carle C. Zimmerman, and Charles Josiah Galpin. *A Systematic Source Book in Rural Sociology*. 3 vols. New York: Russell & Russell, 1930–1932.

Syon, Danny. "Tyre and Gamla: A Study in the Monetary Influence of Southern Phoenicia on Galilee and the Golan in the Hellenistic and Roman Periods." Ph. D. diss., Hebrew University, 2004.

Tacitus, Cornelius. *Dialogus, Agricola, Germania*. Translated by William Peterson and Maurice Hutton. LCL. London: Heinemann; New York: Macmillan, 1914.

Theophrastus. *The Characters of Theophrastus; Herodes, Cercidas, and the Greek Choliambic Poets (Except Callimachus and Babrius)*. Translated by J. M. Edmonds. LCL. Cambridge: Harvard University Press, 1929.

Thorner, Daniel. "Peasantry." Pages 503–11 in vol. 11 of *International Encyclopedia of the Social Sciences*. Edited by David L. Sills. 17 vols. New York: Macmillan, 1968.

Van der Spek, Robartus J. "The Hellenistic Near East." Pages 409–33 in *The Cambridge Economic History of the Greco-Roman World*. Edited by Walter Scheidel, Ian Morris, and Richard Saller. Cambridge: Cambridge University Press, 2007.

Varro, Marcus Terentius. *Marcus Porcius Cato, On Agriculture; Marcus Terentius Varro, On Agriculture*. Translated by William Davis Hooper and Harrison Boyd Ash. Rev. ed. LCL. Cambridge: Harvard University Press, 1935.

Dietze, Constantin von. "Peasantry." Pages 48–53 in vol. 12 of *Encyclopaedia of the Social Sciences*. Edited by Edwin R. A. Seligman and Alvin Johnson. 15 vols. New York: Macmillan, 1930–1935.

Weber, Max. *Economy and Society*. Edited by Günther Roth and Claus Wittich. 2 vols. Berkeley: University of California Press, 1978.

White, K. D. *Greek and Roman Technology*. Ithaca, N.Y.: Cornell University Press, 1984.

Wittfogel, Karl A. *Oriental Despotism: A Comparative Study of Total Power*. New Haven: Yale University Press, 1957.

Wolf, Eric R. *Peasants*. Edited by Marshall D. Sahlins. Foundations of Modern Anthropology Series. Englewood Cliffs, N.J.: Prentice Hall, 1966.

5
Assessing the Economy of Galilee in the Late Second Temple Period: Five Considerations

David A. Fiensy

"It was the best of times; it was the worst of times." Charles Dickens is not the only one who can write this way. This observation also summarizes what the historians of Galilee in the late Second Temple period have written lately. Yet these scholars do not make this observation in order to point out the varied nature of conditions. Scholars seem divided into two groups, and each group concludes only one side of the Dickensian paradox: either Galilee knew the best of times (i.e., economic prosperity and even an egalitarian society), or it witnessed the worst of times (i.e., increasing indebtedness, land losses, and exploitation of the peasants).

It is small wonder that we can read such drastically differing analyses. Each side works with different data, different methodologies, and different assumptions.[1] It reminds me of the story of the sight-impaired persons who discovered an elephant. One person grabbed the tail and said, "This is a rope with which the wealthy of Galilee were strangling the poor." Another felt the elephant's leg and exclaimed, "This is a tree trunk, strong and stout, like the Galilean economy in the late Second Temple period."

So where do we go from here? I would like to survey five considerations for assessing the economy of Galilee in the late Second Temple period. These five considerations have helped me to strike a position mid-way between the polar opposites. I see the economic situation in Lower Galilee in the late Second Temple period as "young." It had not

---

1. See Dennis E. Groh, "The Clash between Literary and Archaeological Models of Provincial Palestine," in *Archaeology and the Galilee* (ed. Douglas R. Edwards and C. Thomas McCollough; Atlanta: Scholars Press, 1997), 29–37.

yet developed into an oppressive society but was perhaps moving in that direction. The five considerations are:

(1) The current broader academic environment, specifically the studies of the ancient economy among classical historians.
(2) The differences, as I see them, between Galilee and other Israelite territories (especially Judea). I observe three important distinctions that influence our evaluation of their economies.
(3) The chronological distinctions. Were the years 6 to 44 C.E. the same as 45 to 66 C.E.? In particular, was indebtedness the same in both of those periods?
(4) The fragmentary nature of the data, especially archaeologically.
(5) The function of social-science models.

Consideration One:
The Current Broader Academic Environment

Scholars of classical history are going through a revolution in their thinking about the ancient economy. In particular, they are debating the usefulness of Moses Finley's assumptions and methods for understanding and researching the Greco-Roman world. One might even observe that in the discipline of classical history, they are now in the post-Finley era. Two significant collections of essays have been published recently, one in 2002 and one in 2005.[2] Each volume received the same title, *The Ancient Economy*, the title Moses Finley had also used,[3] but they might rather have been entitled, *The Study of the Ancient Economy in the Post-Finley Era*. These two recent collections contain essays that assess the legacy of the great historian, sometimes positively, more often critically.

As these authors see it, there are now four (overlapping) approaches to the study of the ancient economy. First, we have the *formalist* versus the *substantivist* positions. Finley (a substantivist) opined that the ancient economy was based more on status and civic ideology than on supply and demand. Economic development was constrained by elite values. For

---

2. Walter Scheidel and Sitta von Reden, eds., *The Ancient Economy* (New York: Routledge, 2002); Joseph G. Manning and Ian Morris, eds., *The Ancient Economy: Evidence and Models* (Stanford, Calif.: Stanford University Press, 2005).

3. Moses I. Finley, *The Ancient Economy* (Berkeley: University of California Press, 1999).

Finley, economic behavior is "embedded in a network of social relationships that determine values, attitudes, and actual behavior."[4]

The formalists maintain that the economic sphere was separate from social relations. They question whether the "elite mentality" played such a significant role in the ancient economy. They now are focusing more and more on trade as an important part of the ancient economy. They find economic growth in the Roman Empire because the empire's structure encouraged markets and trade. These ancient economists maintain that Finley underestimated the power of markets and exchange.[5]

The second polarity is the *primitivists* versus the *modernists*. Finley maintained that the "market economy" was no more than four hundred years old, and thus the modern discipline of economics could be no older. Modern economics textbooks are essentially about modern market economies and thus are of little value in understanding the ancient economy.[6]

Michael Rostovtzeff, however, assumed that "modern capitalistic development differs from the ancients only in quantity and not in quality."[7] Modernists in general affirm that economics is the study of "laws that hold true between humans and goods.... they apply in all periods of history and to all forms of society."[8]

We might with benefit allow Finley and Rostovtzeff to represent the two sides. One classical economist has summarized their differences as follows: "Primitivist versus modernist, no-trade versus long-distance trade, autarky versus integrated markets, technological stagnation versus technological progress, no economic growth versus growth, non-rationalist traditionalist versus rational individualists."[9]

It looks like those who view Galilee in the late Second Temple period as prosperous (mostly archaeologists) are formalists and modernists (like Rostovtzeff). Those who view Galilee as poor and exploited (mostly those using social science models) are substantivists and primitivists (like Finley). The assumptions are quite different, and thus the conclusions, the

---

4. Scheidel and von Reden, *The Ancient Economy*, 1–8.
5. Ibid.
6. Scott Meikle, "Modernism, Economics, and the Ancient Economy," in Scheidel and von Reden, *The Ancient Economy*, 236.
7. Ibid., 239.
8. Ibid., 236.
9. Richard Saller, "Framing the Debate Over Growth and the Ancient Economy," in Scheidel and von Reden, *The Ancient Economy*, 224.

picture of the whole, if you will, must be different. But both sides can benefit from listening in on the conversation among the classical historians.

Consideration Two: The Differences between Galilee and Judea

When constructing a picture of the Galilean economy in the late Second Temple period, we should make geographical distinctions. Too many of us—and I confess my error here as well—have treated Palestine/Israel as one economic unit. There is a sense in which that can be done. All territories were once under Herod the Great; most of the residents were Jewish. One could even treat Palestine and Syria as an economic unit with some success (as Heichelheim has done[10]). They were under the same Roman oversight. But this should be done only to a point. Failure to view Galilee as separate from Judea/Idumea/Samaria masks significant differences. I can think of three distinctions that should always be kept in mind.

Different Political Histories

Judea/Idumea/Samaria came under direct Roman rule in 6 C.E.; Galilee not until 44 C.E. This fact means that the former three territories were taxed directly by Rome from then on. Were their taxes greater than in Galilee? Probably both areas had the *tributum soli*. The rate of the tax on the soil may have increased in Judea. It may have included both a tax on annual produce and a flat tax on land.[11] In addition to the *tributum soli*, the Romans may have added the *tributum capitis* or poll tax (i.e., head tax), though that is now disputed.[12] This tax was levied in Syria (according to Ulpian, *Digest*) on every male between the ages of fourteen and sixty-five, on every female between twelve and sixty-five. For Judea, this tax *might* have been one denarius per person (based on Mark 12:13–17). Or, it could have been one denarius plus a percentage of the movable property

---

10. F. M. Heichelheim, "Roman Syria," in *Economic Survey of Ancient Rome* (ed. Tenney Frank; Baltimore: Johns Hopkins University Press, 1938), 121–257.

11. Fabian E. Udoh, *To Caesar What Is Caesar's* (Providence, R.I.: Brown University, 2005), 222.

12. Ibid., 237, 241. But see Fergus Millar, *The Roman Near East* (Cambridge: Harvard University Press, 1993), 110, who writes, "We have to assume that both a land tax (*tributum soli*) and a 'head-tax' were payable (in Syria)." He bases his conclusion on the third century C.E. evidence from Ulpian and the Roman jurist Paul.

(i.e., animals, slaves, ships, and wagons).[13] There were also house taxes and duties on produce brought into Jerusalem (*Ant.* 18.90, 19.299).[14] The point is, taxation seems to have been a greater burden in Judea than in Galilee. Whether it was so much greater as to lower the standard of living significantly in Judea *vis-à-vis* Galilee, is the question. We know that in 17 C.E. Judea appealed to Tiberius for tax relief (Tacitus, *Annales* 2.42).[15] Thus, direct taxation from Rome seems to have contributed to a lower standard of living.[16]

DIFFERENT ECONOMIC HISTORIES

Galilee was more recently settled than Judea and therefore had a newer economy. There are three hypotheses at present as to the origin of the Galileans. Some have suggested that they were the remnants of the old Israelites, those left behind when the elites were deported in the eighth century B.C.E. Others offer that these folk were converted Iturians, Gentiles who became Jews when Aristobulus conquered the territory in the late second century B.C.E. Finally, a third group of historians posits that the people of Galilee were Jewish colonists (from Judea) who settled in Galilee after Aristobulus annexed the territory for Judea. The data from archaeological surveys support the third view. The surveys indicate an absence of Galilean settlements for over a century after the conquest by the Assyrians (thus ruling out the first hypothesis). Further, the reign of Alexander Jannaeus (103 to 77 B.C.E.) coincides with an increase in population (thus

---

13. David A. Fiensy, *The Social History of Palestine in the Herodian Period: The Land Is Mine* (Studies in the Bible and Early Christianity 20; Lewiston, N.Y.: Mellen, 1991), 100–101. Udoh (*To Caesar*, 222) thinks that the taxes on movable property, if they were assessed, would have been added to the *tributum soli*.

14. Udoh, *To Caesar*, 238.

15. Tacitus described Judea and Syria as *fessae*, "exhausted," by taxes. See Moses I. Finley, *Ancient Economy* (Berkeley: University of California, 1999), 90. Cf. Josephus (*J.W.* 2.85-86; *Ant.* 17.204-205, 306-307), who reports that the people of Palestine/Israel complained about the taxes levied by Herod the Great.

16. "Taxes distort prices and thus the decisions of households and firms" (N. Gregory Mankiw, *Principles of Macroeconomics* [Mason, Ohio: Southwestern, 2004], 9). The author means that a centralized economy—one controlled by the government by heavy taxation—is the opposite of a free-market economy. Thus observations based on free markets may not apply to the ancient Palestinian economy if the taxation was unusually burdensome.

suggesting the third hypothesis). Most archaeologists and historians now support hypothesis number three.[17] The implications of a young economy are very significant. Even if we accept that it was inevitable in the ancient economy that the rich would become richer and the poor, poorer, that more and more land was being concentrated in the hands of fewer and fewer elites, that peasants tended to go into debt during lean years and then to lose their land through foreclosure, these forces were probably not yet well developed in Galilee. They may have been moving in that direction (we can still debate that issue) but were still years from producing those results. The economy was too young in the first half of the first century C.E.

DIFFERENCES IN WEALTH OF THE ELITES

Finally, we can see a gap between the level of wealth of the aristocrats of Galilee and the elites of Judea. If we compare the houses of the aristocrats of Sepphoris, those of the "western domestic quarter" whose inhabitants, according to Eric Meyers,[18] were "well-to-do aristocratic Jews," with aristocratic houses of Jerusalem, we notice some striking differences. The houses in Sepphoris were certainly nice by ancient standards. They had multiple rooms and a courtyard. Many had fresco paintings and some had mosaic floors. Several were multi-storied. They were impressive for their time and place. But compared with the Jerusalem houses (excavated in the Jewish quarter of the old city), they were modest. For example, the "Great Mansion" of Jerusalem had a living area of 600 m^2, while a large house of Sepphoris had an area of 300 m^2. The size difference alone is remarkable. Further, the small finds in the aristocratic houses of Sepphoris indicate modest wealth. They used bone instead of ivory for cosmetic applications. They

---

17. Jonathan Reed, "Galileans, 'Israelite Village Communities' and the Sayings Gospel Q," in *Galilee through the Centuries* (ed. Eric M. Meyers; Winona Lake, Ind.: Eisenbrauns, 1999), 87–108; Eric M. Meyers, James F. Strange, and Dennis E. Groh, "The Meiron Excavation Project: Archeological Survey in Galilee and Golan, 1976," *BASOR* 230 (1978): 1–24; Mordechai Aviam, "Galilee: The Hellenistic to Byzantine Periods," *NEAEHL* 2:453; idem, *Jews, Pagans and Christians in the Galilee* (Rochester, N.Y.: University of Rochester Press, 2004), 41–49; and Seán Freyne, "Archaeology and the Historical Jesus," in *Archaeology and Biblical Interpretation* (ed. J. R. Bartlett; London: Routledge, 1997), 133–34.

18. Eric M. Meyers, "Roman Sepphoris in Light of New Archaeological Evidence and Recent Research," in *The Galilee in Late Antiquity* (ed. Lee I. Levine; New York: Jewish Theological Seminary, 1992), 322.

employed common pottery, not fine ware. They imported no wines.[19] Thus based on the evidence of the houses from first-century Sepphoris discovered so far (Tiberias has not been excavated adequately for such an assessment), we would have to say that the extreme distance between the elites and lower class, found elsewhere in the Roman Empire and evidently in Judea, was diminished in Galilee. While there certainly was an economic distance between the two groups, it was not as great as in other regions.

Consideration Three: The Chronological Distinctions

We must always consider chronology when we present a unified understanding of the Galilean economy in the late Second Temple period. This caveat is especially important with respect to the question of debt. Was peasant indebtedness widespread in Galilee? Was it about at the same level throughout the years 6 to 44 as it was from 45 to 66? Did it surge upward after direct Roman rule? Or did it gradually increase throughout these two periods? I think some scholars have assumed a more or less uniform percentage of debtors throughout the first century C.E. Therefore, the invention of the *prosbul* in the first century B.C.E. and the attack on the debt records in Jerusalem in 66 C.E. serve as backdrop—as historical parentheses really—to the ministry of Jesus. These two events are believed to prove that indebtedness was a major economic problem in the first century C.E. Consequently, any text from the gospels that refers to debts must confirm this conclusion.[20]

But this historical method is imprecise. We need careful definitions of what constitutes widespread indebtedness and hard evidence for it. Elsewhere I have argued[21] that the only valid evidence we have—barring the future discovery of enough data to do a statistical analysis—is a social

---

19. Eric M. Meyers, "The Problems of Gendered Space in Syro-Palestinian Domestic Architecture: The Case of Roman-Period Galilee," in *Early Christian Families in Context* (ed. David L. Balch and Carolyn Osiek; Grand Rapids: Eerdmans, 2003), 54–69, 76; Nahman Avigad, "How the Wealthy Lived in Herodian Jerusalem," *BAR* 2.4 (1976): 22–35.

20. Martin Goodman, "The First Jewish Revolt: Social Conflict and the Problem of Debt," *JJS* 33 (1982): 414–27; Douglas E. Oakman, *Jesus and the Peasants* (Eugene, Ore.: Cascade, 2008), 11–32; Jack Pastor, *Land and Economy in Ancient Palestine* (London: Routledge, 1997), 147–49.

21. David A. Fiensy, "Jesus and Debts: Did He Pray about Them?" *ResQ* 44 (2002): 233–39.

eruption in protest of debts. Social eruptions (i.e., riots, wars, attempts at reform, and petitions for relief) imply a group effort by persons who are at their wits' end with frustration. Where we have social eruption over debts, we have indebtedness as a significant economic factor.

The only case of such a social eruption was in Jerusalem in 66 C.E. during the Feast of Wood-Carrying when the Sicarii broke into the upper city and fired the houses of Ananias the High Priest and Agrippa II. Then the mob turned to the public archives to burn the debt records (*J.W.* 2.427). Josephus speculates at this point that the Sicarii hoped to win to their side a multitude of debtors.

Thus both the act of burning the archives and Josephus's reference to a multitude of debtors compel one to conclude that, in the years leading up to the war of 66 to 73 C.E., Judea experienced ubiquitous peasant anger. Since such outbreaks mark only the boiling point in a gradually heating cauldron of dissatisfaction over spreading indebtedness, it is likely that the problem had existed for some time. The Sicarii knew well of this resentment and directed the rage of the mob toward the archives and the hated documents of indebtedness. A plausible conclusion, then, is that Judea, like many of the Greek cities in the Hellenistic period (highlighted by Rostovtzeff[22]), saw more and more peasants burdened by debt, at least in the years or decades before the war.

There are two problems with using this event as backdrop for the ministry of Jesus. First, this took place in Judea, not Galilee (see Consideration Three above). Second, even if we should use this event as also describing Galilean economics, what should we conclude about how long indebtedness had been a problem? Was indebtedness also a problem forty years prior to this event when Jesus was teaching and preaching? There is simply no way to answer that question based on the evidence. Therefore, one cannot conclude that pervasive indebtedness existed in Galilee in the earlier part of the first century C.E and that it served as a historical and economic backdrop to the ministry of Jesus.

---

22. Michael Rostovtzeff, *The Social and Economic History of the Hellenistic World* (Oxford: Clarendon, 1941), 1:141.

Consideration Four: The Fragmentary Nature of the Data

The nature of the data is fragmentary. This fact should both cause us to be cautious in our conclusions and to press for more data of the appropriate type. The central question in the "economy wars" (i.e., the debates between some Galilean archaeologists and some of those New Testament scholars utilizing social science models) is about the standard of living of the Galilean folk in the late Second Temple period.

Moses Finley, following his mentor Karl Polanyi and influenced by Max Weber, maintained that the ancient economy was not market driven but driven by status and that exchange took place on a small scale among households. Finley reminded us that the "inapplicability to the ancient world of a market-centered analysis was powerfully argued by Max Weber."[23] Polanyi offered that the ancient economies were either redistributive or reciprocal but not market. Some historians of Galilee also refuse to affirm that there was a market economy in the late Second Temple period, arguing for a redistributive or tributary economy instead of a market economy.[24] By this they mean that in Galilee in the late Second Temple period trade did not move goods but taxation and tribute moved them. Thus the movement of goods was under control of the state. This economic system kept the peasantry impoverished and put a brake on market exchange.

Was the standard of living rising, falling, or remaining the same? It is a law of modern economics that standard of living is tied to productivity.[25] Standard of living may be defined not only as the acquisition of possessions but also as nutrition levels and longevity.[26] Only when a society produces more goods and services does standard of living go up. But how does one find data in archaeological remains to inform us about productivity?

---

23. Finley, *Ancient Economy*, 26.
24. Richard A. Horsley, *Archaeology, History and Society in Galilee* (Valley Forge, Pa.: Trinity Press International, 1996), 77; Hanson and Oakman, *Palestine*, 116.
25. Mankiw, *Macroeconomics*, 11–12; and David C. Colander, *Macroeconomics* (Boston: McGraw-Hill, 2008), 177.
26. Mankiw, *Macroeconomics*, 11–12. Here we might add a note of gratitude to Douglas Oakman, who was calculating average daily caloric intake for the ancient Palestinian people before most New Testament scholars even thought about it. See Oakman, *Jesus and the Economic Questions of His Day* (Lewiston, N.Y.: Mellen, 1986), 58–59. Another New Testament scholar who considered this important issue was Joachim J. Jeremias, *Jerusalem in the Time of Jesus* (Philadelphia: Fortress, 1969), 122–23.

Ian Morris[27] has observed that archaeology is undermining what had been called the Finley orthodoxy. He[28] calls for studies of the ancient folk to determine their stature, nutrition, mortality, morbidity, and housing. He asks for more attention to floral, faunal, and pollen remains to determine diet. Although, in the end, he laments the general lack of information in most of these areas and settles on housing alone to make his case, the archaeological remains demonstrate to him that the standard of living increased in Greece from the eighth to the third centuries B.C.E. His study of three hundred houses indicates, remarkably, that house sizes increased five or six fold in that span, and he concludes that there must have been "a dramatic improvement in the standard of living." Therefore, Morris rejects Moses Finley's ancient economy model in which there was "essentially static economic performance."[29] Morris's study is most interesting, and I agree with his call to see more data on the skeletal remains (to determine stature, nutrition, morbidity and mortality) before I conclude that the standard of living for most persons improved in Lower Galilee. I still have questions about primarily using housing as the measure for standard of living: Have poorly constructed houses left any traces? Were not most houses do-it-yourself constructions like the log cabins of the American frontier? To what extent do house sizes reflect cultural as opposed to economic factors?

It seems to me that those arguing for a prosperous Galilee in the late Second Temple period focus like Morris mostly on constructions, especially houses, and secondarily, on market opportunities. I know of no studies like Ian Morris's with respect to Galilee, but it is common to cite the nice houses in Gamla, Khirbet Qana, and Yodefat as evidence that the villagers were not poverty stricken, but, on the contrary, that the economy was booming. The houses were well constructed and did not seem to have deteriorated because of inability to maintain them.[30]

There also may have been more industry in Galilee than elsewhere in Palestine/Israel during this period, indicating more market exchange.

---

27. Morris, foreword to Finley, *Ancient Economy*, xxix. For the Finley "orthodoxy," see xxiv, xxxv, and note 46.

28. Ian Morris, "Archaeology, Standards of Living and Greek Economic History," in Manning and Morris, *The Ancient Economy*, 107.

29. Ibid., 123, 107.

30. Peter Richardson, *Building Jewish in the Roman East* (Waco, Tex.: Baylor University Press, 2004), 57–71.

The pottery of Kefar Hananya and Shikhin has been featured in studies of David Adan-Bayewitz and Isadore Perlman[31] and in studies of James F. Strange, Dennis E. Groh, and Thomas R. W. Longstaff.[32] The pottery was disseminated from those two small villages throughout Galilee and the Golan. That dissemination does not look like a small-scale market among households. Mordechai Aviam rightly stresses the olive-oil industry of Galilee.[33] He discovered oil producing installations that exceeded local needs. Yitzhak Magen has reported on stone vessel factories in Galilee.[34] Factories imply production on a large scale and, therefore, marketing these goods somewhere. Douglas Edwards observed that Capernaum exported basalt grinders as far away as Cyprus;[35] James Strange notes the availability of roads and travel in Galilee and asks what were they for if not for trade.[36]

The conclusions often drawn from this analysis are: (1) the cities with their wealthy elites must not have exploited the peasants who lived in the villages but rather must have given them opportunities for marketing their goods and thus improved their economic opportunities; (2) the villages not only engaged in farming but had industries as well, and these industries elevated the economic life (the standard of living) of the village peasants.[37]

One should not discount this evidence. These data are part of what is needed for us to understand the Galilean economy. But as Morris observes, we need more examination of human remains. I realize in Israel

---

31. David Adan-Bayewitz and Isadore Perlman, "The Local Trade of Sepphoris in the roman Period," *IEJ* 40 (1990): 153–72; David Adan-Bayewitz, *Common Pottery in Roman Galilee* (Ramat-Gan, Israel: Bar-Ilan University Press, 1993).

32. James F. Strange, Dennis E. Groh, and Thomas R. W. Longstaff, "Excavations at Sepphoris: the Location and Identification of Shikhin," *IEJ* 44 (1994): 216–27.

33. Aviam, *Jews, Pagans and Christians*, 51–57.

34. Yitzhak Magen, *The Stone Vessel Industry in the Second Temple Period* (Jerusalem: Israel Exploration Society, 2002).

35. Douglas R. Edwards, "Identity and Social Location in Roman Galilean Villages," in *Religion, Ethnicity, and Identity in Ancient Galilee* (ed. Jürgen Zangenberg, Harold W. Attridge, and Dale B. Martin; Tübingen: Mohr Siebeck, 2007), 366–67.

36. James F. Strange, "First Century Galilee from Archaeology and from the Texts," in *Archaeology and the Galilee* (ed. Douglas R. Edwards and C. Thomas McCollough; Atlanta: Scholars Press, 1997), 39–41.

37. See Adan-Bayewitz, *Common Pottery*, 23–41, 216–36; Strange, "First Century Galilee," 41; Douglas R. Edwards, "First Century Urban/Rural Relations in Lower Galilee: Exploring the Archaeological and Literary Evidence," in *SBL 1988 Seminar Papers* (Atlanta: Scholars Press, 2000), 169–82.

this is much more difficult than in Greece. But some attention to analysis of bones, asking whether there was a protein or iron deficiency, if done in several sites, could be quite revealing.

One reason to ask for human pathological data is because of the Meiron excavation report. Although some of the houses were nice—one elaborate one was dubbed the "Patrician House"[38]—there were interesting results in the examination of the skeletal remains. First, there was a high rate of child mortality.[39] Second, a pathological examination of the children's skulls revealed that most had protein and iron deficiencies. The examiners concluded that these deficiencies were caused either by disease or "socioeconomic conditions," that is, poverty. In other words, the children may have been malnourished.[40] So the presence of nice houses does not necessarily indicate how equitable the economy was and thus may not reveal the overall standard of living. This case is intriguing since Meiron was a village in Galilee, but also ambiguous since this village tomb was used from the first century B.C.E. to the fourth century C.E.[41]

Some recent skeletal examinations have been done by Aviam in his excavations of Yodefat. At the SBL meeting in Boston in 2008, he reported on an examination of around twenty-five skeletons out of the 2,500 found at the site. He reported that they all "looked healthy."[42] This

---

38. Eric M. Meyers, James F. Strange, and Carol Meyers, *Excavations at Ancient Meiron, Upper Galilee, Israel 1971–72, 1974–75, 1977* (Cambridge: American Schools of Oriental Research, 1981), 50–72.

39. See Rachel Hachlili and Patricia Smith, "The Genealogy of the Goliath Family," BASOR 235 (1979): 67–71, esp. 69. The children from 0 to 19 years of age in the Meiron tombs represented 47% of the total. This is roughly the same as the average percentage of children of that age in Greek tombs (49%) but much higher than for the tombs of Jericho (39%, a first century C.E. tomb) and two tombs in Jerusalem (43%, also from the first century).

40. Patricia Smith, Elizabeth Bornemann, and Joe Zias, "The Skeletal Remains," in Meyers, Strange, and Meyers, *Excavations at Ancient Meiron*, 110–20. There were 197 individuals in this tomb. Ninety-five of them were under age eighteen. Seventy percent of the ninety-five persons were younger than five years.

41. One must be cautious even in assessing the nutritional evidence from human remains. Cereal based economies in general could result in deficiencies even though there might be enough food to eat. See Nathan MacDonald, *What Did the Ancient Israelites Eat?* (Grand Rapids: Eerdmans, 2008), 80–87.

42. Mordechai Aviam, "Economy and Social Structure in First-Century Galilee: Evidence from the Ground-Yodefat and Gamla" (paper presented at the Annual Meeting of the Society of Biblical Literature, Boston, November 2008).

report is enormously helpful. But we need to enlarge the sample size to feel comfortable about any statistical results.

Neither housing construction nor evidence of trade is sufficient—though, again, these are important clues—as the determiner of Galilean standard of living. But there is a kind of construction more helpful in determining standard of living. Again—if we are to live by the principles of modern economists—standard of living rises only if productivity rises. Thus finding some nice houses does not alone settle for us the efficiency of the economy (the size of the pie) or the equity of the economy (the size of the slice of the pie the average family received).[43] But there may be a type of construction that would be more relevant. If we could show that family grain silos were increasing in size in the first century C.E., that would go a long way toward settling this issue.

Consideration Five: The Function of Social Science Models

Understanding the function of social-science models should make us more judicious in our use of them. Like economists, sociologists and anthropologists construct models to assist them in interpreting the data. Manning and Morris observe: "While humanists tend to work from a specific body of texts and to focus on particulars, economists tend to begin from propositions, drawing out logical implications that can be operationalized.... The data are there to test the hypothesis, not to be enjoyed or understood in their own terms."[44] We might substitute, in this quotation, Galilean archaeologists for humanists and social science interpreters for economists. Those New Testament scholars utilizing the social-science models operate similarly to the economists in the quotation. They appropriate an existing model and investigate its efficacy in explaining a text in the New Testament. They ask, "Can the disparate data be better understood if they are unified by the construction of a social scintist? They tend to work more deductively (they prefer the term "abduction"[45]), while the archaeologists work more inductively.

---

43. Mankiw, *Macroeconomics*, 5, 11.
44. Ian Morris and Joseph G. Manning, "Introduction," in Manning and Morris, *The Ancient Economy*, 29.
45. See, e.g., Jerome H. Neyrey, preface to *The Social World of the New Testament* (ed. Jerome H. Neyrey and Eric C. Stewart; Peabody, Mass.: Hendrickson, 2008), xxii.

As Morris notes, "the core thesis of Finley's book (*The Ancient Economy*) is that we can build a coherent model of a single ancient economy which sums up the important features of the whole Graeco-Roman Mediterranean from 1000 BC through AD 500."[46] Indeed, Finley was allegedly harshly critical of "practitioners of local histories"[47] or those who compared his model with all the data they could accumulate for their region of specialization. But at some point, if a model is increasingly inconsistent with the data, it must be rejected. Can a model achieve the ambitious goal Finley wanted, or should we discard the use of models altogether?

I would like to propose six caveats to those using the social science models and/ or refusing to use them.

(1) The model should not be based on only one social theory (e.g., functionalism, class conflict, Marxism) but should be eclectic.

(2) The model should have been informed by a study of ancient societies. Models based only on abstractions from contemporary societies may be anachronistic.

(3) The model should be cross-cultural. Those that were formulated from observations only from Western Europe or the United States may not be relevant to the ancient economy.

(4) The model should not become "proxy data." This term is used by classical historians for comparing ancient societies with "relevantly similar" contemporary ones.[48] Proxy data, as I understand them, are hypothetical scenarios not supplied by the ancient evidence but by "likelihood, analogy, or comparison."[49] For example, someone reasoned that Pompeii did not sell much wine outside of its own city limits by calculating the amount of grain needed to feed its citizens.[50] I would say, these methods are interesting and show us possibilities but should not be trusted as hard evidence.[51]

---

46. Morris, foreword to Finley, *Ancient Economy*, xix.
47. Morris, foreword to Finley, *Ancient Economy*, xxvii.
48. Paul Cartledge, "The Economy (Economics) of Ancient Greece," in Scheidel and von Reden, *The Ancient Economy*, 17, 21, 22.
49. See Jean Andreau, "Twenty Years after Moses I. Finley's *Ancient Economy*" in Scheidel and von Reden, *The Ancient Economy*, 39.
50. Ibid.
51. See the model used by the present author: David A. Fiensy, "Ancient Economy and the New Testament," in *Understanding the Social World of the New Testament* (ed. Dietmar Neufeld and Richard E. DeMaris; London: Routledge, 2009), 199. The model

(5) "We should judge a model by how helpful it is in making sense of the data."⁵² If the model must ignore some data to remain consistent, it is probably not useful any longer. Probably no model can accommodate all known data, but the one we use as a heuristic visualization should interpret most of it.

Thus when New Testament scholars assume that more and more land in Galilee was being gobbled up by the wealthy and that, therefore, the average peasant was on the verge of losing his land, we may justifiably ask for evidence. One recent work, for example, states that "estates grew and tenancy increased as economies of scale for cash crops were created."⁵³ We can agree with this statement if one is speaking in general about the ancient Greco-Roman world or even about Palestine/Israel as a whole. But we need to know whether there is hard data (archaeological or literary) that show that there were large estates in Lower Galilee and that these estates were both increasing in size and multiplying.

(6) On the other hand, there needs to be a cautionary note to those rejecting social science models out of hand. We need the models. As Keith Hopkins observes: "The model is a sort of master picture, as on the front of a jigsaw puzzle box; the fragments of surviving ancient sources provide only a few of the jigsaw pieces."⁵⁴

Models help us sketch out the social, economic, or cultural picture much like an artist's reconstruction of an archaeological ruin. Without some kind of model, we are left only to talk about the individual pieces. Models may also help us examine our own bias both in selecting the sources to examine and in interpreting them. The best way to think about a social science model is to regard it as a working hypothesis, a sort of template on which one places data. Any good historian must always be ready to affirm, edit, or reject the hypothesis based on the data.

Thus Seán Freyne has used the model of Thomas Carney, a kind of threefold barometric reading, to conclude that economic changes were happening in first century C.E. Galilee. These three "elements" help Freyne

---

I used was developed from John K. Davies, "Linear and Nonlinear Flow Models for Ancient Economies," in Manning and Morris, *The Ancient Economy*, 150.

52. Morris, foreword to Finley, *Ancient Economy*, xxvii.

53. John Dominic Crossan and Jonathan L. Reed, *Excavating Jesus* (San Francisco: Harper, 2001), 70.

54. Keith Hopkins, "Rome, Taxes, Rents and Trade," in Scheidel and von Reden, *The Ancient Economy*, 191.

to focus his research and to organize his data. They assist him in getting beyond what he calls the "intuitivist" approach (the "hit or miss aspect") which leaves one open to unstated biases.[55]

We all approach the data with some sort of a priori. The classical historians now challenging Finley's primitivist economic theory approach the evidence with modernist theory. It is not a question of whether one will use a model but which model, consciously or not, one will select. As the social science interpreters repeatedly remind us, we need to reflect on the social science models we use because they can guard against the twin errors of "ethnocentrism and anachronism."[56]

I offer one example. When historians infer from Herod the Great's many building projects that they stimulated the economy of Palestine and that the economic prosperity was a rising tide that floated all boats, it gives one pause.[57] It all seems plausible to the modern reader because we would probably experience a bit of economic stimulation if we had construction in our area. But the ancient experience may have been different. In the first place, Herod built large edifices outside of Palestine as well as in Palestine. Those building projects outside Palestine did not benefit the residents of his own nation (Josephus, *J.W.* 1.422–28). Second, the benefit even in the building projects in Palestine is debatable. Such projects almost always required a large supply of imported workers.[58] Thus, the local folk would

---

55. Seán Freyne, "Herodian Economics in Galilee: Searching for a Suitable Model," in *Modeling Early Christianity* (ed. Philip F. Esler; London: Routledge, 1995), 23, 46. See also Thomas Carney, *The Shape of the Past: Models and Antiquity* (Lawrence, Kans.: Coronado, 1975).

56. See the following references from the same volume: Neyrey and Stewart, preface, xxiii; Bruce Malina, "Rhetorical Criticism and Social Scientific Criticism: Why Won't Romanticism Leave us Alone?" 17; Neyrey and Stewart, 201; Malina and Neyrey, "Ancient Mediterranean Persons in Cultural Perspective: Portrait of Paul," 258.

57. See Duane W. Roller, *The Building Program of Herod the Great* (Berkeley: University of California, 1998), 125–238. Roller believes that the building projects were economically beneficial to the village residents. Similarly, F. C. Grant, A. H. M. Jones, and A. Momigliano thought that Herod's excessive taxation was economically beneficial to the nation on the whole. See Grant, *The Economic Background of the Gospels* (London: Oxford University Press, 1926), 46; Jones, *The Herods of Judea* (Oxford: Clarendon, 1938), 87; Momigliano, "Herod of Judea," in *Cambridge Ancient History* (ed. S. A. Cook, F. E. Adcock, and M. P. Charlesworth; Cambridge: Cambridge University, 1966), 10:331.

58. See Alison M. Burford, "The Economics of Greek Temple Building," *Proceedings of the Cambridge Philological Society* 191 (1965): 21–34; and David A. Fiensy,

not necessarily reap the benefits of construction in their region because of increased employment. Finally, one must not forget that all of that construction activity demanded finances. Doubtless Herod had considerable personal estates from which to draw but he also evidently increased taxes to afford all of his activity. We know this because after Herod's death, the Jews of Palestine sent delegates to Rome to report his misdeeds. On the list of his crimes was that he had decorated surrounding non-Jewish cities at the expense of the Palestinian ones. He had impoverished the entire Jewish nation with his building programs both inside Palestine and outside (Josephus, *Ant.* 17.307; *J.W.* 2.285). We must not forget that ancient kings and rulers built buildings and cities not for the benefit of the residents but for their own glory. Therefore, while large construction projects in the modern economy might bring certain benefits to the local residents, it is debatable how much benefit they would have brought to the ancient economy.[59]

Those who argue for economic prosperity in first-century Palestine/Israel need to remember the Jewish War of 66 to 73 C.E. It neither sprang to life overnight nor was it only about religion. In Judea, at least, if we can credit Josephus's account, there was a simultaneous class war alongside the war against the Romans. During the procuratorship of Felix (52–60 C.E.) certain bands of ruffians looted the houses of Jewish nobles, killing their owners (Josephus, *J.W.* 2.264). Once war broke out in 66 C.E., a full scale campaign against the wealthy followed, begun by the Sicarii, Zealots, and the followers of Simon bar Giora (Josephus, *J.W.* 2.426–428, 2.652, 4.140–245, 4.315, 327, 335, 358, 5.309, 5.439–441, 5.527–532). When we see uprisings in the Roman Empire elsewhere (or anywhere else for that matter), we naturally assume socioeconomic factors played at least some role. The question is, of course, whether Judea was at that time significantly more stressed economically than Galilee.

Conclusion

Remarkable gains have been made in understanding Galilee in the late Second Temple period in the last thirty years. This is a credit to both fine

---

"Jesus' Socioeconomic Background," in *Jesus and Hillel* (ed. James H. Charlesworth and Loren Johns; Minneapolis: Fortress, 1997), 249.

59. See Douglas E. Oakman, *The Political Aims of Jesus* (Minneapolis: Fortress, 2012), 53, where he makes the point (following K. A. Wittfolgel) that large ornamental building projects are characteristic of oriental despotism.

archaeological work and to the study of the insights of the social sciences. We must continue to use all of the resources available as we advance this pursuit. I, for one, intend to drink from both wells in assessing Lower Galilee in the late Second Temple period. I have enjoyed immensely sampling the mineral waters of each camp. But neither well alone seems to quench my thirst. Mixed together, however, they form a refreshing draft that strengthens one to move forward in the quest.

Bibliography

Adan-Bayewitz, David. *Common Pottery in Roman Galilee.* Ramat-Gan, Israel: Bar-Ilan University Press, 1993.

Adan-Bayewitz, David, and Perlman, Isadore. "The Local Trade of Sepphoris in the Roman Period." *IEJ* 40 (1990):153–72.

Andreau, Jean. "Twenty Years after Moses I. Finley's *Ancient Economy*." Pages 33–49 in *The Ancient Economy.* Edited by Walter Scheidel and Sitta von Reden. New York: Routledge, 2002.

Aviam, Mordechai. "Economy and Social Structure in First-Century Galilee: Evidence from the Ground-Yodefat and Gamla." Paper presented at the Annual Meeting of the Society of Biblical Literature. Boston, November 2008.

———. "Galilee: The Hellenistic to Byzantine Periods." *NEAEHL* 2:453–58.

———. *Jews, Pagans and Christians in the Galilee.* Rochester, N.Y.: University of Rochester Press, 2004.

Avigad, Nahman. "How the Wealthy Lived in Herodian Jerusalem." *BAR* 2.4 (1976): 22–35.

Burford, Alison M. "The Economics of Greek Temple Building." *Proceedings of the Cambridge Philological Society* 191 (1965): 21–34.

Carney, Thomas. *The Shape of the Past: Models and Antiquity.* Lawrence, Kans.: Coronado, 1975.

Cartledge, Paul. "The Economy (Economics) of Ancient Greece." Pages 12–32 in *The Ancient Economy.* Edited by Walter Scheidel and Sitta von Reden. New York: Routledge, 2002.

Colander, David C. *Macroeconomics.* Boston: McGraw-Hill, 2008.

Crossan, John Dominic, and Jonathan L. Reed. *Excavating Jesus.* San Francisco: Harper, 2001.

Davies, John K. "Linear and Nonlinear Flow Models for Ancient Economies." Pages 127–56 in *The Ancient Economy: Evidence and Models.*

Edited by Joseph G. Manning and Ian Morris. Stanford, Calif.: Stanford University Press, 2005.

Edwards, Douglas. "First Century Urban/Rural Relations in Lower Galilee: Exploring the Archaeological and Literary Evidence." Pages 169–182 in *SBL 1988 Seminar Papers*. Atlanta: Scholars Press, 2000.

———. "Identity and Social Location in Roman Galilean Villages." Pages 357–74 in *Religion, Ethnicity, and Identify in Ancient Galilee*. Edited by Jürgen Zangenberg, Harold W. Attridge, and Dale B. Martin. Tübingen: Mohr Siebeck, 2007.

Fiensy, David A. "Ancient Economy and the New Testament." Pages 194–206 in *Understanding the Social World of the New Testament*. Edited by Dietmar Neufeld and Richard E. DeMaris. London: Routledge, 2009.

———. "Jesus and Debts: Did He Pray about Them?" *ResQ* 44 (2002): 233–39.

———. "Jesus' Socioeconomic Background." Pages 225–55 in *Jesus and Hillel*. Edited by James H. Charlesworth and Loren Johns. Minneapolis: Fortress, 1997.

———. *The Social History of Palestine in the Herodian Period: The Land Is Mine*. Studies in the Bible and Early Christianity 20. Lewiston, N.Y.: Mellen, 1991.

Finley, Moses I. *The Ancient Economy*. Berkeley: University of California Press, 1999.

Freyne, Seán. "Herodian Economics in Galilee: Searching for a Suitable Model." Pages 23–46 in *Modeling Early Christianity*. Edited by Philip F. Esler. London: Routledge, 1995.

———. "Archaeology and the Historical Jesus." Pages 117–44 in *Archaeology and Biblical Interpretation*. Edited by J. R. Bartlett. London: Routledge, 1997.

Goodman, Martin. "The First Jewish Revolt: Social Conflict and the Problem of Debt." *JJS* 33 (1982): 414–27.

Grant, F. C. *The Economic Background of the Gospels*. London: Oxford University Press, 1926.

Groh, Dennis E. "The Clash between Literary and Archaeological Models of Provincial Palestine." Pages 29–37 in *Archaeology and the Galilee*. Edited by Douglas R. Edwards and C. Thomas McCollough. Atlanta: Scholars Press, 1997.

Hachlili, Rachel, and Patricia Smith. "The Genealogy of the Goliath Family." *BASOR* 235 (1979): 67–71.

Hanson, K. C., and Douglas E. Oakman. *Palestine in the Time of Jesus*. Minneapolis: Fortress, 2008.

Heichelheim, F. M. "Roman Syria." Pages 121–257 in vol. 4 of *Economic Survey of Ancient Rome*. Edited by Tenney Frank. Baltimore: Johns Hopkins University Press, 1938.

Hopkins, Keith. "Rome, Taxes, Rents and Trade." Pages 191–230 in *The Ancient Economy*. Edited by Walter Scheidel and Sitta von Reden. New York: Routledge, 2002.

Horsley, Richard A. *Archaeology, History and Society in Galilee*. Valley Forge, Pa.: Trinity Press International, 1996.

Jeremias, Joachim J. *Jerusalem in the Time of Jesus*. Philadelphia: Fortress, 1969.

Jones, A. H. M. *The Herods of Judea*. Oxford: Clarendon, 1938.

MacDonald, Nathan. *What Did the Ancient Israelites Eat?* Grand Rapids: Eerdmans, 2008.

Magen, Yitzhak. *The Stone Vessel Industry in the Second Temple Period*. Jerusalem: Israel Exploration Society, 2002.

Malina, Bruce. "Rhetorical Criticism and Social Scientific Criticism: Why Won't Romanticism Leave Us Alone?" Pages 5–21 in *The Social World of the New Testament*. Edited by Jerome H. Neyrey and Eric C. Stewart. Peabody, Mass: Hendrickson, 2008.

Malina, Bruce, and Jerome H. Neyrey. "Ancient Mediterranean Persons in Cultural Perspective: Portrait of Paul." Pages 255–75 in *The Social World of the New Testament*. Edited by Jerome H. Neyrey and Eric C. Stewart. Peabody, Mass: Hendrickson, 2008.

Mankiw, N. Gregory. *Principles of Macroeconomics*. Mason, Ohio: Southwestern, 2004.

Manning, Joseph G., and Ian Morris, eds. *The Ancient Economy: Evidence and Models*. Stanford: Stanford University, 2005.

Meikle, Scott. "Modernism, Economics, and the Ancient Economy." Pages 233–50 in *The Ancient Economy*. Edited by Walter Scheidel and Sitta von Reden. New York: Routledge, 2002.

Meyers, Eric M. "The Problems of Gendered Space in Syro-Palestinian Domestic Architecture: The Case of Roman-Period Galilee." Pages 44–69 in *Early Christian Families in Context*. Edited by David L. Balch and Carolyn Osiek. Grand Rapids: Eerdmans, 2003.

———. "Roman Sepphoris in Light of New Archaeological Evidence and Recent Research." Pages 321–38 in *The Galilee in Late Antiquity*. Edited by Lee I. Levine. New York: Jewish Theological Seminary, 1992.

Meyers, Eric M., James F. Strange, and Dennis E. Groh. "The Meiron Excavation Project: Archeological Survey in Galilee and Golan, 1976." *BASOR* 230 (1978): 1–24.

Meyers, Eric M., James F. Strange, and Carol Meyers. *Excavations at Ancient Meiron, Upper Galilee, Israel 1971–72, 1974–75, 1977*. Cambridge: American Schools of Oriental Research, 1981.

Millar, Fergus. *The Roman Near East 31 BC–AD 337*. Cambridge: Harvard University Press, 1993.

Momigliano, A. "Herod of Judea." Pages 316–39 in vol. 10 of *Cambridge Ancient History*. Edited by S. A. Cook, F. E. Adcock, and M. P. Charlesworth. Cambridge: Cambridge University Press, 1966.

Morris, Ian. "Archaeology, Standards of Living and Greek Economic History." Pages 91–126 in *The Ancient Economy: Evidence and Models*. Edited by Joseph G. Manning and Ian Morris. Stanford, Calif.: Stanford University Press, 2005.

———. Foreword to Moses I. Finley, *The Ancient Economy*. Berkeley: University of California Press, 1999.

Morris, Ian, and Joseph G. Manning. "Introduction." Pages 1–44 in *The Ancient Economy: Evidence and Models*. Edited by Joseph G. Manning and Ian Morris. Stanford, Calif.: Stanford University Press, 2005.

Neyrey, Jerome H. Preface to *The Social World of the New Testament*. Edited by Jerome H. Neyrey and Eric C. Stewart. Peabody, Mass: Hendrickson, 2008.

Neyrey, Jerome H., and Eric C. Stewart, eds. *The Social World of the New Testament*. Peabody, Mass: Hendrickson, 2008.

Oakman, Douglas E. *Jesus and the Economic Questions of His Day*. Lewiston, N.Y.: Mellen, 1986.

———. *Jesus and the Peasants*. Eugene, Ore.: Cascade, 2008.

———. *The Political Aims of Jesus*. Minneapolis: Fortress, 2012.

Pastor, Jack. *Land and Economy in Ancient Palestine*. London: Routledge, 1997.

Reed, Jonathan. "Galileans, 'Israelite Village Communities' and the Sayings Gospel Q." Pages 87–108 in *Galilee through the Centuries*. Edited by Eric M. Meyers. Winona Lake, Ind.: Eisenbrauns, 1999.

Richardson, Peter. *Building Jewish in the Roman East*. Waco, Tex.: Baylor University Press, 2004.

Roller, Duane W. *The Building Program of Herod the Great*. Berkeley: University of California Press, 1998.

Rostovtzeff, Michael. *The Social and Economic History of the Hellenistic World*. Oxford: Clarendon, 1941.

Saller, Richard. "Framing the Debate Over Growth and the Ancient Economy." Pages 223–238 in *The Ancient Economy*. Edited by Walter Scheidel and Sitta von Reden. New York: Routledge, 2002.

Scheidel, Walter, and Sitta von Reden, eds. *The Ancient Economy*. New York: Routledge, 2002.

Smith, Patricia, Elizabeth Bornemann, and Joe Zias. "The Skeletal Remains." Pages 110–20 in *Excavations at Ancient Meiron, Upper Galilee, Israel 1971-72, 1974-75, 1977*. Edited by Eric Meyers, James F. Strange, and Carol L. Meyers. Cambridge: ASOR, 1981.

Strange, James, Dennis E. Groh, and Thomas R. W. Longstaff. "Excavations at Sepphoris: The Location and Identification of Shikhin." *IEJ* 44 (1994): 216–27.

Strange, James. "First Century Galilee from Archaeology and from the Texts." Pages 39–48 in *Archaeology and the Galilee*. Edited by Douglas R. Edwards and C. Thomas McCollough. Atlanta: Scholars, 1997.

Udoh, Fabian E. *To Caesar What Is Caesar's*. Providence, R.I.: Brown University, 2005.

Contributors

Mordechai Aviam (PhD, Bar Ilan University) is Senior Lecturer in the Kinneret Academic College on the Sea of Galilee, Israel, and the director of the Institute for Galilean Archaeology in the Kinneret College. In his previous position as District Archaeologist for Western Galilee in the IAA, he conducted numerous surveys and several excavations, including that of Yodefat. Among his recent publications are "The Decorated Stone from the Synogogue at Migdal—A Holistic Interpretation and a Glimpse into the Life of Galilean Jews at the Time of Jesus," *NT* 55 (2013): 205–20, and "The Book of Enoch and the Galilean Archaeology and Landscape," in *Parables of Enoch: A Paradigm Shift* (ed. D. L. Bock and J. H. Charlesworth; Edinburgh: T&T Clark, 2013), 159–70.

David A. Fiensy (PhD, Duke University) is Professor of New Testament and Dean of the Graduate School of Bible and Ministry, Kentucky Christian University, in Grayson, Kentucky. Among his previous publications are *The Social History of Palestine in the Herodian Period: The Land Is Mine* (New York: Mellen, 1991) and *Jesus the Galilean: Soundings in a First Century Life* (Piscataway, N.J.: Gorgias, 2007).

Ralph K. Hawkins (PhD, Andrews University) is Chair of the Religious Studies Department and an Associate Professor of Biblical and Archaeological Studies at Averett University, in Danville, Virginia. He has recently published *The Iron Age I Structure on Mt. Ebal: Excavation and Interpretation* (Winona Lake, Ind.: Eisenbrauns, 2012) and *How Israel Became a People* (Nashville: Abingdon, 2013).

Sharon Lea Mattila (PhD, University of Chicago) is an Assistant Professor in the Department of Philosophy and Religion at the University of North Carolina at Pembroke. Her recent publications include "Jesus and the 'Middle Peasants'? Problematizing a Social-Scientific Concept," *CBQ*

72 (2010): 291–313, based on part of her dissertation; she is presently engaged in a larger research project with the proposed title *Rural Socioeconomic Life in Greco-Roman Egypt and Palestine: An Experimental Intersecting Thick Description*.

Thomas McCollough (PhD, University of Notre Dame) is the Nelson and Martha McDowell Rodes Professor of Religion at Centre College in Danville, Kentucky. He is the Director of the Archaeological Excavations at Khirbet Qana and edited (with Douglas Edwards) *The Archaeology of Difference: Gender, Ethnicity, Class, and the "Other" in Antiquity: Studies in Honor of Eric M. Meyers* (Boston: American Schools of Oriental Research, 2007).

Douglas E. Oakman (PhD, Graduate Theological Union) has been with the faculty of Pacific Lutheran University since 1988. He was chair of the Religion Department from 1996 to 2003 and Dean of Humanities from 2004 to 2010. He is the author of *Jesus and the Economic Questions of His Day* (New York: Mellen, 1986), the award-winning *Palestine in the Time of Jesus* (with K. C. Hanson; 2nd ed.; Minneapolis: Fortress, 2008), *Jesus and the Peasants* (Eugene, Ore.: Cascade, 2008), and *The Political Aims of Jesus* (Minneapolis: Fortress, 2012).

Ancient Sources Index

Hebrew Bible

Nehemiah
13:4–9 — 104 n. 84
13:15–22 — 104 n. 84

Zechariah
13:5 — 152

Deuterocanonical Books

Jesus ben Sirach
38:24–26 — 142

Josephus

Antiquities
12.119–124 — 108
13.401–415 — 104
14.71–73 — 104 n. 84
17.149–165 — 97
17.151–152 — 97
17.204–205 — 169 n. 15
17.271 — 16
17.306–307 — 169 n. 15
17.307 — 181
18.16 — 104
18.27 — 17
18.38 — 17
18.90 — 169
19.299 — 169

Contra Apionem
1.60 — 139

Jewish War
1.110–114 — 104
1.152–153 — 104 n. 84
1.303 — 15
1.307–313 — 15
1.328 — 15
1.422–28 — 180
1.651–655 — 97
2.85–86 — 169 n. 15
2.264 — 181
2.285 — 181
2.426–428 — 181
2.427 — 172
2.503–504 — 43
2.562–568 — 29
2.591–592 — 107, 108
2.652 — 181
3.10 — 18
3.27–28 — 37
3.42–43 — 142
4.104 — 9, 104
4.140–245 — 181
4.315 — 181
4.316–317 — 37
4.327 — 181
4.335 — 181
4.358 — 181
5.309 — 181
5.439–441 — 181
5.527–532 — 181

Josephus, *Vita*
38	54, 158
43–45	104
65–66	97
73–74	107, 108
86	59

New Testament

Mark
12:13–17	168

Acts
12:20	109

Greco-Roman Literature

Cato, *De agricultura*
1.2–4	106

Cicero, *De officiis*
1.150–51	106

Columella, *De re rustica*
1.1–17	106

Tacitus, *Agricola*
30	159 n. 53

Tacitus, *Annales*
2.42	169

Theophrastus, *Characters*
4.4–11	141

Ulpian, *Digest* — 168

Varro, *De re rustica*
2.10.1–3	106
3.1.4	141

Rabbinic Works

m. Arakhin
9:6	11

B. Bat.
1:1	125

Qoheleth Rabbah
1.8	111

t. Shevi'it
4:14	11

Early Christian Writings

Epiphanius, *Panarion*
30.11.9–10	111

Modern Authors Index

Adan-Bayewitz, David   11, 11 n. 9, 22 n. 35, 34, 35 n. 49, 46, 102 n. 74, 108 n. 95, 130, 131, 175, 175 nn. 31 and 37, 182
Akerlof, George   72 n. 31
Alston, Richard   128 n. 156, 131
Amitai, Aharoni   6, 9 n. 5, 46
Andreau, Jean   178 n. 49, 183
Applebaum, Shimon   151 n. 31, 160
Arav, Rami   81 n. 9, 82 n. 11, 111 n. 110, 137
Arensberg, Conrad M.   143 n. 15, 162.
Ariel, Donald T.   9 n. 4, 102 n. 75, 131
Atrash, Walid   18 n. 26, n. 27, 47
Asaro, Frank   35 n. 49, 46
Avigad, Nahman   23 n. 38, 47, 48, 97 n. 54, 100 n. 66, 101 n. 67, 108 n. 96, 131, 137, 171 n. 19, 182
Aviam, Mordechai   2, 3, 4, 6, 6 n. 1, 8, 9 n.5, 10, 10 n. 7, 11 n. 8, 15 n. 20, 19, 20, , 22 n. 35, 25, 26, 27 n. 40, 33, 38 n. 53, 39, 46, 47, 49, 49 n. 1, 57, 65, 65 n. 22, 68, 68 n. 26, 71, 72, 101 nn. 70–71, 102 n. 74, 103, 103 nn. 79–80, 105 n. 86, 107 nn. 92–95, 109 nn. 101–102, 130, 131, 133, 139, 152, 154, 155, 156 n. 44, 159, 159 n. 54, 170 n. 17, 175, 175 n. 33, 176, 176 n. 42, 182
Avshalom-Gorni, Dina   38 n. 52
Bar Nathan, Rachel   99 n. 60, 100 n. 63, 102 n. 74, 108 n. 97, 131

Barag, Dan 23 n. 39, 31, 31 n. 42, 34 n. 47, 46
Batey, Richard A.   52 n. 6
Becker, Marc   153, 153 n. 36, 154, 160
Ben David, H.   43 n. 55, 46
Berlin, Andrea M.   9 n. 6, 16 n. 21, 33, 33 nn. 43–44, 46, 47, 91, 91 nn. 40–41, 92 nn. 41–43. 94, 99, 100 n. 65, 101, 101 nn. 68 and 72, 104 n. 81, 105 n. 84, 109 n. 98, 125 n. 146, 131, 155, 155 n. 41, 160
Bernstein, Henry   140 n. 10, 154, 154 n. 38, 160
Bloedhorn, Hanswulf   81 n. 9, 131
Boak, Arthur E. R.   125 n. 150, 126, 127 nn. 150–51, 128 n. 154, 132
Bösen, Willibald   75 n. 2, 132
Bornemann, Elizabeth   176 n. 40, 186
Burford, Alison M.   180 n. 58, 182
Byres, Terence J.   140 n. 10, 154, 154 n. 38, 160
Capp, C.   27
Carney, Thomas   151 n. 29, 154 n. 39, 160, 179, 180 n. 55, 182
Cartledge, Paul   105 n. 87, 178 n. 48, 182
Chancey, Mark A.   91 n. 38, 98 n. 57, 105 n. 85, 111 n. 111, 112 n. 112, 132
Charlesworth, James H.76.   89, 89 nn. 32 and 34, 120, 120 n. 141, 120, 132
Christian, David   151, 151 n. 30, 153, 153 n. 37, 160

Colander, David C.   173 n. 25, 182
Corbo, Virgilio C.   23 n. 36, 46, 81, 81 n. 10, 82 n. 13, 83, 83 nn. 14 and 15, 86 n. 27, 91 n. 39, 96 n. 51, 115, 115 nn. 125 and 128, 117 nn. 129 and 133, 118 n. 136, 119 n. 138, 122 n. 144, 132
Crossan, John Dominic 1 n. 2, 4, 76, 76 n. 3, 84, 84 n. 16, 85, 85 nn. 22–23 and 25, 86, 86 nn. 25–26 and 28, 88, 88 n. 30, 90, 90 nn. 35–36, 92 n. 41, 94, 94 n. 45, 95, 95 n. 50, 96, 120, 120 n. 140, 129, 132, 179 n. 53, 182
Dagani, Avi   6
Dalman, Gustaf   140, 140 n. 7, 160
Danby, Herbert   125 n. 149, 132
Dar, Shimon   138 n. 1, 155, 155 n. 43, 160
Davies, John K.   179 n. 51, 182
Degani, Avi   6 n. 1, 47, 109 n. 102, 133
De Luca, S.   13, 13 n. 14, n. 16, 46
Dietze, Constantin von   142 n. 12, 152, 152 n. 35, 163
Edwards, Douglas R.   1 n. 3, 4, 17 n. 32, 22 n.35, 46, 50, 50 n. 2, 57, 57 nn. 15–16, 58, 59 n. 17, 61, 63, 64, 67, 67 n. 24, 68, 68 nn. 25 and 27, 69, 69 nn. 28–29, 70, 72, 73, 106 n. 91, 109, 109 nn. 99–100, 110, 110 n. 105, 113 n. 122, 114, 132, 175, 175 nn. 35 and 37, 183
Elliott, Carolyn   109 n. 99, 138
Eschebach, Hans   84 n. 18, 133
Fiensy, David   3, 4, 39, 51, 53, 148, 148 n. 23, 149 n. 27, 152, 154, 160, 169 n. 13, 171 n. 21, 178 n. 51, 189 n. 58, 183
Finley, Moses I.   1, 1 n.1, 4, 166, 166 n. 3, 167, 169 n. 15, 173, 173 n. 23, 174, 174 n. 27, 178, 178 nn. 46–47 and 49, 179 n. 52, 180, 182, 183, 185
Fischer, Alysia A.   59 n. 17, 73
Fischer, Moshe   7, 7 n. 3, 46

Foster, George   140 n. 5, 143, 143 n. 14, 144, 144 nn. 17, 19, 160
Foster, Gideon   81 n. 11, 112 n. 114, 133
Foss, Pedar W.   117 n. 130, 133
Frankel, Rafael   6 n. 1, 7, 7 n. 2, 47, 109 n. 102, 133
Freyne, Séan 2 n.4, 4, 70, 70 n. 30, 73, 76, 88, 89 n. 31, 120, 120 n. 141, 129, 133, 170 n. 17, 179, 180 n. 55, 183
Gal, Zvi   156 n. 44, 159
Garcia, Jeffrey   38 n. 52
Gazda, Elaine K.   125 n. 147, 128 n. 154, 133
Getzov, Nimrod   6 n. 1, 47, 109 n. 102, 133
Giauque, Robert   35 n. 49, 46
Goodblatt, David   109, 110 nn. 103 and 107, 112 n. 117, 133
Goodman, Martin   151 n. 31, 160, 171 n. 20, 183
Grant, Elihu   140, 140 n. 6, 161
Grant, F. C.   180 n. 57, 183
Green, William Scott   22 n. 35
Greene, Kevin   148 n. 22, 161
Groh, Dennis E.   2 n.3, 4, 96 n. 52, 106 n. 91, 113 n. 122, 114 n. 124, 133, 136, 165 n. 1, 170 n. 17, 175, 175 n. 32, 183, 185, 186
Gunneweg, Jan   34 n. 48, 47
Gutman, Shemaryahu   7, 35 n. 51, 47, 101 n. 69, 107 n. 93, 133
Habas, Li-hi   41 n. 54, 47
Hachlili, Rachel   176 n. 39, 183
Halpern, Joel M.   148, 148 n. 24, 161
Hamel, Gildas   149 n. 27, 161
Hanson, K. C. 150 n. 28, 154 n. 40, 155 n. 42, 161, 173 n. 24, 184
Harland, Philip 105 n. 86, 106 n. 90, 133
Hartal, Moshe   18 nn. 28–29, 47
Hayes, Christine E.   104 n. 84, 112 n. 118, 134
Heichelheim, F. M. 168, 168 n. 10, 184

MODERN AUTHORS INDEX

Herbert, Sharon C.   9 n. 6, 47, 99 nn. 59 and 61, 109 n. 98, 134
Hershkovovitz, Malka   23 n. 39, 34 n. 47, 46
Hirschfeld, Yizhar   115 nn. 127–128, 119, 119 n. 138, 125, 125 n. 148, 127, 127 n. 153, 134
Hobsbawm, Eric J.   143, 143 n. 14, 153, 153 n. 37, 161
Hopkins, Keith   179, 179 n. 54, 184
Horden, Peregrine   71 n. 31, 73
Horsley, Richard A.   1 n. 2, 4, 12, 12 n.11, 47, 55, 56 n. 11, 73, 76, 89, 89 nn. 33–34, 118, 118 n. 137, 120, 121 n. 142, 134, 152 n. 32, 161, 174 n. 24, 184
Husselman, Elinor M.   125 n. 147, 128 nn. 154 and 156, 134
Isaac, Benjamin   52 n. 4
Jensen, Morten Hørning   20 n. 30, 47, 56, 56 n. 12, 73, 89 n. 32, 124 n. 145, 134
Jeremias, Joachim   142 n. 11, 161, 173 n. 26, 184
Johnson, Barbara   128 n. 155, 134
Jull, A.J. Timothy   59 n. 17, 73
Kazen, Thomas   98 n. 56, 104 nn. 82–83, 134
Kautsky, John H.   143, 143 n. 13, 144, 145 n. 21, 161
Kearney, Michael   142 n. 12, 153, 154 n. 38, 161
Kim, H. S.   105 n. 87, 134
Kingsley, Sean A.   96, 96 n. 53, 134
Klausner, Joseph   142 n. 11, 161
Klawans, Jonathan   104 n. 84, 134
Kloner, Amos   22 n. 34, 47
Kloppenborg, John S.   156 n. 45, 161
Lapin, Hayim   113 n. 119, 135
Laughlin, John C. H.   78 n. 6, 85 n. 22, 121, 121 n. 143, 135
Lenski, Gerhard E.   143, 143 n. 13, 148, 148 n. 25, 155, 161

Lenski, Jean   148 n. 25, 161
Levine, Lee I.   112 nn. 112 and 116, 135
Liebner, Uzi   11 n. 10, 12, 13, 13 n. 13, 14, 14 n. 18, 21 n. 33, 30 n. 41, 47
Loffreda, Stanislao   76 n. 4, 78 n. 9, 82 nn. 12–13, 85 n. 21, 86 n. 27, 87, 89 n. 32, 90 n. 37, 91 nn. 39 and 41, 92, 92 nn. 41 and 44, 93, 94, 94 n. 46, 96 nn. 51 and 52, 99 n. 58, 108, 128 n. 155, 130 n. 157, 132, 135
Longstaff, Thomas R. W.   51, 175, 175 n. 32, 186
McCollough, C. Thomas   3, 4, 17 n. 23, 18, 46, 50 n. 2, 64, 66, 67, 73, 75 n.1, 85 n. 19
MacDonald, Nathan   176 n. 41, 184
MacDonald, William   53 n. 8
Magen, Yitzhak   102 n. 77, 107 n. 94, 135, 175, 175 n. 39, 184
Magness, Jodi   95 n. 47, 97 nn. 54–55, 99 n. 62, 102 n. 76, 135
Malina, Bruce   180 n. 56, 184
Mankiw, N. Gregory   169 n. 16, 173 nn. 25–26, 177 n. 43, 184
Manning, Joseph G.   177, 177 n. 44, 184, 185
Malpas, John G.   109 n. 99, 138
Ma'oz, Zvi Uri   78 n. 8, 81 n. 9, 111 n. 110, 135
Mattila, Sharon   3, 79, 80, 81, 84, 116, 123, 136, 152, 152 n. 32, 154, 158 n. 50, 161
Mazor, Gabriel   18 n. 27, 47
Meier, John P.   98 n. 56, 136
Meikle, Scott   167 n. 6, 184
Meshorer, Yaakov   114 n. 123, 137
Meyers, Carol L.   96 n. 52, 114 n. 123, 116, 118 n. 136, 136, 176 nn. 38 and 40, 185
Meyers, Eric M.   52 n. 5, 54 n. 10, 56, 56 n. 14, 71 n. 30, 73, 74, 75 n. 1, 84 n. 17, 96 n. 52, 97 n. 54, 106 n. 91,

Meyers, Eric M. (cont.)
 112 n. 108, 112 nn. 113 and 115, 113 n. 121, 114 nn. 122 and 123, 116, 118 n. 136, 136, 170, 170 nn. 17–18, 171 n. 19, 176 nn. 38 and 40, 184, 185
Millar, Fergus 168 n. 12, 185
Millett, Paul C. 155 n. 42, 161
Mintz, Sidney 140, 140 n. 8, 152 n. 34, 153, 162
Mizzi, Dennis J. 95 nn. 47–48, 136
Momigliano, A. 180 n. 57, 185
Moore, Barrington 143, 143 n. 14, 144, 14 n. 18, 162
Moreley, Neville 162
Morris, Ian 166 n. 2, 174, 174 nn. 27–28, 175, 177, 177 n. 44, 178, 178 nn. 46–47, 179 n. 52, 184, 185
Moxnes, Halvor 2 nn. 4–5, 4
Nagy, Rebecca Martin 112 n. 113, 136
Netzer, Ehud 52 n. 5, 85 n. 20, 99 n. 61, 100 n. 64, 136, 138
Neyrey, Jerome H. 156 n. 46, 162, 177 n. 45, 180 n. 56, 184, 185
North, Douglas C. 162
Oakman, Douglas E. 3, 4, 148 n. 23, 150 n. 28, 154 n. 40, 156 n. 46, 161, 162, 171 n. 20, 173 nn. 24 and 26, 181 n. 59, 184, 185
Olyan, Saul M. 104 n. 84, 136
Overman, J. Andrew 1 n.3, 4
Pearson, Harry W. 143 n. 15, 162
Perlman, Isadore 34 n. 48, 47, 107 n. 95, 131, 175, 175 n. 31, 182
Peterson, Enoch E 126, 127 nn. 150–151, 128 n. 154, 132
Pirson, Felix 115 n. 127, 136
Plattner, Stuart 140 n. 10, 162
Poirier, John C. 98 n. 56, 137
Polanyi, Karl 143, 143 n. 15, 162, 173
Porath, Yosef 23 n. 37, 48
Purcell, Nicholas 71 n. 31, 73
Rabinowitz, A.H. 125 n. 149, 137
Rapinchuk, Mark 2 n. 5, 4
Rathbone, Dominic W. 158 n. 52, 162
Raynor, Joyce 114 n. 123, 137
Rech, Jason A. 59 n. 17, 60 n. 19, 73
Redfield, Robert 140, 140 n. 9, 143, 143 n. 14, 162
Reed, Jonathan 56 n. 13, 73, 75, 76, 76 n. 3, 78 n. 6, 84, 84 nn. 16–17, 85, 85 nn. 19 and 22–25, 86, 86 nn. 25–26 and 28, 88, 88 nn. 29–30, 89, 89 n. 34, 90, 90 nn. 35–36, 92 n. 41, 94, 94 n. 45, 95, 95 n. 50, 96, 98 n. 58, 104, 120, 120 n. 140, 129, 132, 137, 149 n. 27, 162, 170 n. 17, 179 n. 53, 182, 185
Richardson, Peter 16 n. 22, 48, 60 n. 18, 62, 62 n. 21, 65, 65 n. 23, 73, 83, 83 n. 15, 111 n. 108, 118, 118 n. 135, 124 n. 145, 137, 174 n. 30, 185
Roll, Israel 52 n. 4
Ronen, Avraham 156 n. 44, 159
Rosenberg, Silvia 32 n. 38, 48
Rosenthal-Heginbottom, Renate 34 n. 45, 48, 100 n. 66, 102 n. 74, 137
Rostovtzeff, Michael 155 n. 42, 157, 157 n. 47, 162, 167, 172, 172 n. 22, 186
Rousseau, John J. 81 n. 9, 82 n. 11, 111 n. 110, 137
Safrai, Zeev
 110 nn. 103–104, 113 n. 120, 132
Saller, Richard 143 n. 12, 147 n. 22, 158 nn. 51–52, 167 n. 9, 186
Saller, Sylvester 82 n. 13, 132
Schneider, Helmut 147, 147 n. 22, 163
Scott, James C. 140, 143, 143 n. 14, 144, 144 n. 20, 163
Segal, Arthur 53, 53 n. 7, 54, 54 n. 9, 73
Shalem, D. 40, 42
Shanin, Teodor 140 nn. 4 and 9, 143, 143 n. 14, 144 n. 16, 163
Shanks, Hershel 81, 81 n. 10, 83 n. 13, 138

Shiller, Robert 72 n. 31
Sjøberg, Gideon 143, 143 n. 13, 163
Slane, Kathlene Warner 99 n. 59, 100 n. 65, 138
Smith, Adam 72 n. 31
Smith, Patricia 176 nn. 39–40, 183, 186
Sorokin, Pitirim Aleksandrovich 140, 140 n. 4, 163
Stern, Ephraim 12 n. 12, 48
Stewart, Eric C. 180 n. 56, 185
Strange, James F. 18, 52n. 5, 54 n. 10, 55, 73, 81, 81 n. 10, 82 n. 13, 83 n. 13, 84 n. 17, 86 n. 27, 96 n. 52, 106 n. 91, 112 n. 115, 115 n. 123, 116, 118 n. 136, 138, 170 n. 17, 175, 175 nn. 32, 36 and 37, 176 n. 38, 185, 186
Strikovsky, Aryeh 102 n. 75, 131
Susser, Bernard 125 n. 149, 137
Syon, Danny 9 n. 5, 15 n. 19, 17, 35, 35 nn. 50–51, 48, 130, 130 n. 27, 101 nn. 69 and 71, 138, 157, 157 n. 48, 163
Taylor, Joan E. 83 n. 13, 89, 89 nn. 33–34, 111 n. 109, 120, 121, 121 n. 142, 138
Thorner, Daniel 148, 149, 149 n. 26, 163
Tsafrir, Yoram 81 n. 9, 82 nn. 11 and 13, 138
Tsuk, Tsvika 18, 18 n. 24, 20, 20 n. 32, 48
Tzaferis, Vassilios 76 nn. 4–5, 138
Udoh, Fabian E. 168 n. 11, 169 nn. 13–14, 186
Van der Spek, Robartus J. 143 n. 12, 163
Wallace-Hadrill, Andrew 115 n. 127, 117 nn. 130–131, 128 n. 156, 138
Weber, Max 139, 140 n. 4, 143, 143 n. 13, 146, 147, 163
Weiss, Zeev 18, 18 n. 25, 48, 52 n. 5, 85 n. 20, 138
White, K. D. 148 n. 22, 164
Wieder, Moshe 35 n. 49, 46
Wittfogel, Karl A. 143, 143 n. 13, 164
Wolf, Eric R. 140, 143, 143 n. 14, 144, 164
Xenophontos, Costas 109 n. 99, 138
Yanchula, George 79, 80, 116, 119 n. 139, 123
Zias, Joe 176 n. 40, 186
Zissu, Boaz 62 n. 22, 74
Zussman, Varda 34 n. 46, 48

Subject Index

abecedary, 69, 69 n. 28
Agrippa I, 28, 44, 109
Agrippa II, 172
animal bones, 15, 16, 27, 27 n. 40
Antipas, 14, 15, 16, 17, 18, 20, 22, 43, 45, 50, 53, 55, 56, 97, 109, 155
basilica, 17, 20, 54, 55, 56, 111
burials, 35, 36–37. *See also* human bones
Byzantine period, 6 n. 1, 17, 23, 28, 60, 76, 78, 83, 85, 86, 86 n. 27, 87, 88, 90, 95, 96, 97, 109, 109 n. 101, 110, 111, 112, 112 n. 113, 113, 114, 114 n. 124, 115, 115 n. 127, 120, 121, 122, 124, 129, 130
Cardo, 17, 18, 50, 51, 54, 56, 88
Cana/Khirbet Qana, 3, 12, 21, 32, 49, 57–69, 70, 71, 118, 125 n. 145, 174
Capernaum, 3, 12, 75–138, 158 n. 50, 175
carbon dating, 59, 59 n. 17, 60, 65
cistern, 17, 22, 28, 36, 37, 59, 60
coins, 7, 9,10, 12, 15, 16, 21, 22, 29, 35, 42, 45, 49, 50, 54, 56, 58, 59, 68, 69, 97, 102, 103, 105, 105 n. 87, 111, 156, 157
Early Roman period, 11, 13, 27, 50, 52, 56, 58, 60, 60 n. 20, 62 n. 20, 69, 82, 82, 84, 85, 86, 90, 92, 92 nn. 41 and 44, 93, 94, 95 n. 47, 98, 100, 102, 108, 109, 110, 114, 122, 124, 124 n. 145, 129, 130, 147, 149, 155, 156, 157, 159

Eastern Terra Sigillata, 67, 91, 92, 92 n. 41, 94, 96, 97–103, 104, 104 n. 84, 106 n. 91, 108, 113 n. 122, 114, 129
fine ware pottery, 86, 86 n. 27, 87, 88, 91, 92, 92 n. 41, 96, 96 n. 51, 99 n. 59, 100, 100 nn. 65–66, 101 102 n. 74, 104, 106 n. 91, 107, 110, 113, 114, 120, 128, 129, 130, 171
fresco, 9, 20, 22, 23, 25, 29, 36, 38, 41, 44, 55, 100, 101. 101 n. 71, 124, 170
Galilean Coarse Ware, 6, 7, 9, 42, 103
Gamla, 7, 7 n. 3, 11, 12, 15, 16, 17, 21, 26, 27, 28–29, 30, 31, 32, 33, 34, 35, 37, 38, 39, 41, 42, 43, 44, 58, 60, 62, 65, 76, 92, 94, 101, 101 n. 71, 102, 107, 107 n. 95, 118, 129, 151, 157, 158, 158 n. 50, 159, 174
glassware, 62, 79, 80, 86, 93, 94, 94 n. 46, 95, 95 nn. 47–48, 100, 122, 124, 128, 129, 130, 142 n. 11
Herod the Great, 15, 16, 18, 19, 20, 43, 97, 99, 104, 155, 168, 169 n. 15, 180
Hasmonean, 5, 7, 9, 10. 11, 12, 13, 14, 15, 16, 16, 21, 22, 31, 32, 35, 42, 43, 45, 58, 68, 92, 97, 98, 98 n. 57, 99, 99 nn. 61–62, 100, 101. 102, 103, 105, 106, 107 n. 93, 111, 114, 155, 157
Hellenistic period, 6, 7, 9, 10, 11, 12, 58, 60, 90, 91, 92, 92 n. 44, 99, 102, 142, 172
Herodian, 14, 16, 22, 23, 31, 34, 45, 53, 55, 92, 93, 95, 97, 99 n. 62, 100, 101, 101 n. 67, 102, 103, 105, 106, 111, 114, 148, 149

SUBJECT INDEX

human bones, 36, 174, 176. *See also* burials
Jerusalem, 22, 23, 29, 31, 32, 34, 35, 37, 41, 43, 44, 45, 85, 90, 92, 95, 99 n. 62, 100, 101 n. 67, 102, 103, 104 n. 84, 105, 107, 107 n. 95, 108, 111 n. 111, 149, 158, 169, 170, 171, 172, 176 n. 39
Jotapata. *See* Yodefat
Karanis (Egypt), 124, 125, 126, 127, 128, 129, 130
Kefar Hananya, 12, 27, 28, 62 n. 20, 65, 67, 69, 107, 107 n. 95, 109, 175
Khirbet Qana. *See* Cana
kiln, 27, 29, 44, 86, 107 n. 95
lamps, 9, 16, 23, 25, 29, 33–35, 38, 45, 93, 107, 107 n. 95
loom weights, 27, 44
luxury items, 24, 29, 86, 90, 95, 96, 101, 128, 129
Migdal/Magdala, 13, 14, 15, 37, 40, 41, 42, 45, 155
miqweh (ritual bath), 10, 15, 16, 23, 26, 32, 44, 45, 59, 63, 65, 66, 62, 97, 97 n. 55, 98, 102 n. 77, 103, 104, 107
money, 142, 146, 150, 155, 156, 157, 158, 159
Nazareth, 12, 21, 32, 73, 107 n. 94, 158 n. 50, 159
olive press, 13, 15, 16, 26, 28, 29, 32, 44
opus sectile, 20, 23, 101
ostracon, 69, 70
Patrician House (Meiron), 116, 118, 118 n. 136, 119, 120, 124, 128, 129, 130, 176
peasants, 2, 3, 29, 43, 44, 71, 86 n. 25, 96, 139–164, 165, 170, 171, 172, 173, 175, 179
ritual purity, 26, 32, 65, 97, 98, 98 n. 56, 99 n. 62, 102, 103, 103 n. 81, 104, 104 nn. 82–84, 108, 114
Rhodian jars/amphorae, 9, 90, 96, 114

Sepphoris/Zippori, 3, 11, 12, 15, 16, 17, 21, 28, 30, 32, 42, 43, 49, 50–57, 65, 68, 69, 71, 84, 85, 85 n. 19, 90, 111, 112 n. 113, 149, 150 n. 27, 158 n. 50, 170, 171
Shikhin, 21, 62 n. 20, 65, 67, 107, 107 n. 65, 175
socioeconomic models, 2, 3, 4, 139, 154, 147, 149, 150, 150 n. 28, 151, 151 n. 29, 152, 154, 154 n. 39, 155, 165 n. 1, 166, 167, 173, 174, 177, 178, 178 n. 51, 179, 179 n. 51, 180, 180 n. 55
spindle whorls, 27, 44
stone table, 23, 38, 39, 40, 42, 45, 100
stoneware vessels, 31, 32–33, 45, 97, 98, 98 n. 58, 103
synagogue, 14, 17, 37–41, 45, 62, 64, 77–82, 83, 89, 94, 111, 112, 112 n. 114, 114, 117, 122
taxes, taxation, 29, 43, 44, 96, 105, 105 n. 87, 139, 145, 146, 150, 155, 156, 168, 168 n. 12, 169, 169 nn. 13, and 15–116, 173, 180 n. 57, 181
theaters, 18, 19, 20, 23, 52, 52 n. 5, 53, 54, 56
Tiberias, 6, 12, 15, 17, 18, 19, 20, 30, 31, 42, 43, 50, 52, 68, 71, 78, 85, 85 n. 19, 90, 97, 111, 149, 149 n. 27, 158, 158 n. 50, 171
Triple Courtyard House (Capernaum), 79, 80, 115, 116, 117, 117 n. 132, 118, 119, 119 n. 138, 120, 121, 122, 123, 128, 130
Yodefat/Jotapata, vii, 3, 6, 9, 11, 12, 21–28, 29, 30, 30 n. 41, 31, 32, 33, 34, 35, 36, 42, 43, 44, 49, 56, 57, 58, 59, 60, 62, 62 n. 20, 65, 68, 71, 101, 107, 107 n. 95, 118, 125 n. 145, 157, 158 n. 50, 159 n. 54, 174, 176

www.ingramcontent.com/pod-product-compliance
Lightning Source LLC
Chambersburg PA
CBHW031313150426
43191CB00005B/206